# CONTENTS

# Young and Active?

**Young people and health-enhancing physical activity – evidence and implications**

# Young and Active?

## Young people and health-enhancing physical activity – evidence and implications

Edited by

*Stuart Biddle, James Sallis and Nick Cavill*

*A report of the Health Education Authority symposium Young and Active?*

Health Education Authority
Trevelyan House
30 Great Peter Street
London SW1P 2HW

Cover design Moore Lowenhoff

Printed in England

ISBN 0 7521 1199 X

## Acknowledgements

The HEA would like to thank the authors, co-ordinators, discussants and all the delegates at the Young and Active? symposium for the wealth of expertise and experience they brought to the event and the preparation of this report.

## Authors, co-ordinators and discussants

**Len Almond**, Senior Lecturer in Physical Education, Loughborough University, UK

**Professor Neil Armstrong**, Professor of Health and Exercise Science, University of Exeter, UK

**Professor Stuart Biddle**, Professor of Sport and Exercise Psychology, Loughborough University, UK

**Dr Ilse De Bourdeaudhuij**, Researcher, Department of Psychology, University of Ghent, Belgium

**Nick Cavill**, Programme Manager, Physical Activity, Health Education Authority, London, UK

**Dr Ken Fox**, Reader in Exercise and Public Health, University of Exeter, UK

**Dr Jo Harris**, Lecturer in Physical Education, Loughborough University, UK

**Professor Leo Hendry**, Professor of Education, University of Aberdeen, UK

**Dr Roger Ingham**, Reader in Health and Community Psychology, Southampton University, UK

**Dr Willem Van Mechelen**, Associate Professor of Social Medicine, Vrije University, Amsterdam, Netherlands

**Dr Nanette Mutrie**, Senior Lecturer, Institute of Biomedical and Life Sciences, University of Glasgow, UK

**Dr Gaynor Parfitt**, Lecturer in Exercise Pyschology and Sport Psychology, University of Wales, Bangor, UK

**Professor Russell Pate**, Professor and Chairman, Department of Exercise Science, University of South Carolina, USA

**Dr Chris Riddoch**, Senior Lecturer in Exercise and Health Science, University of Bristol, UK

**Professor James F Sallis**, Professor of Psychology, San Diego State University, USA

**Stuart Trost**, Graduate Research Assistant, University of South Carolina, USA

**Dr Craig Williams**, Senior Lecturer in Sport and Exercise Science, University of Brighton, UK

**Dr Bente Wold**, Research Director, Research Centre for Health Promotion, Bergen University, Norway

## Delegates

**Sue Ball**, Department of Health, London, UK

**Professor Colin Boreham**, Professor of Sport and Exercise Science, University of Ulster, UK

**Annette Burgess**, Education Development Officer, The Exercise Association of England

**Dr Lorraine Cale**, Lecturer in Physical Education, Loughborough University, UK

**Dr Carlton Cooke**, Reader in Sport and Exercise Science, School of Leisure and Sports Studies, Leeds Metropolitan University, UK

**Alana Diamond**, Research Manager, Physical Activity, Health Education Authority, London, UK

**Dr Dawn Edwards**, Research Co-ordinator, St Mary's University College, Twickenham, UK

**Jill Elbourn**, Education Exercise Consultant, Physical Education Association, UK

**Dr Roger Eston**, Senior Lecturer in Human Physiology, University of Wales, Bangor, UK

**Debra Hall**, Project Officer, Physical Activity, Health Education Authority, London, UK

*Acknowledgements*

**Carol Healy**, Project Manager, European Network of Health Promoting Schools, Health Education Authority, London, UK

**Frank Kelly**, Programme Manager, Physical Activity, Health Promotion Agency for Northern Ireland, Belfast, UK

**Helen King**, International Technical Assistance, Health Education Authority, London, UK

**Bob Laventure**, Manager Field Liaison, Physical Activity, Health Education Authority, London, UK

**Dr Martin Lee**, Principal Research Fellow, Chelsea School of Physical Education, Sports Science, Dance and Leisure, University of Brighton, UK

**Paul Lincoln**, Director, Health Education Authority, London, UK

**Alan Lindsay**, Advisory Teacher for Physical Education, representing British Association of Advisers and Lecturers of Physical Education, UK

**Dr David Markland**, Director of Postgraduate Studies, University of Wales, Bangor, UK

**Dr Victor Matsudo**, Secretaria de Estado da Saude/Celafiscs, Brazil

**Karen McColl**, Consumers Association, UK

**Sonia McGeorge**, Project Manager, Exercise and Health Group, Loughborough University, UK

**Dr Thomas McKenzie**, Professor, Department of Exercise and Nutritional Sciences, San Diego State University, USA

**Dr Dawn Milner**, Department of Health, London, UK

**Dr Angie Page**, Lecturer, Exercise and Health Research Unit, University of Bristol, UK

**Dr Claire Paisley**, Senior Research Officer, Health Promotion Wales, Cardiff, UK

**Gillian Prior**, Social Community and Planning Research, UK

**David Rivett**, Project Co-ordinator, Health Promoting Schools, WHO Europe, Copenhagen, Denmark

**Professor Ken Roberts**, Professor of Sports Science, Brunel University, UK

**Nick Rowe**, Senior Research Officer, English Sports Council, London, England

**Professor Craig Sharp**, Professor of Sports Science, Brunel University, UK

**Mike Sleap**, Lecturer in Education, University of Hull, UK

**Dr Andy Smith**, Senior Lecturer in Sports Science and Health Studies, University College of Ripon and York St John, representing British Association of Sport and Exercie Sciences, UK

**Professor Andrew Steptoe**, Professor of Psychology, St George's Hospital Medical School, London, UK

**Dr Gareth Stratton**, Senior Lecturer in Exercise Physiology and Physical Education, Liverpool John Moores University, UK

**Di Swanston**, Manager, *ACTIVE* for LIFE Campaign, Health Education Authority, London, UK

**Alison Walker**, Independent Research Consultant

**Dr Hilarie Williams**, Department of Health, London, UK

**Angela Wortley**, Director of Physical Education, University of Leicester, UK

**Adele Wright**, Research Co-ordinator, National Adolescent and Student Health Unit, UK

The HEA also thanks those individuals and organisations who commented on earlier drafts of the policy framework.

# INTRODUCTION

Much progress has been made in recent years on the promotion of physical activity among adults. There is a wealth of data on the health benefits of physical activity and strong international consensus on the amount and type of physical activity that is beneficial for health. The same, however, cannot be said for young people. The evidence base is weaker than that for adults and there continues to be great debate about the nature and extent of any public health problem, and the range of possible solutions.

In 1997 the Health Education Authority began to tackle this issue by initiating a process of expert consultation and review of the evidence surrounding the promotion of health-enhancing physical activity for young people. The aim of this process was to produce a policy framework from a public health perspective that would maximise the opportunity for young people to participate in a lifetime of regular health-enhancing physical activity. To produce such a framework, the following objectives were identified:

- Investigate the key issues affecting young people's participation in physical activity.

- Establish expert consensus on the recommended level and type of physical activity for young people.

- Identify the most effective strategies to ensure participation throughout life.

- Identify future research priorities.

- Seek views from key sectors, organisations and practitioners on their potential contribution.

Eight distinguished experts were commissioned to prepare review papers on key aspects of the field of physical activity and young people. Following a review process drafts of these papers were presented at a two-day symposium, 'Young and Active?' in June 1997. This meeting brought together over 50 academics and experts from a range of disciplines within the field of young people and physical activity. Led by a chair and discussants, they examined the key papers and made recommendations, based on the evidence presented. A final session drew on the evidence available, and discussed the main recommendations of the meeting. Where evidence was unavailable or insufficient, expert opinion was drawn upon.

Following the meeting a draft policy framework was prepared and issued for consultation to a wide body of practitioners in the field of young people and physical activity. Over 40 consultation responses were received, and a number of people attended a subsequent consultation meeting. These responses focused on the practical implications of the experts' recommendations and the potential roles of key sectors and organisations.

This book presents the full outcomes of this review process plus the review papers. Chapter 1 covers the full policy framework and recommendations for action and Chapters 2 to 9 are the review papers. It thus provides the most up-to-date review of the evidence available, and a consensus view of current expert opinion. It aims to inform the work of anyone interested in promoting health-enhancing physical activity for young people.

# DEFINITIONS

*Exercise*: planned, structured and repetitive bodily movement done to improve or maintain one or more components of physical fitness.

*Health*: The World Health Organization (1948) has defined health as 'a state of complete physical, mental and social well-being and not merely the absence of disease or infirmity'. It is now seen more broadly as a 'resource for everyday life, not the objective for living, and a positive concept emphasising social and personal resources as well as physical capacities' (WHO, 1984).

*Health-related exercise*: is the term adopted within the physical education National Curriculum for the area of work associated with health and physical fitness. Health-related exercise is physical activity associated with health enhancement and disease prevention. The teaching of health-related exercise would typically include the teaching of knowledge, understanding, competence and motor skills, behavioural skills and the creation of positive attitudes and confidence for lifelong participation in physical activity.

*Moderate intensity physical activity*: activity usually equivalent to brisk walking, which might be expected to leave the participant feeling warm and slightly out of breath.

*Physical activity*: any bodily movement produced by skeletal muscles that results in energy expenditure.

*Physical education*: the part of the school curriculum that aims to educate young people through physical activity. An important aim is to promote the adoption of a physically active lifestyle that persists through adulthood.

*Physical fitness*: a set of attributes that people have or achieve that relates to the ability to perform physical activity.

*Vigorous intensity physical activity*: activity usually equivalent to at least slow jogging, which might be expected to leave the participant feeling out of breath and sweaty.

*Young people*: all people aged 5–18 years.

# Policy framework for young people and health-enhancing physical activity

## Recommended level and type of physical activity for young people

From a health perspective, there are three main rationales for encouraging young people to take part in regular physical activity (PA):

■ To optimise physical fitness, current health and well-being, and growth and development.

■ To develop active lifestyles that can be maintained throughout adult life.

■ To reduce the risk of chronic diseases of adulthood.

The recommendations are intended to take into account the current physical activity patterns and lifestyles of young people, so that they do not represent unattainable goals that discourage young people from trying to achieve them. They are based on current scientific evidence and expert opinion, but it is acknowledged that neither the minimal nor the optimal amount of PA for young people can be precisely defined at this time. Expert opinion strongly supports these recommendations until further research leads to refinements.

> ### RECOMMENDATIONS FOR YOUNG PEOPLE AND PHYSICAL ACTIVITY
>
> #### Primary recommendations
> ■ All young people should participate in physical activity of at least moderate intensity for *one hour per day*.
>
> ■ Young people who currently do little activity should participate in physical activity of at least moderate intensity for *at least half an hour per day*
>
> #### Secondary recommendations
> ■ *At least twice a week*, some of these activities should help to enhance and maintain muscular strength and flexibility, and bone health.

### Rationale – primary recommendation

An average of one hour of PA per day is the preferred recommendation because,

3

although the majority of young people are currently meeting the criterion of 30 minutes of moderate PA per day on most days of the week (Verschuur, Kemper and Besseling, 1984; Atomi *et al*, 1986; Sleap and Warburton, 1992, 1994, 1996; Pate, Long and Heath, 1994; Armstrong and Welsman, 1997), childhood overweight and obesity is increasing in the UK (Chinn and Rona, 1994). Many young people have been shown to possess at least one modifiable coronary heart disease risk factor (Baranowski *et al*, 1992), and many young people have symptoms of psychological distress (Kurtz, 1992).

For all young people, participating in at least 30 minutes of PA per day should be seen as a minimum. One hour of activity per day represents a more favourable level and is particularly appropriate for children of primary school age.

Examples of moderate intensity activities for all young people may include brisk walking, cycling, swimming, most sports or dance. Activities may be carried out as part of transportation, physical education, games, sport, recreation, work or structured exercise. For younger children, activities can be carried out as part of active play. Such activity may be performed in a continuous fashion or intermittently accumulated throughout the day. Given that young people have demonstrated patterns of intermittent activity, emphasising the accumulation of PA over the day seems a more practical approach.

Methods of meeting the recommendation may vary according to stage of maturation. Young children may achieve the recommendation during play, by alternating short bouts of moderate to vigorous PA with rest periods or bouts of lower intensity activity. Teenagers are more likely to be active by performing structured continuous bouts of moderate to vigorous PA through sports, active trans-

portation, dance or structured exercise. While young people should be physically active nearly every day, PA can vary from day to day in type, setting, intensity, duration, and amount.

## Rationale – secondary recommendation

Participation in strength and weight-bearing activities is positively associated with bone mineral density and is believed to be related to a reduced long-term risk of osteoporosis (Grimston, Willows and Hanley, 1993; Slemenda *et al*, 1994; Valimaki *et al*, 1994; Cooper *et al*, 1995; VandenBergh *et al*, 1995). Muscular strength is particularly important, as it is required to perform activities of daily life such as lifting and carrying, bending and twisting. Trunk strength and muscular flexibility may be associated with reduced risk of injury and back pain in later life (Plowman, 1992).

Activities for younger children that enhance strength include play, such as climbing, skipping or jumping, whereas for adolescents they might include structured exercise such as body conditioning or resistance exercises. Weight-bearing activities that promote bone health include gymnastics, dance, aerobics, skipping, and sports such as basketball. A variety of activities are important to develop strength in a wide range of muscles and bones.

## ▨ Benefits of physical activity for young people

PA can have multiple beneficial health outcomes in young people:

- *Psychological well-being:* PA can enhance psychological well-being

(Gruber, 1986; Steptoe and Butler, 1996; Gordon and Grant, 1997) and reduce symptoms of depression and anxiety (Calfas and Taylor, 1994).

■ *Self-esteem:* PA can enhance self-esteem. This is particularly marked in disadvantaged groups such as those with learning difficulties and those with initially low self-esteem (Gruber, 1986). The potential psychological benefits for some young people can be limited by an over-emphasis on competitive performance (Bredemeier and Shields, 1984; Shields and Bredemeier, 1994).

■ *Moral and social development:* if appropriately structured, PA may enhance social and moral development (Sage, 1986; Shields and Bredemeier, 1994).

■ *Overweight and obesity:* there are small but significant beneficial effects of increased PA on reducing body fat (Bar-Or and Baranowski, 1994). Evidence supports the role of PA as part of an effective obesity treatment for young people, when combined with appropriate dietary modification (Bar-Or and Baranowski, 1994).

■ *Chronic disease risk factors:* PA has a small but beneficial association with serum lipid and lipoprotein concentrations (Craig *et al*, 1996; Boreham *et al*, 1997) and blood pressure (Armstrong and Simons-Morton, 1994). Recent research has also identified a favorable relationship between PA and a range of factors associated with metabolic syndromes (hypertension, obesity, insulin resistance, impaired lipid and lipoprotein profile (Kahle *et al*, 1996). In addition, weight-bearing and strength-enhancing PA can promote skeletal health in young people (Grimston, Willows and Hanley, 1993; Welten *et al*,

1994). The health outcomes for physical activities that enhance strength, flexibility and anaerobic components of fitness in young people are, unfortunately, not known.

■ *PA 'tracking':* There is a moderate relationship between the amount and type of PA in childhood with that in youth. Current evidence indicates low levels of tracking from youth into young adulthood (Malina, 1996).

■ *Negative effects of PA:* PA can increase the risk of musculo-skeletal injuries. Most injuries that do occur are the result of over-exercise, particularly around puberty. However, some activities and sports can increase the risk of accidents, including road accidents, falls, collisions and other trauma.

## ▨ Current levels of physical activity and fitness

Objective measures have shown that most young people accumulate 30 minutes or more of moderate intensity PA on most days of the week (Armstrong and Welsman, 1997). Young people's PA patterns are characterised by short, rather than sustained, bouts of activity (Armstrong *et al*, 1990). Using a variety of different criteria, research shows that some young people are very active while others are inactive. Boys are more active than girls from an early age, and both boys and girls reduce their PA as they mature (Sallis, 1993a). This decline is more marked in girls than boys, and is steeper in adolescence than in childhood (Armstrong and Welsman, 1997).

It is not possible to determine objectively whether there has been a decline in PA in recent years in young people, although data on energy intake and body mass indirectly suggest that adolescents in the UK have reduced their energy expenditure (Durnin, 1992). There is no evidence that young people's aerobic fitness levels are low or have declined over the past 50 years (Armstrong and Welsman, 1997).

The most accurate estimates of PA participation in young people come from objective measures used over several days (Sallis, 1993a; Armstrong and Welsman, 1997). For public health purposes, it is more important to monitor the PA of young people than to monitor fitness.

## ■ Determinants of young people's participation in physical activity

There are a number of determinants affecting young people's participation in PA.

### Psychological determinants

Enjoyment is particularly important and is consistently associated with participation in PA (Wankel and Kreisel, 1985). The factors that influence enjoyment of PA will, however, vary between individuals and groups. There is a consistent association between some key psychological variables and PA in youth: feelings of competence (Duda, 1987; Klint and Weiss, 1987), control and autonomy; self-efficacy (confidence) (Sallis *et al*, 1992); the existence of positive attitudes to PA (Godin and Shephard, 1986); having personal goals that focus on personal effort and improvement (Duda, 1987); and perceptions of increased benefits and decreased barriers

to PA (Sallis *et al*, 1996). Major differences exist between boys and girls on some of these variables, with girls showing lower levels of perceived competence (Weiss *et al*, 1990; Lirgg, 1991; Brustad, 1992), higher levels of perceived barriers or costs (Sallis *et al*, 1996; Trost *et al*, 1996) and lower levels of enjoyment.

The importance of determinants may change across the lifespan of young people, with psychological variables being more important in adolescence. A full understanding of determinants can only be achieved through studying the interaction of psychological, social and environmental factors. These determinants should guide the implementation of, and research into, interventions.

### Social and environmental determinants

There is substantial evidence that family and peer modeling and support correlate with PA levels of young people (Wold and Anderssen, 1992), and that access to appropriate environments can enhance their participation (Sallis *et al*, 1990; Sallis, 1993b). Mass media, cultural factors and youth sports organisations can influence PA in young people, but direct data are lacking.

Gender and socio-economic inequalities in PA in young people appear to reflect inequalities in the broader society (Wold *et al*, 1994).

## ■ Recommended interventions to promote physical activity

The most thoroughly evaluated interventions are health-related physical education (PE) programmes for primary school pupils, although most data come from the United States. While studies have tended to focus on physiological outcomes, there is recent evidence that an appropriately designed, delivered and supported PE curriculum can enhance current levels of physical activity and can improve physical skill development (Shephard *et al*, 1980; Simons-Morton, Parcel and O'Hara, 1988; Pieron *et al*, 1996; Harris, 1997).

Correlational evidence suggests that families can influence young people's participation in PA, but to date trials of interventions in healthy families have been uniformly ineffective (Nader, *et al*, 1992).

Observational data show that young people benefit from access to suitable and accessible facilities and opportunities for PA (Sallis *et al*, 1990, 1993). This implies the need for environmental and policy interventions to increase these opportunities.

There is consensus that interventions are likely to be more effective when young people are involved in decision-making and planning of programmes.

## Targeting interventions

There is general consensus that interventions are needed to encourage adequate PA for all young people, beginning at a young age, and with a specific focus on the inactive. However, young people are not a homogenous group. Therefore, in the light of the scientific data available and from a public health perspective, priority groups are:

■ girls aged 12–18 years.

■ young people of low socio-economic status.

■ older adolescents (16–18 years).

Priority groups for further investigation of targeted strategies to increase PA include young people:

■ from black and minority ethnic groups;

■ with physical or mental disabilities;

■ with clinical conditions such as obesity, clinical depression or diabetes.

Evidence suggests that interventions should be differentiated on the grounds of gender, age/life-stage and socio-economic status.

## Research needs

More research is needed to investigate the relationship between the PA patterns of young people and the contribution PA makes to health. This research should involve different methods and disciplines including quantitative, qualitative and multidisciplinary approaches. Research priorities can be grouped under four headings.

### Methods

■ To develop reliable and valid measures of various types of PA.

■ To develop reliable and valid measures of a range of health outcomes of PA, including mental and skeletal health.

### Relationship between PA and health

■ To conduct prospective population studies which identify the physiological, psychological and developmental health benefits of PA of different types, intensities, duration and frequency; and test their appropriateness for different stages of development.

- To investigate which types of PA track over time and to identify factors that affect tracking.

### Determinants of PA

- To conduct prospective population studies on the socio-economic, environmental, cultural, developmental and behavioural determinants of PA and inactivity in young people.

### PA interventions

- To monitor and evaluate the contribution that schools, and in particular PE, make to PA in young people.

- To monitor and evaluate the implementation and effectiveness of the new PA recommendations among young people, parents, PE teachers, health care providers and other relevant professionals.

- To identify, develop and evaluate interventions in a variety of community and family settings that promote PA.

## ◻ The role of key organisations

A range of agencies at national and local level have a vital role to play in promoting health-enhancing PA for young people. All of these should recognise the need for greater co-ordination of effort across a broad range of agencies. Where appropriate, programmes should be designed to meet the specific needs of young people, for example, those with disabilities, those from black and minority ethnic groups and those from a lower socio-economic background.

### The education sector

This includes schools, further and higher education (FE & HE) colleges, youth services, local education authorities (LEAs), advisory and support services and professional bodies.

Those involved in the education of young people, including governors and senior managers, can make a major contribution towards enabling young people to develop lifetime habits of PA. To achieve this, schools and LEAs will need to work with a range of organisations including local government, leisure and recreation, the health services and environmental and voluntary groups to develop local strategies to increase levels of PA of young people.

Their role relates to:

- The planning, delivery and support of the curriculum in health education and physical education.

- The delivery of whole-school approaches to promoting PA.

- Developing sustained links with providers in the local community.

### *Recommendations*

- Schools should enable young people of all ages to take part in PA for the recommended time, both in the PE curriculum and at other times.

- PE programmes should take into account both the perceived needs of young people and those expressed by young people themselves.

- Schools should recognise the importance of health-related exercise within the National Curriculum and ensure that the requirements are fully implemented in practice.

- Health-related exercise should take the form of an effectively planned, delivered and evaluated programme of study.

- Professional development, training and support services, including FE and HE colleges, should provide appropriate training (including initial teacher and in-service training) that includes the teaching of health-related exercise.

- Schools and FE colleges should develop the concept of the health promoting school/college, which includes the contribution that physical activity can make to health.

- Extra-curricular programmes should be designed to provide a broad range of health-enhancing activities to meet the needs of all young people.

- Schools should form partnerships with other agencies to increase opportunities for participation in PA both in and out of school.

- Schools, colleges and universities should ensure wider access to their facilities for all young people in their local community.

- Schools and LEAs should encourage young people to walk or cycle by developing safe routes to schools.

- Schools and LEAs should work with planners and other agencies to develop safe and attractive environments that encourage young people to be physically active (e.g. safe playgrounds, changing rooms, playing fields).

- Schools should develop programmes that involve parents and encourage them to support participation in physical activity.

## Local authorities

These include leisure and recreation, community, planning and transport, social and environmental services. Local authorities (LAs) can play a vital role in the promotion of health-enhancing PA with young people. To achieve this LA departments will need to work in partnership with each other and also with a wide range of external organisations including health services and environmental and voluntary groups.

### *Recommendations*

- LAs should provide a range of easily accessible, attractive and appropriate environments including parks, open spaces and play grounds in which young people are encouraged to play safely.

- LAs should ensure that the contract specification for the management of local leisure facilities includes appropriate policies, prices and programming to encourage participation among young people, including those with low levels of participation in PA.

- LAs should design programmes to provide a broad range of health-enhancing PA for young people (e.g. sport and dance development, play, outdoor education).

- LAs should assist in the development of safe and attractive walking and cycling routes to schools within local authority development plans.

- LAs should ensure that those who work with young people (including leaders, coaches, recreation, health, youth workers and other community personnel), are appropriately trained and qualified for their role as PA promoters to educate, motivate and build confidence.

9

- LAs should ensure the development of policies for the protection of school playing fields.

- LAs are in a position to lead strategic alliances with education and health professionals in their area to promote PA to young people.

- LAs should develop partnerships with non-statutory organisations who provide a broad range of PAs for young people (e.g. sports and youth clubs, playgroups).

## Organisations concerned with sport and recreation and young people

These may be statutory and non-statutory bodies including youth groups, clubs, church and religious organisations, sport and recreation bodies, consumer groups and private sector agencies.

These organisations and agencies have the potential to access a variety of groups who work with young people and provide opportunities for increased participation in PA at a local level.

### *Recommendations*

- These organisations should ensure that those who work with young people are aware of the health benefits of PA for young people and where appropriate are trained and qualified in the delivery of health-enhancing PA.

- These organisations should ensure the inclusion of a broad range of health-enhancing PAs for young people in their programme of activities (e.g. sport and dance development, play, outdoor education).

- Health, transport and environmental groups should work with planners and other agencies to develop safe and attractive environments that encourage young people to be physically active (e.g. safe playgrounds, walking and cycling routes).

- Funding agencies should commission research into PA for young people, and the effectiveness of interventions.

- Funding agencies should provide resources for local interventions to improve the opportunities available for participation in PA by young people.

- Private sector agencies should develop appropriate policies, pricing and programming to encourage participation among young people, including those with low levels of participation in PA.

## Health services

These include health promotion, primary health care and directors of public health.

Health professionals and those in the health services are in a position to provide leadership in promoting PA to young people, both in developing and implementing PA policies and through professional education and training. As well as providing services and education for young people and their parents, health professionals can act as advocates for PA, including advocating PA in other settings.

### *Recommendations*

- Health authorities and trusts should develop and co-ordinate PA policies for young people and support local interventions and campaigns that target young people.

- Health authorities and trusts should develop policy agreements with health promotion units and LAs on the promotion of PA for young people.

- Health authorities and trusts should ensure that those who work with young people are aware of the health benefits of PA for young people and where appropriate are trained and qualified in the delivery of health-enhancing PA.

- Health authorities in partnership with LAs, schools and other partners, should design school and community-based physical activity schemes that target young people and their parents. A special emphasis should be placed on those groups of young people with low levels of participation in PA.

- Health professionals, in partnership with LAs, should provide information for young people and parents on local opportunities for participation in PA by young people including safe and attractive play areas, walking and cycling routes, and sports and recreation programmes and facilities.

- Health authorities should commission research to evaluate the effectiveness of local PA promotion interventions that target young people.

- Health professionals including primary health-care teams, nurses and community health workers should target young people with specific needs (e.g. overweight or obese, people with diabetes, asthma and mild depression).

## Mass media

These include broadcasting, newspapers and magazines and the world of advertising.

The media has a key role in raising public and professional awareness of the benefits of PA for young people. TV, radio and magazines are particularly effective for reaching young people and can have a huge impact on young people's perceptions.

### *Recommendations*

- All forms of media should be encouraged to promote positive and health-enhancing images of participation in a range of activities by young people, placing in perspective the relative dangers of traffic and 'stranger danger'.

- All forms of media should be encouraged to use accurate data to present the key issues relating to young people and PA.

- Local media, including press and radio, should be encouraged to publicise a range of opportunities for young people to participate in PA, including safe play areas, walking and cycling routes.

- If celebrities are used to promote regular PA to young people, non-sport role models should be used, avoiding the use of stereotypical images associated with PA which emphasise appearance, beauty and muscularity.

## Government departments

These include the Departments of Health; Education and Employment; Environment, Transport and the Regions; Culture, Media and Sport; Agriculture, Fisheries and Food; and the Treasury.

Government departments play a key role in promoting health-enhancing PA with young people. Their role relates to policy development – legal and fiscal legislation and research.

## Recommendation

- Inter-departmental strategies and policies should be agreed that ensure a co-ordinated approach to the promotion of PA among young people.

- The government should identify and provide human and financial resources to support PA policies that target young people.

- National Lottery Funds (including capital costs) should be allocated to a range of initiatives targeting young people which promote and sustain PA (e.g. safe play, cycling, walking).

- The Department for Education and Employment (DfEE) should, through the review of the National Curriculum, encourage the development of PA promoting policies in schools.

- The Department of Environment, Transport and the Regions (DETR) should work with interested parties to develop safe play, cycling and walking policies that target young people.

- The Department for Culture, Media and Sports (DCMS) should adopt a broad approach towards sport and recreation policies for young people.

- The Department of Health (DoH) should expand its programme of PA promotion aimed at adults to include young people.

- The DoH should work with the DfEE to expand the programme of Health Promoting Schools, and include PA as a core topic area among the other health topics.

- The DoH should establish a taskforce involving the DfEE, DCMS, DETR and other agencies to promote health-enhancing PA.

- The DoH should consider the importance of schools and colleges in developing the plans for Healthy Living Centres and Health Action Zones.

# ■ References

**Armstrong, N., Balding, J., Gentle, P. and Kirby, B.** (1990) 'Patterns of physical activity among 11-16 year-old British children', *British Medical Journal*, **301**, 203–5.

**Armstrong, N. and Simons–Morton, B.** (1994) 'Physical activity and blood lipids in adolescents', *Pediatric Exercise Science*, **6**, 381–405.

**Armstrong, N. and Welsman, J.R.** (1997) *Young people and physical activity*. Oxford: Oxford University Press.

**Atomi, Y., Iwaoka, K., Hatta, H., Miyashita, M. and Yamamoto, Y.** (1986) 'Daily physical activity levels in preadolescent boys related to $\dot{V}O_2$ max and lactate threshold', *European Journal of Applied Physiology*, **55**, 156–61.

**Baranowksi, T., Bouchard, C., Bar–Or, O., Bricker, T., Heath, G., Kimm, S.Y.S., Malina, R., Obarzanek, E., Pate, R., Strong, W.B., Truman, B. and Washington R.** (1992) 'Assessment, prevalence, and cardiovascular health benefits of physical activity and fitness in youth', *Medicine and Science in Sports and Exercise*, **24** (Suppl.), S237–S247.

**Bar–Or, O. and Baranowski, T.** (1994) 'Physical activity, adiposity and obesity among adolescents', *Pediatric Exercise Science*, **6**, 348–60.

**Boreham, C.A., Twisk, J., Savage, M.J., Cran, G.W. and Strain, J.J.** (1997) 'Physical activity, sports participation and risk factors in adolescents', *Medicine and Science in Sports and Exercise*, **29**, 788–93.

**Bredemeier, B.J. and Shields, D.L.** (1984) 'Divergence in moral reasoning about sport and everyday life', *Sociology of Sport Journal*, **1**, 348–57.

**Brustad, R.** (1992) 'Integrating socialization influences into the study of children's motivation in sport', *Journal of Sport and Exercise Psychology*, **14**, 59–77.

**Calfas, K. J. and Taylor, C.** (1994) 'Effects of physical activity on psychological variables in adolescents', *Pediatric Exercise Science*, **6**, 406–23.

**Chinn, S. and Rona, R.J.** (1994) 'Trends in weight-for-height and triceps skinfold thickness for English and Scottish children, 1972–82 and 1982–1990', *Paediatric and Perinatal Epidemiology*, **8** (1), 90–106.

**Cooper, C., Cawley, M., Bhalla, A., Egger, P., Ring, F., Morton, L. and Barker, D.** (1995) 'Childhood growth, physical activity and peak bone mass in women', *Journal of Bone and Mineral Research*, **10** (6), 940–7.

**Craig, S.B., Bandini, L.G., Lichtenstein, A.H., Schaefer, E.J. and Dietz, W.H.** (1996) 'The impact of physical activity on lipids, lipoproteins and blood pressure in preadolescent girls', *Pediatrics*, **98** (3), 389–95.

**Duda, J.** (1987) 'Toward a developmental theory of children's motivation in sport', *Journal of Sport and Exercise Psychology*, **9**, 130–45.

**Durnin, J.V.G.A.** (1992) 'Physical activity levels past and present', in: N. Norgan (ed.), *Physical activity and health*, pp.20–7. Cambridge: Cambridge University Press.

**Godin, G. and Shephard, R.** (1986) 'Psychosocial factors influencing intentions to exercise of young students from grades 7–9', *Research Quarterly for Exercise and Sport*, **57**, 41–52.

**Gordon, J., and Grant, G.** (eds.) (1997) *How we feel*. London: Jessica Kingsley Publishers.

**Grimston, S.K., Willows, N.D. and Hanley, D.A.** (1993) 'Mechanical loading regime and its relationship to bone mineral density in children', *Medicine and Science in Sports and Exercise*, **25** (11):1203–10.

**Gruber, J. J.** (1986) 'Physical activity and self-esteem development in children: a meta-analysis', in: Stull, G. and Eckert, H. (eds.) *Effects of physical activity on children*, pp.330–48. Champaign: Human Kinetics.

**Harris, J.** (1997) *Physical education: A picture of health? The implementation of health–related exercise in the National Curriculum in secondary schools in England and Wales*. Unpublished doctoral dissertation, Loughborough University.

**Kahle, E.B., Zipf, W.B., Lamb, D.R., Horswill, C.A. and Ward, K.M.** (1996) 'Association between mild, routine exercise and improved insulin dynamics and glucose control in obese adolescents', *International Journal of Sports Medicine*, **17**,1–6.

**Klint, K. and Weiss, M.** (1987) 'Perceived competence and motives for participating in youth sports: a test of Harter's Competence Motivation Theory', *Journal of Sports and Exercise Psychology*, **9**, 55–65.

**Kurtz, Z.** (ed), (1992) *With health in mind*. London: Action for Sick Children.

**Lirgg, C.** (1991) 'Gender differences in self–confidence in physical activity: a meta–analysis of recent studies', *Journal of Sport and Exercise Psychology*, **8**, 294–310.

**Malina, R.M.** (1996) 'Tracking of physical activity and physical fitness across the lifespan', *Research Quarterly for Exercise and Sport*, **67** (3) (Suppl.), S1–S10.

**Nader, P.R., Sallis, J.F., Abramson, I.S., Broyles, S.L., Patterson, T.L., Senn, K., Rupp, J.W. and Nelson, J.A.** (1992) 'Family-based cardiovascular risk reduction education among Mexican– and Anglo-Americans', *Family and Community Health*, **15**, 57–74.

**Pate, R.R., Long, B.J. and Heath, G.** (1994) 'Descriptive epidemiology of physical activity in adolescents', *Pediatric Exercise Science*, **6**, 434–47.

**Pieron, M., Cloes, M., Delfosse, C. and Ledent, M.** (1996) 'An investigation of the effects of daily physical education in kindergarten and elementary schools', *European Physical Education Review*, **2**, 116–32.

**Plowman, S.A.** (1992) 'Physical activity, physical fitness, and low back pain', *Exercise and Sport Sciences Reviews*, **20**, 221– 42.

**Sage, G.** (1986) 'Social development' in: Seefeldt, V. (ed.), *Physical activity and well-being*, pp. 343–71. Reston: American Alliance for Health, Physical Education and Dance.

**Sallis, J.F.** (1993a) 'Epidemiology of physical activity and fitness in children and adolescents', *Critical Reviews in Food Science and Nutrition*, **33**, 403–8.

**Sallis, J.F.** (1993b) 'Promoting healthful diet and physical activity', in: Millstein, S.G., Petersen, A.C. and Nightingale, E.O. (eds.), *Promoting the health of adolescents*, pp.209–41. New York: Oxford University Press.

**Sallis, J.F., Hovell, M.F., Hofstetter, C.R., Elder, J.P., Hackley, M., Caspersen, C.J. and Powell, K.E.** (1990) 'Distance between homes and exercise facilities related to frequency of exercise among San Diego residents', *Public Health Reports*, **105**, 179–85.

**Sallis, J.F., Nader, P.R., Broyles, S.L., Berry, C.C., Elder, J.P., McKenzie, T.L., and Nelson, J.A.** (1993) 'Correlates of physical activity at home in Mexican-American and Anglo-American preschool children', *Health Psychology*, **12**, 390–8.

**Sallis, J., Simons–Morton, B., Stone, E., Corbin, C., Epstein, L., Faucette, N., Iannotti, R., Killen, J., Klesges, R., Petray, C., Rowland, T. and Taylor, W.** (1992) 'Determinants of physical activity and interventions in youth', *Medicine and Science in Sports and Exercise*, **24**, S248–S257.

**Sallis, J., Zakarian, J., Hovell, M. and Hofstetter, R.** (1996) 'Ethnic, socio-economic, and sex differences in physical activity among adolescents', *Journal of Clinical Epidemiology*, **49**(2), 125–34.

**Shephard, R.J., Jequier, J-C., Lavallee, H., La Barre, R. and Rajic, M.** (1980) 'Habitual physical activity: effects of sex, milieu, season and required activity', *Journal of Sports Medicine*, **20**, 55–66.

**Shields, D.L.L. and Bredemeier, B.J.L.** (1994) *Character development and physical activity*. Champaign: Human Kinetics.

**Simons–Morton, B.G., Parcel, G.S. and O'Hara, N.M.** (1988) 'Implementing organizational changes to promote healthful diet and physical activity at school', *Health Education Quarterly*, **15** (1), 115–30.

**Sleap, M. and Warburton, P.** (1992) 'Physical activity levels of 5–11-year-old children in England determined by continuous observation', *Research Quarterly for Exercise and Sport*, **63**, 238–45.

**Sleap, M. and Warburton, P.** (1994) 'Physical activity levels of preadolescent children in England', *British Journal of Physical Education Research Supplement*, **14**, 2–6.

**Sleap, M. and Warburton, P.** (1996) 'Physical activity levels of 5–11-year-old children in England: cumulative evidence from three direct observation studies', *International Journal of Sports Medicine*, **17**, 248–53.

**Slemenda, C.W., Reister, T.K., Hui, S.L., Miller, J.Z., Christian, J.C. and Johnston, C.C.** (1994) 'Influences on skeletal mineralization in children and adolescents: evidence for varying effects of sexual maturation and physical activity', *Journal of Pediatrics*, **125**, 201–7.

**Steptoe, A. and Butler, N.** (1996) 'Sports participation and emotional well-being in adolescents', *Lancet*, **347**, 1789–92.

**Trost, S., Pate, R., Dowda, M., Saunders, R., Ward, D. and Felton, G.** (1996) 'Gender differences in physical activity and determinants of physical activity in rural fifth grade children', *Journal of School Health*, **66** (4), 145–50.

**Valimaki, M.J., Karkkainen, M., Lamberg-Allardt, C., Laitinen, K., Alhava, E., Heikkinen, J., Impivaara, O., Makela, P., Palmgren, J., Seppanen, R. and Vuori, I.** (1994) 'Exercise, smoking and calcium intake during adolescence and early adulthood as determinants of peak bone mass', *British Medical Journal*, **309**, 230–5.

**VandenBergh, M.F., DeMan, S.A., Witteman, J.C., Hofman, A., Trouerbach, W.T. and Grobbee, D.E.** (1995) 'Physical activity, calcium intake and bone mineral content in children in the Netherlands', *Journal of Epidemiology and Community Health*, **49** (3), 299–304.

**Verschuur, R., Kemper, H.C.G. and Besseling, C.W.M.** (1984) 'Habitual physical activity and health in 13 and 14-year-old teenagers', in: Ilmarinen, J. and I. Valimaki, I. (eds.), *Children and Sport*, pp. 255–61. New York: Springer–Verlag.

**Wankel, L. and Kreisel, P.** (1985) 'Factors underlying enjoyment of youth sports: sport and age group comparisons', *Journal of Sport Psychology*, **7**, 51–64.

**Weiss, M., McAuley, E., Ebbeck, V. and Wiese, D.** (1990) 'Self-esteem and causal attributions for children's physical and social competence in sport', *Journal of Sport and Exercise Psychology*, **12**, 21–36.

**Welten, D.C., Kemper, H.C.G., Post, G.B., Van Mechelen, W., Twisk, J., Lips, P. and Teule, G.J.** (1994) 'Weight-bearing activity during youth is a more important factor for peak bone mass than calcium intake', *Journal of Bone and Mineral Research*, **9**, 1089–96.

**Wold, B. and Anderssen, N.** (1992) 'Health promotion aspects of family and peer influences on sport participation', *International Journal of Sport Psychology*, **23**, 343–59.

**Wold, B., Oeygard, L., Eder, A. and Smith, C.** (1994) 'Social reproduction of physical activity: implications for health promotion in young people', *European Journal of Public Health*, **4**, 163–8.

**World Health Organization** (1948), quoted in: WHO (1998) *Health promotion glossary*. Geneva: WHO.

**World Health Organization** (1986), quoted in: WHO (1998) *Health promotion glossary*. Geneva: WHO.

# Relationships between physical activity and physical health in young people

Chris Riddoch
*Senior Lecturer in Exercise and Health Science,*
*University of Bristol, UK.*

McNeill Alexander (1991) has argued that all mammals have a maximum rate of oxygen consumption that is optimum for the species. The optimum level has evolved to balance the biological costs of improved running performance (more viscous blood, greater muscle mass, lack of outer protection) and its benefits (hunting, escape from predators). For many well-protected animals, for example the tortoise, running ability is simply not required. Interestingly, tortoises are among the most long-lived of mammals, with the giant tortoise living for up to 180 years. For the majority of mammals, the balance of advantage probably favours those with less extreme ability – in other words it may be better to be an inferior performer – or, to use McNeill Alexander's phrase:

It may be better to be a wimp.

Must we therefore question whether the pursuit of high levels of running ability is the panacea for improving health? The notion of optimum balance, above or below which the costs are greater and the benefits lower, is certainly attractive, and might be applied to physical activity that, at least partly, determines fitness. Interestingly, Starnes and Bowles (1995) have suggested that most of the potential cardiovascular benefit of exercise training is attained at a 'relatively low' threshold – 75% maximal aerobic power ($\dot{V}O_2$ max.), 60 min·day$^{-1}$. However, this level does exceed the physical demands of most routine daily activities.

To ascertain an optimal health-related level of activity in children is more problematic. It is a sobering thought that the major morbidities of childhood are unwanted pregnancy, substance abuse, physical and sexual abuse and anxiety disorders, and that the primary cause of death is violence (accidents, homicides, suicides) (Blum, 1987). It is difficult to see how physical activity can affect such factors in any meaningful way. There are, however, other compelling arguments that childhood is important in terms of disease prevention. While children are relatively free of disease and have extremely low mortality rates, it is possible, if not likely, that degenerative biological processes are initiated during infancy and childhood and manifest themselves as chronic disease in later life. Further, there is evidence to suggest that adult health status may be determined, at least in part, by biological events that occur *in utero* (Barker, 1990). It is argued that early biological events trigger a morphological and/or functional change (e.g. damage to the arterial wall) which subsequently becomes a chronic and worsening condition (e.g., atherosclerosis, hypertension), leading to overt signs and symptoms of disease and ultimately death. The individual is effectively 'programmed' to succumb to a disease through an early biological event. The biological event may itself be triggered by an environmental influence (e.g., inadequate maternal nutrition, smoking) and be reflected in infant characteristics (e.g., low birth-weight). A key finding is that children from areas with high levels of adult cardiovascular disease (CVD) mortality have elevated CVD risk factors compared with children from areas with lower mortality (Whincup *et al.*, 1996). This difference is independent of birthweight, which suggests that the childhood environment is more important than the intrauterine environment. It may also be argued that the presence of childhood CVD risk factors is of great significance, as this has been shown to predict the extent of arterial fatty streaks in young adulthood (Newman, Freedman and Voors, 1986).

Whatever the merits of such biological arguments, it might also be argued that childhood activity is important from a behavioural perspective, the concern being that inactivity in childhood will lead to inactivity in adulthood and subsequent elevated risk of adult disease (Riddoch *et al.*, 1991). There are now strong arguments that the health status of adults has its origins in behaviours which are thought to be established during childhood (Coronary Prevention Group, 1988; Loucks, 1995). Despite the fact that exchanging an inactive lifestyle for a more active one during adulthood has significant health benefits (Paffenbarger *et al.*, 1993; Blair *et al.*, 1995), it may be more

appropriate to prevent the development of sedentary living than to attempt to reverse the situation in adulthood (World Health Organization, 1990). As Strong (1978) has stated:

> To allow children to develop habits which, when they become adults, must be altered is absurd.

Physical activity may also be necessary for children in order to promote and maintain optimal growth and development, and to alleviate some medical disorders (Rowland, 1990). Further, it may be important for children to be active for social, psychological and developmental reasons.

There are, therefore, three compelling reasons why we should be interested in physical activity as an important childhood behaviour: (a) to enhance social, physical and cognitive development and quality of life; (b) to modify the evolution of health risk factors in order to minimise future degenerative disease; and (c) to establish a healthy behaviour at an early stage of life in order that it might be continued into adult life (Blair *et al.*, 1989a; Astrand, 1994; Blair and Meredith, 1994; Malina, 1994b).

There is no doubt that with the current epidemic of lifestyle-related chronic disease, contemporary lifestyles have become a matter of concern (Department of Health and Social Services, 1992; US Department of Health and Human Services, 1996). The purpose of this review, therefore, is to assess the evidence relating physical activity to a range of health-related parameters in children, and to interpret the evidence in the light of the major issues which surround it. It should be noted that the social and psychological benefits, while being considered no less important, will not be addressed in this chapter.

# ■ Background

## Activity and health in adults

In adults, both physical activity and physical fitness levels are strongly and inversely related to all-cause mortality and in particular to CVD mortality (Paffenbarger *et al.*, 1986; Blair *et al.*, 1989). A consistent finding across many observational studies is the existence of a graded dose-response relationship, with risk of mortality from CVD and all causes being greatest at the lower end of the activity spectrum and a reduced risk at the higher end (Paffenbarger *et al.*, 1986). This suggests that: (a) avoiding the lower end of the spectrum carries the greatest reduction in risk; (b) an optimum level of activity may exist beyond which there are few further benefits; and (c) high levels of activity may be unnecessary for the achievement of most health benefits (Blair *et al.*, 1992).

This evidence is consistent with the view that there may exist for humans a level of physical activity that is optimal for the species, above or below which the costs may outweigh the benefits. Although the evidence from observational studies clearly indicates that low activity is related to increased mortality, there is little evidence to suggest that very high levels of activity, for example cardiovascular fitness training, are associated with increased mortality. Close scrutiny of the available literature suggests that at the higher end of the activity spectrum, some body systems react adversely when compared to more moderate activity. Examples of this are musculo-skeletal injuries, gastrointestinal disturbances, immune system suppression and menstrual irregularities. Although such problems are largely transient and not life-threatening, there appear to be few additional health benefits for individuals who exercise at very high levels, compared to those who practise more moderate levels of activity.

In terms of mortality, it is now clear that physical activity, which may not be reflected in measurable increases in cardiorespiratory fitness, is indeed beneficial to health (Leon *et al.*, 1987). Additionally, there is strong evidence to suggest that the volume of activity is the key health-related dimension, irrespective of individual permutations of intensity, frequency or duration (Blair *et al.*, 1992).

## Activity and health in children

In children, relationships between activity and health are less clear. The topic has been reviewed by many authors. (For comprehensive reviews see Monotoye, 1985; Vaccaro and Mahon, 1989; Baranowski *et al.*, 1992; Bar-Or 1994; Barnard and Wen, 1994; Borer, 1995; Chilibeck Sale and Webber, 1995; Ward and Evans, 1995; Faulkner and McKay, 1996.) The most comprehensive set of reviews are those conducted for the 1994 International Consensus Conference, which established physical activity guidelines for adolescents (Sallis and Patrick, 1994). In contrast to the compelling adult data, scrutiny of the evidence in children is not encouraging – a consistent conclusion across all reviews. A synopsis of opinion is that although there are indications of beneficial associations in some areas, there is no compelling evidence that unambiguously relates childhood physical activity to childhood health, a more favourable childhood risk profile, or to later adult health (Rowland, 1991; Blair and Meredith, 1994). This is in contrast to the conventional wisdom that activity is beneficial for children.

## ◼ **Methods**

This review incorporates the results of empirical research published since the 1994 International Consensus Conference, together with relevant reviews and expert comment, in order to provide a critical overview of current knowledge in this field.

### Selection of health parameters

The major health parameters selected for review are:

- Overweight, fatness and obesity.
- Main biological CVD risk factors (lipid and lipoprotein metabolism, blood pressure).
- Skeletal health and growth.
- Other health-related risk factors.
- Tracking characteristics of physical activity.
- Musculo-skeletal injuries.

Use of the term 'fitness' is controversial. Numerous studies have used fitness as the outcome measure of choice in exercise training studies, but its role as a predictor of health status, especially in children, is unclear. Papers using fitness as a health parameter have not been included.

### The search process

Papers published during and after 1992 were located, thus providing a degree of overlap with the 1994 Consensus Conference reviews. The following search strategy was utilised:

- Search of Medline electronic database, using search headings: child/adolescence; exercise; obesity; lipids; skeletal health; blood pressure; and injury.

Various combinations of terms were used. Health was not included as a search category as interpretations of the term's meaning varies, and key papers can be missed. Rather, personal judgement was used to decide on each paper's relevance to health. Further searches using the key word 'exercise' and the various health parameters were also made.

- Search of personal files.
- Cross-checking of reference lists in key papers.
- Cross-checking of reference lists in major reviews.
- Personal requests to known authors in the field.

From the original search, covering 1992 to 1997, over 1000 titles were located and examined for relevant health contexts. Approximately 200 papers were identified as having a health context, and the abstracts were obtained and scrutinised. Additional titles were located from conference proceedings and book chapters. Full papers were obtained as appropriate.

### Inclusion criteria

Papers were examined according to the following criteria:

- Empirical papers published in peer-reviewed sources, and clearly measuring either an *association* between physical activity (or surrogate measure) and one of the selected health parameters, or measuring *tracking* of physical activity. Papers 'in press' were also included.

- Non-empirical papers (reviews, editorials and informed comment) were included if they were clearly based on empirical evidence.

■ Materials from other related fields of study were included where they helped to clarify major issues.

A final selection process was undertaken according to originality, design, methodology, size, population group, scope and interpretation of results. The evidence presented is therefore a representative synopsis of previous reviews, more recent empirical studies and informed comment. Although not exhaustive, the data reviewed are representative of this diverse field of study.

## ▦ Results

### Physical activity and childhood health status

#### *Overweight and obesity*
Bar-Or and Baranowski (1994) concluded that controlled trials and cross-sectional studies showed small but significant beneficial effects of activity for both general adolescent population and obese adolescents. No effect was apparent in prospective observational studies. The authors also pointed out the considerable methodological problems associated with the assessment of activity, adiposity and energy expenditure and the problems associated with interpreting multifactor intervention studies (e.g., diet and exercise). This latter point is important, as caloric intake may be a more powerful influence on body weight than physical activity, but studies that address both parameters are sparse. Both physical activity and diet demonstrate high variability, and to measure both in the same study is logistically and analytically difficult. In the light of these limitations, Bar-

Or and Baranowski (1994) concluded that some weak associations were evident, but no threshold 'dose' of activity could be identified. They particularly emphasised the low motivation of obese adolescents for a fitness training programme, despite the evidence that fat loss can be achieved via exercise training. The results of studies published since 1992 are summarised in Table 2.1.

Although the more recent evidence is insubstantial and methodologically diverse, it does add some strength to the conclusions of previous reviewers that there may be small but significant beneficial effects, in terms of reduced fatness, as a result of increased physical activity. Interestingly, only two studies (Du Rant *et al.*, 1994; 1996) observed no effect, while others (Du Rant *et al.*, 1993; Robinson *et al.*, 1993; Wolf *et al.*, 1993; Gutin *et al.*, 1995; Boreham *et al.*, 1997) observed some effect. However, it should be pointed out that in most studies beneficial effects were not observed in all assessed parameters of obesity, and there appears to be no clear pattern across studies concerning which parameters respond consistently. The data must therefore be treated as suggestive rather than definitive.

Of particular note is the work of Must and colleagues (1992), which emphasises the importance of avoiding being overweight during adolescence. In this large, prospective study with 55 years of follow-up, being overweight in adolescence predicted a broad range of adverse health effects in adulthood that were independent of adult weight. Being overweight during adolescence appears to be a more significant predictor of a range of future diseases than being overweight as an adult. The relationships were stronger in men. These findings suggest that being overweight during adolescence is indeed a

**Table 2.1.** *Studies assessing physical activity and dimensions of overweight/obesity, 1992–97*

| Authors | Year | N | Type of subjects (years of age) | Study design | Dependent variable(s) | Independent variable(s) | Main finding(s) |
|---|---|---|---|---|---|---|---|
| **Du Rant et al.** | 1996 | 138 | Children (5–6) | Longitudinal (1 year follow-up) | Sum 7 skinfolds Waist: hip ratio | TV viewing | No significant associations Thinnest children did not watch any more television than fattest children |
| **Gutin et al.** | 1995 | 22 | Obese girls (7–11) | Intervention | Skinfold Circumferences | Physical training | Significant improvement in skinfolds and circumferences |
| **Du Rant et al.** | 1994 | 191 | Children | Observation | 7 skinfolds | TV viewing and PA | PA not associated with body composition TV watching weakly associated with PA |
| **Clarke and Lauer** | 1993 | 2631 | Children (9–18) | Longitudinal (10 year follow-up) | BMI, triceps skinfold | TV viewing and PA | Tracking coefficients: BMI 0.58–0.91, Triceps 0.26–0.58 Majority obese children became obese adults 30% obese children became lean adults |
| **Du Rant et al.** | 1993 | 123 | Children (4–5) | Cross-sectional and longitudinal | Waist:hip ratio | PA | Mean activity level inversely associated with waist:hip ratio |
| **Robinson et al.** | 1993 | 671 | Children (12 at baseline) | Cross-sectional and longitudinal | Adiposity | TV viewing | TV viewing had weak, if any, meaningful association with adiposity or change in adiposity over time |
| **Wolf et al.** | 1993 | 522 | Girls (grades 5–12) | Cross-sectional | Obesity (85th percentile BMI) | TV viewing PA (self-report) | BMI inversely associated with PA Obesity not associated with TV viewing |
| **Must et al.** | 1992 | 508 | Lean and overweight adolescents | Longitudinal | CVD morbidity CVD mortality | Overweight during adolescence | CVD mortality associated with adolescent overweight in men, but not women. CVD morbidity associated with adolescent overweight in men and women Overweight in adolescence is a more powerful predictor of CVD than overweight in adulthood |

BMI: body mass index; PA: physical activity; CVD: cardiovascular disease.

prime target from both prevention and treatment perspectives. The study of Clarke and Lauer (1993) is important as it suggests strongly that measures of obesity persist into adulthood, making overweight during adolescence a prime target for early intervention. The work done by both Must *et al.* (1992) and Clarke and Lauer (1993) indicate that obesity in childhood is significant for health. This lends credence to the view that even weak statistical associations between activity and obesity in children might be of considerable biological importance.

The studies of Du Rant *et al.* (1994, 1996), and Robinson *et al.* (1993) are also interesting as they report data relating to the influence of TV watching. However, the data are equivocal and we cannot confirm the conventional wisdom that children who watch more TV have lower activity levels. In general, studies of this kind, which evaluate activity as a preventive measure for obesity and have relevance to the majority of the child population, are sparse. It must be concluded that although there are some encouraging indications of a positive role for physical activity in the treatment of obesity, its preventive role is largely ignored and therefore dose-related recommendations are not currently possible.

There are indications that overweight and obesity in children is increasing in both the United States (Campaigne *et al.*, 1994; Troiano *et al.*, 1995; Freedman *et al.* 1997) and the UK (Chinn and Rona, 1994). There are three reasons why an increased prevalence of childhood obesity might be a major source of concern: (1) obesity is a major risk factor for insulin resistance and diabetes, hypertension, cancer, gall bladder disease and atherosclerosis (Schonfeld-Warden and Warden, 1997); (2) obesity tends to track into

adulthood (Clarke and Lauer, 1993); and (3) adults who were obese children have increased morbidity and mortality, irrespective of adult weight (Must *et al.*, 1992). For these reasons, childhood obesity should be a major target from both primary prevention and treatment perspectives.

## Physical activity and risks to the child

Concern has been expressed (van Mechelen, 1997) regarding the added potential for childhood injury resulting from a shift from free play in various types of sports to competitive participation in just one or two sports. Free play activity increases the risk of traumatic (acute) injury and it might be argued that this is acceptable in the light of the potential physical, social and psychological benefits of activity. However, too strong a focus on training for competition in a limited range of physical activities can result in the additional risk of overuse (chronic) injury. Whereas both types of injury normally heal without permanent disability, the costs must be considered in terms of activity-time lost, school-time lost, predisposition to re-occurrence, the risk (albeit small) of permanent damage and the financial cost of treatment.

Baxter-Jones, Maffulli and Helms (1993) have estimated, in elite child athletes, a one-year incidence rate of 40 injuries per 100 children, equivalent to fewer than one injury per 1000 hours of training. However, about one-third of injuries were overuse injuries, which were in turn more severe than the traumatic injuries (20 days lay-off v. 13 days). It should be emphasised that all sports and active recreational pursuits carry increased injury risk, for both adults and children, and it is a matter of personal

**Table 2.2.** *Studies assessing physical activity and cardiovasular disease risk factors, 1992–97*

| Authors | Year | N | Type of subjects (years of age) | Study design | Dependent variable(s) | Independent variable(s) | Main finding(s) |
|---|---|---|---|---|---|---|---|
| **Boreham** *et al.* | 1997 | 1015 | Children (12 and 15) | Cross-sectional | Blood pressure, TC, TC:HDL-C fatness | PA Sports participation | 12-year-olds: no associations observed 15-year-olds: Males – PA beneficially associated with systolic BP and TC:HDL-C Females – sports participation negatively associated with fatness |
| **Craig** *et al.* | 1996 | 49 | Girls (8–11) | Cross-sectional | TC, HDL-C, LDL-C, apo B, apo A-1 Lp (a) | (a) Moderate PA (self-report) (b) PA energy expenditure (doubly-labelled water) | Hours of PA predicted LDL-C and apo B PA energy expenditure predicted nothing |
| **Gutin** *et al.* | 1996 | 22 | Obese black girls (7–11) | Intervention | Insulin, glucose, glycohemoglobin, TC, HDL-C, TC:HDL, TG, LDL-C: apo B, Lp(a) | (a) Physical training (b) Lifestyle education | Both interventions similarly effective in improving some diabetogenic indices |
| **Harrel** *et al.* | 1996 | 1274 | 3rd and 4th grade children | Intervention | Blood pressure, TC | 8 weeks of aerobic training | No change |
| **Rowland** *et al.* | 1996 | 31 | Boys and girls (10–12) (normolipemic) | Intervention | TC, HDL-C, LDL-C, TG | 13 weeks aerobic training | No change |
| **Twisk** *et al.* | 1996 a, b, c | 181 | Boys and girls (13 at entry) | Longitudinal (15 year follow-up) | TC, HDL-C, TC:HDL-C | | Long-term exposure to PA associated with low risk profile for fatness in boys, but high risk profile for girls Tracking coefficients 0.51–0.71 Development of HDL-C positively related to daily PA |
| **Webber** *et al.* | 1996 | 4019 | Boys and girls | Intervention | TC, HDL-C, apo B | 30-month diet, exercise and non-smoking programme | No significant changes |

*continued on next page*

**Table 2.2.** continued

| Authors | Year | N | Type of subjects (years of age) | Study design | Dependent variable(s) | Independent variable(s) | Main finding(s) |
|---|---|---|---|---|---|---|---|
| **Bistritzer** *et al.* | 1995 | | Children from 40 families with parental history of MI/CVD before age 40 years | Cross-sectional | TC, LDL-C, HDL-C, TG | PA | No relationship for TC or LDL-C Relationship for TG(-ve) and HDL-C(+ve) |
| **Al-Hazzaa** *et al.* | 1996 | 91 | Preadolescent boys | Cross-sectional | TC, TG, HDL-C, LDL-C, glucose, BP | PA (HR telemetry) | No associations with lipids Inverse relationship between PA and systolic and diastolic BP |
| **Anderson** *et al.* | 1996 | 4416 | Adolescents (17) | Cross-sectional | BP | PA Sports activity | No association between PA or sports activity and BP |
| **de Visser** *et al.* | 1994 | – | Offspring of hypertensive and non-hypertensive parents | Cross-sectional | Habitual PA (self-report) | Hypertension | No difference between 'at risk' and 'not at risk' children |
| **Dwyer and Gibbons** | 1994 | 1919 | Boys and girls (9, 12 and 15) | Cross-sectional | TC, TG, HDL-C | PWC 170/kg LBM | No association with lipids Weak, negative association with systolic BP |
| **Raitakari** *et al.* | 1994 | 961 | Children (12, 15 and 18 at baseline) | Longitudinal (6 year follow-up) | Insulin, TG, HDL-C, HDL-C:TC | PA (self-report) | Children classified inactive at all three measurements had higher insulin and TG, and worse HDL:TC (boys) and higher adiposity and TG (girls) Change in PA over 6 years inversely related to change in insulin and TG (boys) |
| **Suter and Hawes** | 1993 | 97 | Boys and girls (10–15) | Cross-sectional | TC, TG, HDL-C, LDL-C, VLDL-C, TC:HDL-C, Apo A-1, Apo B, Lp (a) | PA (self-report) | Boys: PA related to HDL-C (+ve), VLDL-C (-ve), TG (-ve), and TC:HDL-C (-ve) Girls: PA related to HDL-C (+ve), PA a significant predictor of HDL-C, apo A-1, TG and VLDL-C |
| **Jenner** *et al.* | 1992 | 1311 | Boys and girls (12) | Cross-setional | BP | PA (self-report) | Inverse relationship in boys but not in girls |

TC: total cholesterol; TG: triglyceride; apo A: apoprotein A; apo B: apoprotein B; HDL-C: high density lipoprotein cholesterol; LDL-C: low density lipoprotein-cholesterol; LDL-C: low density lipoprotein cholesterol; PA: physical activity; BP: blood pressure; Lp (a) lipoprotein (a); HR: heart rate; PWC: physical work capacity; LBM: lean body mass; MI: myocardial infarction; CVD: cardiovasular disease.

judgement as to how the risks and benefits are balanced. However, there is the moral issue of at what stage the child is capable of making such personal judgements. With younger children, parents and coaches have to make such decisions.

## Physical activity and childhood health risk factors

### *Modifiable, biological risk factors for CVD*

Blood pressure and lipids/lipoproteins are included in this section as many studies assess these parameters concurrently. Armstrong and Simons-Morton (1994) concluded in their review that data suggesting a beneficial effect of activity on lipids and lipoproteins are minimal, although there is a suggestion in some studies that high-density lipoprotein cholesterol (HDL-C) concentrations might be enhanced. Alpert and Wilmore (1994) concluded that exercise training had only a weak relationship with blood pressure within the normal range, but aerobic-type training consistently reduced both systolic and diastolic blood pressure in hypertensive adolescents, but not to normal levels. The results of studies published since 1992 are summarised in Table 2.2.

For lipids and lipoproteins, six studies (Al-Hazzaa, *et al.*, 1994; de Visser *et al.*, 1994; Dwyer and Gibbons, 1994; Harrell *et al.*, 1996; Rowland *et al.*, 1996; Webber *et al.*, 1996) show no association with measures of activity. Five studies (Suter and Hawes, 1993; Bistritzer *et al.*, 1995; Boreham *et al.*, 1997; Craig *et al.*, 1996; Gutin *et al.*, 1996) show some associations, but the patterns of association are inconsistent. There is no suggestion that associations are more likely if initial levels are abnormal.

For blood pressure, two studies (Anderson, 1994; de Visser *et al.*, 1994) report no association. Six studies (Jenner, Vandongen and Beilin, 1992; Al-Hazzaa *et al.*, 1994; Dwyer and Gibbons, 1994; Harrell *et al.*, 1996; Webber *et al.*, 1996; Boreham *et al.*, 1997) report a positive association. Again, there is no suggestion that associations are more likely in subjects with initially abnormal levels.

Two studies are of particular note. Boreham *et al.*, 1997 investigated a large, nationally representative probability sample of over 1000 children in Northern Ireland. No associations between activity and either blood pressure or lipid/lipoprotein levels were detected in 12-year-olds and only weak associations in 15-year-olds. The Child and Adolescent Trial for Cardiovascular Health (CATCH) study (Webber *et al.*, 1996) assessed total cholesterol and blood pressure in over 4000 children in a 30-month multicentre, multidisciplinary intervention study. No significant differences between control and intervention schools were observed. That these two large and rigorous studies, carrying high levels of statistical power, detected either no or weak associations is striking, and we have to conclude that, in children and youth, physical activity as defined and assessed in these studies, has only weak associations with serum lipid and lipoprotein concentrations and with blood pressure.

### *Skeletal health and growth*

Bailey and Martin (1994) concluded that our knowledge about the long-term effects of physical activity on bone accretion is incomplete, although they identified some beneficial effects of activity on children's skeletal health. Comparison of sports groups with non-sports groups led the authors to comment that physical activity must be vigorous if it is to enhance bone mineral density (BMD) in children.

**Table 2.3.** *Studies assessing physical activity and dimensions of skeletal health/growth, 1992-97*

| Authors | Year | N | Type of subjects (years of age) | Study design | Dependent variable(s) | Independent variable(s) | Main finding(s) |
|---|---|---|---|---|---|---|---|
| **Cooper et al.** | 1995 | 153 | Women (21) (retrospective data obtained from birth and school records) | Retrospective | Bone mass | Outdoor sports at school | Outdoor sports at school associated with higher bone mass at 21 years of age |
| **VandenBergh et al.** | 1995 | 1359 | Boys and girls, (7–11) | Cross-sectional | BMC | PA (self-report) | No association between PA and BMC Significant difference in BMC between extremes of activity (boys only) |
| **Malina et al.** | 1994 | 332 | Active and inactive boys and sports participation | Longitudinal | Attained stature Timing of PHV Rate of growth in stature Age at menarche | Regular PA Sports partipation Training for sport | No differences between active and inactive boys in any parameter |
| **Slemenda et al.** | 1994 | 90 | White children (6–14 at entry) | Longitudinal | BMD | PA (self-report) | PA associated with more rapid bone mineralisation |
| **Valimaki et al.** | 1994 | 264 | Children (9–18) | Longitudinal | BMD | Lifestyle factors (inc. PA) | Regular exercise is an independent predictor of BMD |
| **Welten et al.** | 1994 | 182 | Children (13 at entry) | Longitudinal | BMD | Weight bearing PA | Regular weight bearing activity in adolescence and young adulthood is more strongly associated with BMD than dietary calcium intake |
| **Conroy et al.** | 1993 | 36 | Junior weightlifters (17) | Cross-sectional | BMD | Weightlifting | BMD values greater than controls |
| **Grimston et al.** | 1993 | 34 | Children (13) | Cross-sectional | BMD | Impact sports v. non-impact sports | Impact sports children had higher BMD |
| **Rice et al.** | 1993 | 35 | Girls (14–18) | Cross-sectional | BMC | PA | No association between habitual PA and BMC |
| **Beunen et al.** | 1992 | 64 | Boys (13) | Longitudinal (3 year follow -up) | Somatic growth, biological maturation and physical performance | Sports participation | No association between increased sports participation and any outcome measure |

BMC: bone mineral content; PA: physical activity; BMD: bone mineral density; PHV: peak height velocity.

They also noted the deleterious effects of immobility and inactivity, especially the absence of weight bearing activity on the skeleton, and recommended that regular short bursts of intense activity were better than irregular, prolonged activity. The results of studies published since 1992 are summarised in Table 2.3.

The studies listed in Table 2.3, with a few exceptions, lend support to the view that activity can enhance a range of parameters related to skeletal health in children. Although three studies (Beunen *et al.*, 1992; Rice *et al.*, 1993; Malina, 1994a) show no association, seven studies (Conroy *et al.*, 1993; Grimston, Willows and Hanley, 1993; Slemenda *et al.*, 1994; Valimaki *et al.*, 1994; Cooper *et al.*, 1995; Welten *et al.*, 1994; VandenBerg *et al.*, 1995) show positive associations. It is tempting to presume that low impact activity or lifestyle activity – more easily misreported than vigorous activity – might have weaker associations, but this is not the case. Beneficial associations, although weak, can be observed for activities related to lifestyle as well as for impact sports.

In a large study (n=1359), Vanden-Bergh *et al.* (1995) found no association between skeletal health and physical activity when the whole group was assessed, but a significant difference in bone mineral content (BMC) was observed when extremes of activity in boys were examined. It may be that large volumes of activity need to be performed in order to produce a measurable response, or that large volumes of activity are more likely to contain significant amounts of high impact activity which might be more effective in promoting bone growth. Although there are limited data to illustrate this in children, whose skeletons are still maturing, the study of Grimston *et al.* (1993) suggests that the

impact load of an activity may indeed be of considerable significance. In this cross-sectional study 17 children aged 12-13 years, who were regularly competing in weight-bearing sports producing impact loads of at least three times body weight (running, gymnastics, tumbling and dance) were compared with 17 competitive swimmers matched for race, gender, pubertal stage, body weight and average daily training time. In effect, equal volumes of external impact (striking) activities were being compared with internal muscular strain activities. 'Impact load' children were found to have significantly higher BMD at the femoral neck, and a tendency for higher BMD at the lumbar spine. In the light of these findings, the authors suggest that for a sport/activity to have the potential to maximise BMD in children, it must exceed an as yet unknown threshold level of strain. It may be that activities which produce strain on the bone by impact have a higher capacity to approach this threshold than activities which produce strain solely through muscular contraction.

It can be concluded that although associations between activity and various measures of skeletal health in children are weak, there are indications that some of the more natural play-like activities of children that involve running, skipping and jumping may indeed be beneficial to bone health.

### Other risk factors

A number of papers were located that assess health-related parameters not covered in the preceding sections. These are summarised in Table 2.4.

These studies again offer limited evidence of a beneficial association with physical activity. It may be of particular importance to note the existence of

**Table 2.4.** *Studies assessing physical activity and other health risk factors, 1992–97*

| Authors | Year | N | Type of subjects (years of age) | Study design | Dependent variable(s) | Independent variable(s) | Main finding(s) |
|---|---|---|---|---|---|---|---|
| **Kahle et al.** | 1996 | 7 | Obese adolescent males (mean 13.3) | Intervention | Glucose, insulin C-peptide | PA (15 week mild intensity exercise) | PA resulted in increased hepatic insulin clearance |
| **Norgren et al.** | 1994 | 88<br>55 | Adolescents (12–22)<br>IDDM adolescents | Lab. test – experimental | BP response to exercise | Exercise | IDDM subjects had more marked BP increase as a response to exercise than healthy controls |
| **Taimela et al.** | 1994 | 2464 | Children and young adults (9–24) | Longitudinal Cross-sectional data reported in this paper) | Lp(a) | PA | PA is associated with favourable levels of Lp(a) |
| **Saito et al.** | 1992 | 2136 | Young obese subjects with hypertension Normotensive controls | Lab. test – experimental | Glucose: insulin (G:I) ratio Fasting insulin concentation Insulin response to oral glucose | PA | PA positively associated with G:I ratio and fasting insulin |

IDDM: insulin dependent diabetes mellitus; Lp(a) lipoprotein(a); PA: physical activity; BP: blood pressure.

studies that show a beneficial effect of physical activity on parameters related to insulin metabolism (Saito *et al.*, 1992; Kahle *et al.*, 1996). While insulin-related parameters may not be considered classical risk factors, they may have significant health consequences. This is a rapidly developing field of research. In particular there is now a recognised 'metabolic syndrome' or 'syndrome X' (Reaven, 1988), encompassing obesity, hypertension, hypertriglyceridaemia, depressed HDL-C and glucose intolerance or hyperinsulinaemia. It may be that this clustering of abnormal metabolic parameters will be an important aspect of future physical activity research, as activity has been shown to impact on each of these factors, at least in adults.

## Tracking characteristics of physical activity

In the preceding sections, physical activity has been considered as an independent variable that influences other health parameters. However, physical activity is also a behavioural risk factor for CVD in its own right. Strictly speaking, it is not the lack of activity that is the risk factor but the associated adverse biological effects of the inactivity. However, because the specific biological mechanisms through which inactivity exerts its effects are unknown, the assessment of physical activity as an independent risk factor *per se* is important. Despite weak associations between physical activity and the classical risk factors in youth, the case for measuring activity remains strong because of potential biological actions via other, as yet unidentified, pathways.

For this reason, the phenomenon of tracking of physical activity over time is potentially of great importance. Tracking of activity has been comprehensively

reviewed by Malina (1996). He concludes that activity tracks at weak to moderate levels during adolescence, from adolescence into adulthood and across various ages during adulthood. Studies assessing the tracking characteristics of physical activity are summarised in Table 2.5.

All of the studies reported in Table 2.5 show at least weak levels of tracking. These data demand careful examination, as the majority of studies have used self-report methodology. It might be presumed that children's cognitive abilities improve during longitudinal studies, which in turn will be reflected in their performance on self-report physical activity questionnaires. There is a logical argument that differential rates of cognitive development between individuals might be reflected in large differences in measurement error between individuals, thus adversely affecting tracking correlations. It is therefore interesting to note that the study with the strongest tracking correlations (Pate *et al.*, 1996) is the only study to use an objective measure of physical activity (heart rate).

## ■ Discussion

### The overall picture

The most striking feature of the available research is that there exists some evidence of positive associations between children's activity and certain health parameters, but these are usually weak. Tracking data, although exhibiting some consistency, also show weak effects. No single study, or set of studies, provides definitive evidence for a meaningful health gain through being an active child. In other words, we cannot yet provide strong empirical evidence that activity during childhood has a

**Table 2.5.** *Studies assessing tracking characteristics of physical activity, 1992-97*

| Authors | Year | N | Type of subjects (years of age) | Study design | Dependent variable(s) | Independent variable(s) | Main finding(s) |
|---|---|---|---|---|---|---|---|
| **Malina et al.** | 1996 | | | Review | PA | | PA tracks at low to moderate levels during adolescence, from adolescence into adulthood and through various stages of adulthood |
| **Pate et al.** | 1996 | 47 | Children (3–4 at entry) | Longitudinal (3 year follow-up) | PA (HR telemetry) | | Tracking correlations 0.57–0.66 |
| **Sallis et al.** | 1995 | 351 | Children (mean 4.4) | Longitudinal (2 year follow-up) | PA | | Weak tracking of PA (r = 0.15–0.36) |
| **Van Mechelen and Kemper** | 1995 | 182 | Chidren (13 at entry) | Longitudinal (15 year follow-up) | PA | | No tracking over total period in boys (r = 0.10) or girls (r = 0.21) Weak tracking over shorter time periods within study period (max. r = 0.58) |
| **Kelder et al.** | 1994 | 237 | Children (6th grade at entry – 1983) | Longitudinal (6 year follow-up) | PA | | Significant tracking reported for tertiles of activity |
| **Raitakari et al.** | 1994 | 961 | Children (12, 15 and 18 at baseline) | Longitudinal (6 year follow-up) | Physical activity (self-report) | | Significant tracking of PA (0.35–0.54 boys; 0.33–0.39 girls) |
| **Telama et al.** | 1994 | 3596 | Children and adolescents (3–18 at entry; 9–18 year-olds only used in this analysis) | Longitudinal (9 year follow-up) | PA (self-report) | | PA during youth is weak predictor of PA 9 years later |
| **Kuh and Cooper** | 1992 | 3000+ | Men and women followed from birth | Longitudinal (36 year follow-up) | Adult PA Sports ability at 13 years, energy level at 15 years | | Teacher rating of sports ability at 13 years and 'energy level' at 15 years are associated with PA at 36 years |
| **Twisk et al.** | 1997 | 181 | Boys and girls (13 at entry) | Longitudinal (14 year follow-up) | PA (interview) | | Stability coefficients: lifestyle factors (except smoking) 0.33–0.42 (PA 0.34) |

PA: physical activity; HR: heart rate.

major impact on the current or future health status of children.

The inconclusive nature of the evidence might be construed as disappointing, but it should also be pointed out that the associations which do exist tend to be in the 'healthy' direction, and also that in no case is there evidence of no association. The weakest evidence is that relating activity to lipid and lipoprotein levels and to blood pressure when the children's baseline levels are in the normal range, a result which might be expected.

In the absence of definitive data on children, and in the face of strong adult data, it is important to rationalise exactly why the data are not more compelling. In particular, we need to address the issue of whether the weak associations seen in children are an indication that it is adult activity levels which are the most important, or whether the existence of even small associations at such an early age is of considerable biological importance. In order to do this, the evidence needs to be considered with respect to concepts and issues which directly impinge on this field of study.

## Why are the data so weak?

### *Are we measuring at an inappropriate life stage?*

The primary morbidities which affect humans occur almost exclusively in middle and old age, and cannot be used as endpoints in paediatric studies. The possible exception to this might be obesity, which can be considered a health-compromising condition for children in its own right. However, temporarily ignoring social and psychological factors, it is probably the physiological consequences of chronic obesity (e.g. diabetes, hyperlipidemia, joint problems) that are the true physical health endpoints. Compared to

adults, most children are inherently healthy, even in the face of a sedentary lifestyle. It is clear that the majority of lifestyle-related chronic diseases have had insufficient time to become apparent, and it may also be that the classical risk factors themselves are an incomplete set of markers for future disease.

Within this uncertainty it is normal to use the classical risk factors, especially those for CVD, as the main health-related endpoints in children. As previously discussed, there are three main reasons for assessing activity levels during childhood: promoting healthy growth and development; retarding the development of precursors of chronic disease; and establishing a health habit that can be maintained throughout life. The latter reason may be particularly significant because the strongest relationships between activity and health are seen in adults, and if activity levels track, then interventions during childhood will be of great importance. Although there exist some data to indicate moderate tracking of physiological risk factors (Berenson *et al.*, 1980), there are only two studies that have measured tracking of activity in a rigorous manner over an appreciable length of time (Raitakiri *et al.*, 1994; Twisk *et al.*, 1997). Both the Amsterdam Growth and Health Study and the Cardiovascular Risk in Young Finns Study report weak to moderate, but significant, tracking coefficients. They are, however unable to provide conclusive evidence of meaningful levels of persistence in this behaviour.

### *Are we measuring inappropriate dimensions of physical activity?*

As pointed out by previous authors (Corbin, Pangrazi and Welk, 1994; Riddoch and Boreham, 1995; Pangrazi,

Corbin and Welk, 1996), the selection of differing dimensions of activity as 'health-related parameters', and the selection of arbitrary levels within those dimensions as 'health-related thresholds', can lead to gross inconsistencies between studies, and possibly erroneous interpretation of results by the authors. In this respect, the work of Welk (1994) has shown only 17% of children achieved a criterion level of activity based on exercise training criteria (heart rate sustained above 140 bpm for 20 min.). However, when a health-related criterion level is applied to the same data (activity equivalent to 4 $kcal \cdot kg^{-1} \cdot day^{-1}$), 99% of boys and 98% of girls achieved this level (Corbin *et al.*, 1994). Such discrepancies are common within the paediatric exercise literature and relate to how the results of the studies reviewed in this chapter should be interpreted. Of particular note is the ubiquitous use of adult cardiovascular fitness training criteria as the level for intervention or threshold, compared to the very few studies that adopt volume of activity as the criterion. If inappropriate criteria are applied, misclassification of individuals will be a significant problem which will distort both the results and their interpretation.

In this respect, the last decade has seen a 'paradigm shift' regarding the type and amount of physical activity which is necessary to achieve and maintain optimal health status, at least in adults. In the light of accumulating evidence from observational studies, guidelines for healthy activity now relate more to the accumulation of activity than to a specific, fitness-oriented exercise prescription (Sallis and Patrick, 1994; Pate *et al.*, 1995; Department of Health and Social Services, 1996; US Department of Health and Human Services, 1996). Such a change of emphasis is crucial to the way in which the evidence relating to children should be

interpreted. Most of the studies included in this review have concentrated on the effects of exercise training. We now have a greater need for evidence relating to other dimensions of physical activity, in particular accumulated moderate intensity activity. The four classical elements of activity, as encompassed by the FITT principle, are frequency, intensity, time and type – each of which can be manipulated within a fitness-training programme. In terms of health, it might be augmented, or even replaced, by the 'volume' dimension of activity. This is crucial if we are to understand children's health-related activity, because of the unique and spontaneous nature of children's activity patterns. Although not the brief of this chapter it is important to note that children's activities tend to be sporadic rather than sustained (see Chapter 4). Further, as this type of activity involves numerous short, eminently forgettable activity bouts, it probably cannot be assessed via activity recall methodology. Objective methods are probably the only valid measure of children's activity patterns. Thus, it is likely that studies based on self-reports greatly underestimate associations between physical activity and health parameters.

### Are we barking up the wrong tree?

Simple observation tells us that young children are highly and spontaneously active (Rowland, 1990; Astrand, 1994), and Blair (1992) has suggested that not only are the majority of children generally fitter and more active than adults, but also they are active enough to receive most of the important health benefits from their activity. Strong *et al.* (1992) have defined the active child as one who 'participates in physical education classes, plays sports, performs regular household chores, spends recreational time outdoors, and regularly travels by foot or bicycle.' Therefore, an alternative explanation for the weak associations in this field might be that most children are already optimally active, as reflected by their high levels of aerobic fitness (Blair and Meredith, 1994; Corbin *et al.*, 1994).

As previously discussed, the application of inappropriate activity thresholds to children may have seriously distorted our interpretation of the available 'evidence' relating to how active children are. If this is the case, and levels of activity are at or near the optimum level, then the addition of a physical activity programme will have little further impact on health status or risk factor profile. However, it is currently unclear whether children under- or overestimate their activity as assessed by self-report. It is interesting to note that the previous reviews of activity and lipids (Armstrong and Simons-Morton, 1994) and activity and blood pressure (Alpert and Wilmore, 1994) have suggested that it is the children with initially poor levels who tend to achieve benefit. While such observations may reflect a degree of regression to the mean, it is also possible that initially normal levels of risk factors, as observed in the majority of children, are not modifiable – they are already optimal, and expectations of 'improvement' are misplaced. This relates importantly to the concept of an optimal level of activity as an alternative to the frequently held assumption that 'more is always better'. As Blair and Meredith (1994) have stated, 'there is something illogical about an emphasis on striving to develop high levels of fitness in children and youth when most are already active and fit'.

However, despite the above, there is evidence of substantial declines in activity post-puberty, until by the end of adolescence children exhibit the low activity levels of adults (Riddoch *et al.*, 1991). This decline in activity can partly be considered a natural phenomenon, and can be seen throughout the animal kingdom (Fagan, 1981), and therefore the true health implications are unclear. However, it may be the case that even active children are gradually socialised, as they grow up, into a sedentary adult lifestyle. It should also be stated that the supposition that most children are sufficiently active is not the conventional wisdom. For example, Bar-Or and Baranowski (1994) conclude that 'the increase in adiposity of North American adolescents in the 1970s and 1980s suggests that current levels of activity are insufficient'.

Whichever is the case, there is a need for more accurate methods for assessing levels of children's physical activity. In particular, there is a need to assess more accurately, via objective methods, the type of activity accumulated by children via their typically sporadic activity patterns.

### Is the exercise training philosophy too pervasive?

The suggestion that exercise training is not a cornerstone of health-related activity is based on epidemiological evidence of relatively recent origin, which may be the reason why habitual 'free living' activity has been largely ignored. It is therefore important to consider how both exercise training and moderate activity may trigger different physiological responses, and to discuss the potential health effects of each. The primary physiological aims of exercise training are to improve the capacity of the heart to deliver fuel and oxygen, and the capacity of the skeletal muscles to extract them. The structural and functional changes in the heart may carry health benefits in their own right (Starnes and Bowles, 1995), but there are other important health-related parameters that can be affected. Such parameters include lipid, lipoprotein and apoprotein concentrations, insulin resistance, clotting factors, fibrinolytic factors, blood pressure, bone health, excessive fatness and psychological factors. Many of the latter group of adaptations are thought to occur at levels of activity below those necessary to achieve improvements in cardiovascular fitness. While the two categories of adaptation to activity may occur concurrently with vigorous exercise training, it is entirely possible that the physiological stimuli and threshold levels for each may differ. The exercise training adaptations may not be directly related to, nor necessary for, disease prevention (Cureton, 1987; Seefeldt and Vogel, 1987; Haskell, 1994b ). Haemodynamic and biochemical changes, termed 'metabolic fitness' by Barnard and Wen (1994), may not manifest themselves as improvements in cardiovascular fitness, but may be the crucial links between activity and health.

Bailey and Martin (1994) have argued that, for skeletal health, regular short bursts of intense activity are better than irregular, prolonged activity. This is supported by data from animal studies which suggest that optimal growth is encouraged by spontaneous activity, rather than extremes of caging or enforced activity (Ring, Bosch and Chu-Shek, 1970). Further, Haskell (1994a) has suggested that the health benefits of activity may accrue from repeated acute physiological responses to individual bouts of activity, rather than from true chronic adaptations to long-term activity. If this 'last bout effect' is real, this would indicate that the frequency of activity may be the key variable, rather than the intensity or the duration. Children, therefore, might be optimally active in health terms because of the sporadic nature of their activity.

Cale and Harris (1993) have pointed out that from a behavioural perspective physical activity needs to be seen by children as an achievable and positive experience, and that adult fitness training guidelines, emphasising continuous bouts of vigorous exercise, do not fulfil this. The studies of Epstein, Wing and colleagues (Epstein *et al.*, 1982, 1985; Jakicic, Wing and Robertson, 1995) indicate that intermittent activity promotes better adherence than sustained activities in both children and adults. The American Heart Association (Strong *et al.*, 1992) have issued a special report which suggests that integrated cardiovascular health promotion in childhood should emphasise play, rather than exercise. It seems, therefore, that we have strong arguments, if not evidence, that the sporadic, spontaneous activity patterns of children may be fundamentally healthy and more efficacious than exercise training.

We might ask whether exercise training is a behaviourally viable recommendation, as it is not part of the lifestyle of many individuals. Less than 10% of adults perform this type of exercise (Caspersen, Christenson and Pollard, 1986; Health Education Authority and Sports Council, 1992; Stephens and Caspersen, 1994) and it is becoming increasingly clear that neither will children (Armstrong and Bray, 1991; Armstrong *et al.*, 1991). Corbin *et al.* (1994) have pointed out that it is only in the last few decades that the scientific community has accepted that children are actually capable of performing vigorous exercise safely. We appear to have imposed a recently discovered form of being active upon children and forgotten about their more natural and spontaneous form of exercise – play. Of further note is that where exercise training has been studied, it is equally plausible that any observed effects are due to the *volume* of activity, rather than the specific combination of frequency, intensity and time. In addition it is not clear whether exercise training results in 'compensatory sloth'. In other words, does the fatigue resulting from strenuous exercise compromise the volume of lifestyle activity? However, Blaak *et al.* (1992) have suggested that this is not the case.

## Is the methodology weak?

The weakness of the observed associations is further compounded by our inability to infer cause and effect in all but a few small-scale intervention studies. In order to infer cause and effect we must apply the following criteria (Bradford Hill and Hill, 1991):

■ Strength of the observed association.

■ Specificity of the association.

■ Existence of a dose-response relationship.

■ Consistency of findings between studies.

■ Independence of effect from recognised confounding variables.

■ Correct temporal sequencing.

■ Biological plausibility.

It is doubtful whether the data currently available satisfy the majority of these criteria.

The assessment of activity – a complex and infinitely variable behaviour – is also problematic and as previously mentioned many studies rely on self-report methodology, which may be inappropriate for many children. The cognitive abilities of children are more limited than adults and the related problems of inaccurate recall are well known. In large epidemiological studies there is no alternative, but it is disturbing to see self-report used in many smaller studies, where misclassification is a serious limiting factor. A related issue is the use of recall methods *per se*. They can only assess the type of activity which is memorable – for example, premeditated exercise sessions, sports, games or long walks and rides. Many questionnaires are designed specifically to do this. Shorter sessions, for example, walking between classes, or upstairs, will not be recalled. As children generally exercise sporadically it is apparent that self-report has particular weaknesses for assessing children's activity patterns. It is likely that such methodological weaknesses, possibly resulting in high levels of measurement error, will misclassify many children, inevitably reducing the strength of any observed associations. It might also be argued that the lack of sensitivity in all current methods of assessing activity is a major limiting factor in that we are unable to detect subtle differences in activity which, in health terms, may be of importance. For example, the addition of a short daily walk to one's daily routine may be masked by measurement deficiencies, but important health benefits might accrue, such as weight reduction.

A final limitation of studies reported to date is the tendency for authors to discuss only the significant changes or associations observed in their studies, and to deal very briefly with, or ignore, the non-significant findings. While this is understandable, there is an inescapable need to explain why various health-related parameters show associations in some studies but not in others, and also why few consistent patterns can be observed across studies.

## Healthy levels of activity

In terms of future research efforts, there is a need to establish a common health-related level of activity. Blair *et al* (1989b) have suggested that a minimum activity energy expenditure of 3-4 kcal·kg⁻¹·day⁻¹, a level known to be associated with a variety of health benefits and with reduced mortality in adults (Paffenbarger *et al.*, 1986; Leon *et al.*, 1987), may also be considered appropriate for children. Cureton (1994) suggests that this represents approximately 100 kcal of activity energy expenditure per day for a 34 kg boy or girl, or alternatively 20-40 min of accumulated moderate intensity activity per day. High intensity activity is not required in order to meet this guideline. Corbin *et al.* (1994) have suggested that 6-8 kcal·kg⁻¹·day⁻¹ is more appropriate for children, and is easily achievable as it translates into approximately 60 minutes of activity per day. This level carries additional health benefits and may be close to an optimum level, at least in adults.

## The need for an ecological perspective

Children accrue activity through sporadic engagement in a wide variety of activities – chasing, climbing, wrestling, playground games – all of which may contribute to improvement in many aspects of health. It is a challenge for investigators to assess children's physical activity taking full account of its true nature. Sallis, McKenzie and Alcaraz (1993) have highlighted the need for studies that assess the variety of activities in which children engage and the environments in which they are naturally performed. Measurement of the multifaceted nature of children's play, recreation and habitual activity must feature prominently in future research. It may be that addressing the nature of children's activity in their natural environment will provide common ground and the strongest links

between physiology, epidemiology, behavioural psychology and public health.

It is an attractive and plausible thought that the optimal level of physical activity for humans may be, in reality, a full day's play as a child, and a full day's physical labour as an adult. There are powerful influences to restrict both of these, but maybe these are the activity goals, or at least an activity equivalent, for which children and adults should strive.

## Interpretation and evaluation

There is a compelling logic which dictates that because we have substantial evidence from adult studies indicating the significant health impact of physical activity on the human organism, it would be a mistake to presume that young age negates such benefits. The lack of strong relationships in childhood does not mean that activity will fail to prevent the development of risk factors, and the improvement of health status, in adulthood. It might be said that, with respect to activity/health relationships in children, absence of evidence should not be taken as evidence of absence. Gutin and Owens (1996) have pointed out the consequences of being wrong in each of two possible scenarios. The presumption that physical activity promotes health in children will involve commitment of scarce resources that will be wasted if subsequent research indicates no health effect. Alternatively, if we presume no health effect, and do not promote activity, then the future health of children may be compromised if research indicates an effect.

## Related issues

It is difficult to find any studies that have compared the effects of more than one 'dose' of activity in children. Notable exceptions are those of Epstein *et al.* (1982, 1985), who have reported that programmed aerobic exercise was less effective in promoting weight loss than lifestyle activity, principally through improved adherence. Bailey (1995) has observed that children are often resistant to high intensity activity. Further, Pangrazi *et al.* (1996) have observed that children's activity is characterised by alternating movement and recovery; and it is interesting to note that this form of activity is conducive to optimal growth and development (Bailey and Martin, 1994).

Also it should be borne in mind just where physical activity is located within the wide range of influences on children's health. Without a grasp of the 'wider picture' it is difficult to determine a role for physical activity. If we are positively to affect the health of children through physical activity, it is crucial to understand that the behavioural and environmental influences on risk factors are established early in life (World Health Organization, 1990). Currently there is an incomplete understanding of the nature and strength of such influences in childhood, their synergistic effects, how they influence risk factors and how they vary with age, sex, culture and ethnicity. In order to improve the long-term health of youth and adults it is both prudent and critical to adopt primary prevention strategies during childhood (World Health Organization, 1990).

There is a need discover and explain: (a) the complex relationships between personal, lifestyle and environmental parameters that influence health risk; (b) the relationships between these parameters and the physiological risk factors; and (c) how these relationships vary between cultures and ethnic groups. In this way a more complete understanding of health risk in children can be ascertained and the scientific rationale for future primary prevention initiatives in children can be retained.

# ◼ Conclusions

The lack of definitive evidence on physical activity and its association with the physical health of youth is disappointing, but, as already discussed, it can be rationalised from a combination of biological, epidemiological, behavioural and conceptual perspectives. Blair *et al.* (1989a) have stated that the specific goal of exercise promotion in children is not the production of health outcomes. Rather, it is to establish regular exercise habits that will persist throughout life. Rowland (1991) has argued that only regular exercise, which is conducted over many years into adulthood can be expected to produce long-term salutary effects, and the lack of current definitive evidence is not inconsistent with this concept.

It is likely that, at least for the foreseeable future, we must rely at least as much on theory, common sense, observation and expert opinion as on hard evidence. This is necessary because, as Newman and Strong (1978) have stated,

> Prevention of the development of fibrous plaques in the coronary arteries would stop the modern epidemic of coronary heart disease ... The time to initiate programs of prevention is, at the latest, the third decade, probably the second decade, and perhaps even the first decade of life.

It may be that, as Blair *et al.*, (1989a) have suggested, activity guidelines for children should focus primarily on the establishment of activity *habits*. This avoids the thorny question of how much activity is *necessary* (Rowland, 1996) and the temptation to adopt definitive guidelines based on weak and inconsistent evidence. It also avoids the need to demonstrate significant associations between activity and health risk factors at a stage of life where such associations may not be observable, at least using current methodologies.

## What we know

- The conceptual, biological and behavioural plausibility that physical activity is a healthful pursuit for children is high.

- The evidence confirming a positive association between childhood activity and the immediate or future health status of children is suggestive, but weak.

- Methodological and conceptual problems may partly explain the weak evidence.

- The most positive evidence comes from studies of children with abnormal levels of the health-related parameters. This may be informative in terms of activity as treatment (the minority), but does not inform us about activity as prevention (the majority).

- There is a lack of definitive evidence that active children will become active adults.

- All activity carries an element of risk, especially for musculo-skeletal injury. However, the incidence in children is low and should be balanced against the potential physical, social and psychological health benefits.

## What we need to know

- Do the tracking characteristics of various dimensions of activity differ?

- What are the health benefits of different types and volumes of activity?

- There is a need to investigate children's activity from an ecological perspective – that is, assessing total activity in natural settings. This demands the use of objective measures of activity, rather than self-report questionnaires

- Can we base recommendations for activity on the limited evidence, when there are so many factors that limit its interpretation?

- Is fitness important for health in youth, independent of physical activity?

- How much trust should we place in the strong adult data, compared to the weak child data? Are the biological effects of activity (or inactivity) likely to differ between adults and children?

- What are the relationships between physical activity and other, newly identified, health-related physiological parameters?

# ■ References

**Al-Hazzaa, H.M., Sulaiman, M.A., Al-Matar, A.J. and Al-Mobaireek, K.F.** (1994). Cardiorespiratory fitness, physical activity patterns and coronary risk factors in preadolescent boys. *International Journal of Sports Medicine*, **15**, 267–72.

**Alpert, B.S. and Wilmore, J.H.** (1994). Physical activity and blood pressure in adolescents. *Pediatric Exercise Science*, **6**, 361-80.

**Anderson, L.B.** (1994). Blood pressure, physical fitness and physical activity in 17-year-old Danish adolescents. *Journal of Internal Medicine*, **236**, 323–30.

**Armstrong, N. and Bray, S.** (1991). Physical activity patterns defined by continuous heart rate monitoring. *Archives of Disease in Childhood*, **66**, 245–7.

**Armstrong, N. and Simons-Morton, B.** (1994). Physical activity and blood lipids in adolescents. *Pediatric Exercise Science*, **6**, 381–405.

**Armstrong, N., Williams, J., Balding, J., Gentle, P. and Kirby, B.** (1991). Cardiopulmonary fitness, physical activity patterns, and selected coronary risk factor variables in 11- to 16-year-olds. *Pediatric Exercise Science*, **3**, 219–28.

**Astrand, P.-O.** (1994). Physical activity and fitness: evolutionary perspective and trends for the future. In C. Bouchard, R.J. Shephard and T. Stephens (eds.). *Physical activity, fitness, and health*, pp. 98–105. Champaign: Human Kinetics.

**Bailey, D.A.** (1995). The role of mechanical loading in the regulation of skeletal development during growth. In C.J.R. Blimkie and O. Bar-Or (eds.). *New horizons in pediatric exercise science*. pp. 97–108. Champaign: Human Kinetics.

**Bailey, D.A., Faulkner, R.A. and McKay, H.A.** (1996). Growth, physical activity and bone mineral acquisition. *Exercise and Sport Sciences Reviews*, **24**, 233–66.

**Bailey, D.A. and Martin, A.D.** (1994). Physical activity and skeletal health in adolescents. *Pediatric Exercise Science*, **6**, 330–47.

**Baranowski, T., Bouchard, C., Bar-Or, O., Bricker, T., Heath, G., Kimm, S.Y.S., Malina, R., Obarzanek, E., Pate, R., Strong, W.B., Truman, B. and Washington, R.** (1992). Assessment, prevalence, and cardiovascular benefits of physical activity and fitness in youth. *Medicine and Science in Sports and Exercise*, **24** (6)S, S237-S247.

**Barker, D.J.P.** (1990). The fetal and infant origins of adult disease. *British Medical Journal*, **301**, 1111.

**Barnard, R.J. and Wen, S.J.** (1994). Exercise and diet in the prevention and control of the metabolic syndrome. *Sports Medicine*, **18**, 218–28.

**Bar-Or, O.** (1994). Childhood and adolescent physical activity and fitness and adult risk profile. In R.R. Pate and R.C. Hohn, (eds.) *Health and fitness through physical education*, pp. 931–42. Champaign: Human Kinetics.

**Bar-Or, O. and Baranowski, T.** (1994). Physical activity, adiposity and obesity among adolescents. *Pediatric Exercise Science*, **6**, 348–60.

**Baxter-Jones, A., Maffulli, N. and Helms, P.** (1993). Low injury rates in elite athletes. *Archives of Disease in Childhood*, **68**, 130–2.

**Berenson, G.S., McMahan, C.A., Voors, A.W. and Webber, L.S.** (1980). *Cardiovascular risk factors in children. The Bogalusa Heart Study.* Oxford: Oxford University Press.

**Beunen, G.P., Malina, R.M., Renson, R., Simons, J., Ostyn, M. and Lefevre, J.** (1992). Physical activity and growth, maturation and performance: a longitudinal study. *Medicine and Science in Sports and Exercise,* **24**, 576–85.

**Bistritzer, T., Rosenzweig, L., Barr, J., Mayer, S., Lahat, E., Faibel, H., Schlesinger, Z. and Aladjem, M.** (1995). Lipid profile with paternal history of coronary heart disease before age 40. *Archives of Disease in Childhood,* **73** (1), 62–5.

**Blaak, E.E., Westerterp, K.R., Bar-Or, O., Wouters, L.J. and Saris, W.H.** (1992). Total energy expenditure and spontaneous activity in relation to training in obese boys. *American Journal of Clinical Nutrition,* **55**, 777–82.

**Blair, S.N.** (1992). Are American children and youth fit? The need for better data. *Research Quarterly for Exercise and Sport,* **63** (2), 120–3.

**Blair, S.N., Clark, D.G., Cureton, K.J. and Powell, K.E.** (1989a). Exercise and fitness in childhood: implications for a lifetime of health. In C.V Gisolfi and D.R Lamb (eds.), *Perspectives in exercise science and sports medicine,* pp. 401–30. Indianapolis: Benchmark Press.

**Blair, S.N., Kohl, H.W., Gordon, N.F. and Paffenbarger, R.S.** (1992). How much physical activity is good for health? *Annual Review of Public Health,* **13**, 99–126.

**Blair, S.N., Kohl, H.W., Barlow, C.E., Paffenbarger, R.S., Gibbons, L.W. and Maccra, C.A.** (1995). Changes in physical fitness and all-cause mortality: a prospective study of healthy and unhealthy men. *Journal of the American Medical Association,* **273**, 1093–8.

**Blair, S.N., Kohl, H.W., Paffenbarger, R.S.J., Clark, D.G., Cooper, K.H. and Gibbons, L.W.** (1989b). Physical fitness and all-cause mortality: a prospective study of healthy men and women. *Journal of the American Medical Association,* **262**, 2395-2401.

**Blair, S.N. and Meredith, M.D.** (1994). The exercise–health relationship: does it apply to children and youth? In R.R. Pate and R.C. Hohn (eds.), *Health and fitness through physical education,* pp. 11–19. Champaign: Human Kinetics.

**Blum, R.** (1987). Contemporary threats to adolescent health in the United States. *Journal of the American Medical Association,* **257**, 3390–5.

**Boreham, C.A., Twisk, J., Savage, M.J., Cran, G.W. and Strain, J.J.** (1997). Physical activity, sports participation and risk factors in adolescents. *Medicine and Science in Sports and Exercise,* **29**, 788–93.

**Borer, K.T.** (1995). The effects of exercise on growth. *Sports Medicine,* **20** (6), 375–97.

**Bradford Hill, A. and Hill, I.D.** (1991). *Bradford Hill's principles of medical statistics.* London: Edward Arnold.

**Cale, L. and Harris, J.** (1993). Exercise recommendations for children and young people. *Physical Education Review,* **16**, 89–98.

**Campaigne, B.N., Morrison, J.A., Schumann, B.C., Falkner, F., Lakatos, E., Sprecher, D. and Schreiber, G.B.** (1994). Indexes of obesity and comparisons with previous national survey data in 9- and 10-year-old black and white girls: The National Heart, Lung, and Blood Institute Growth and Health Study. *Journal of Pediatrics*, **124**, (5) Part I, 675–80.

**Caspersen, C.J., Christenson, G.M. and Pollard, R.A.** (1986). Status of the 1990 physical fitness and exercise objectives – evidence from NHIS 1985. *Public Health Reports*, **101**, 587-592.

**Chilibeck, P.D., Sale, D.G. and Webber, C.E.** (1995). Exercise and bone mineral density. *Sports Medicine*, **19**, 103–22.

**Chinn, S. and Rona, R.J.** (1994). Trends in weight-for-height and triceps skinfold thickness for English and Scottish children, 1972–82 and 1982–1990. *Paediatric and Perinatal Epidemiology*, **8** (1), 90–106.

**Clarke, W.R. and Lauer, R.M.** (1993). Does childhood obesity track into adulthood? *Critical Reviews in Food Science and Nutrition*, **33** (4/5), 423-30.

**Conroy, B.P., Kraemer, W.J., Maresh, C.M., Fleck, S.J., Stone, M.H., Fry, A.C., Miller, P.D. and Dalsky, G.P.** (1993). Bone mineral density in elite junior Olympic weightlifters. *Medicine and Science in Sports and Exercise*, **25** (10), 1103–09.

**Cooper, C., Cawley, M., Bhalla, A., Egger, P., Ring, F., Morton, L. and Barker, D.** (1995). Childhood growth, physical activity and peak bone mass in women. *Journal of Bone and Mineral Research*, **10** (6), 940–7.

**Corbin, C.B., Pangrazi, R.P. and Welk, G.J.** (1994). Toward an understanding of appropriate physical activity levels for youth President's Council of Physical Fitness and Sports. *Physical Activity and Fitness Research Digest*, **1** (8), 1–8.

**Coronary Prevention Group** (1988). *Children at risk: should prevention of coronary heart disease begin in childhood?* London: Scientific and Medical Advisory Committee.

**Craig, S.B., Bandini, L.G., Lichtenstein, A.H., Schaefer, E.J. and Dietz, W.H.** (1996). The impact of physical activity on lipids, lipoproteins and blood pressure in preadolescent girls. *Pediatrics*, **98** (3), 389–95.

**Cureton, K.J.** (1987). Commentary on 'Children and fitness: A public health perspective'. *Research Quarterly for Exercise and Sport*, **58**, 315–20.

**Cureton, K.J.** (1994). Physical fitness and activity standards for youth. In R.R. Pate and R.C. Hohn (eds.) *Health and fitness through physical education.* pp. 129–36. Champaign: Human Kinetics.

**Department of Health** (1992). *The Health of the Nation.* London: HMSO.

**Department of Health** (1996). *Strategy statement on physical activity.* London: Department of Health.

**de Visser, D.C., van Hooft, I.M., van Doornen, L.J., Hofman, A., Orlebeke, J.F. and Grobbee, D.E.** (1994). Anthropometric measures, fitness and habitual physical activity in offspring of hypertensive parents. Dutch hypertension and offspring study. *American Journal of Hypertension*, **7** (3), 242–8.

**Du Rant, R.H., Baranowski, T., Johnson, M. and Thompson, W.O.** (1994). The relationship among television watching, and body composition of young children. *Pediatrics*, **94**, 449–55.

**Du Rant, R.H., Baranowski, T., Rhodes, T. et al.** (1993). Association among serum lipid and lipoprotein concentrations and physical activity: physical fitness and body composition in young children. *Journal of Pediatrics*, **123**, 185–92.

**Du Rant, R.H., Thompson, W.O., Johnson, M. and Baranowski, T.** (1996). The relationship among television watching, physical activity, and body composition of 5- or 6-year-old children. *Pediatric Exercise Science*, **8**, 15–26.

**Dwyer, T. and Gibbons, L.E.** (1994). The Australian Schools Health and Fitness Survey. Physical fitness related to blood pressure but not lipoproteins. *Circulation*, **89** (4), 1539–44.

**Epstein, L.H., Wing, R.R., Koeske, R., Ossip, D.J. and Beck, S.** (1982). A comparison of lifestyle change and programmed aerobic exercise on weight and fitness changes in obese children. *Behavior Therapy*, **13**, 651–65.

**Epstein, L.H., Wing, R.R., Koeske, R. and Valoski, A.** (1985). A comparison of lifestyle exercise, aerobic exercise, and calisthenics on weight loss in obese children. *Behavior Therapy*, **16**, 345–56.

**Fagan, R.** (1981). *Animal play behavior*. Oxford: Oxford University Press.

**Freedman, D.S., Srinivasan, S.R., Valdez, R.A., Williamson, D.F. and Berenson, G.S.** (1997). Secular increases in relative weight and adiposity among children over two decades: The Bogalusa Heart Study. *Pediatrics*, **99** (3), 420–6.

**Grimston, S.K., Willows, N.D. and Hanley, D.A.** (1993). Mechanical loading regime and its relationship to bone mineral density in children. *Medicine and Science in Sports and Exercise*, **25** (11), 1203–10.

**Gutin, B., Cucuzzo, N., Islam, S., Smith, C., Mofatt, R. and Pargman, D.** (1995). Physical training improves body composition of black obese 7- to 11-year-old girls. *Obesity Research*, **3** (4), 305–312.

**Gutin, B., Cucuzzo, N., Islam, S., Smith, C. and Stachura, M.E.** (1996). Physical training, lifestyle education and coronary risk factors in obese girls. *Medicine and Science in Sports and Exercise*, **28** (1), 19–23.

**Gutin, B. and Owens, S.** (1996). Is there a scientific rationale supporting the value of exercise for the present and future cardiovascular health of children? *Pediatric Exercise Science*, **8**, 294–302.

**Harrell, J.S., McMurray, R.G., Bangdiwala, S.I., Frauman, A.C., Gansky, S.A. and Bradley, C.B.** (1996). Effects of a school-based intervention to reduce cardiovascular disease risk factors in elementary-school children: The Cardiovascular Health in Children (CHIC) Study. *Journal of Pediatrics*, **128**, 797–805.

**Haskell, W.L.** (1994a). Health consequences of physical activity. *Medicine and Science in Sports and Exercise*, **26**, 649–60.

**Haskell, W.L.** (1994b). Dose-response issues from a biological perspective. In C. Bouchard, R.J. Shephard and T. Stephens (eds.), *Physical activity, fitness and health*, pp. 1030–39. Champaign: Human Kinetics.

**Health Education Authority and Sports Council** (1992). *Allied Dunbar National Fitness Survey*. London: Health Education Authority/Sports Council.

**Jakicic, J.M., Wing, R.R. and Robertson, R.J.** (1995). Prescribing exercise in multiple short bouts versus one continuous bout: effects on adherence, cardiorespiratory fitness and weight loss in overweight women. *International Journal of Obesity*, **19**, 893–901.

**Jenner, D.A., Vandongen, R. and Beilin, L.J.** (1992). Relationships between blood pressure and measures of dietary energy intake, physical fitness, and physical activity in Australian children aged 11-12 years. *Journal of Epidemiology and Community Health*, **46**, 108–13.

**Kahle, E.B., Zipf, W.B., Lamb, D.R., Horswill, C.A. and Ward, K.M.** (1996). Association between mild, routine exercise and improved insulin dynamics and glucose control in obese adolescents. *International Journal of Sports Medicine*, **17**, 1-6.

**Kelder, S.H., Perry, C.L., Klepp, K.-I. and Lytle, L.L.** (1994). Longitudinal tracking of adolescent smoking, physical activity and food choice behaviours. *American Journal of Public Health*, **84**, 1121–6.

**Kuh, D.J.L. and Cooper, C.** (1992). Physical activity at 36 years: patterns and childhood predictors in a longitudinal study. *International Journal of Epidemiology*, **46**, 114–19.

**Leon, A.S., Connett, J., Jacobs, D.R.J. and Raurama, R.** (1987). Leisure-time physical activity levels and risk of coronary heart disease and death: Multiple Risk Factor Intervention Trial. *Journal of the American Medical Association*, **258**, 2388–95.

**Loucks, A.B.** (1995). The reproductive system and physical activity in adolescents. In C.J.R. Blimkie, and O. Bar-Or, (eds.), *New horizons in pediatric exercise science*, pp. 27-37. Champaign: Human Kinetics.

**Malina, R.M.** (1994a). Physical activity and training: effects on stature and the adolescent growth spurt. *Medicine and Science in Sports and Exercise*, **26** (6), 759–66.

**Malina, R.M.** (1994b). Physical activity: relationship to growth, maturation, and physical fitness. In C. Bouchard, R.J. Shephard and T. Stephens (eds.), *Physical activity, fitness, and health*, pp. 918–30. Champaign: Human Kinetics.

**Malina, R.M.** (1996). Tracking of physical activity and physical fitness across the lifespan. *Research Quarterly for Exercise and Sport*, **67** (Supplement to No. 3), S1–S10.

**McNeill Alexander, R.** (1991). It may be better to be a wimp. *Nature*, **353**, 696.

**Montoye, H.** (1985). Risk indicators for cardiovascular disease in relation to physical activity in youth. In R.J. Binkhorst, H.C.G. Kemper and W.H.M. Saris (eds.). *Children and exercise*, XII pp. 3–25. Champaign: Human Kinetics.

**Must, A., Jacques, P.F., Dallal, G.E., Bajema, C.J. and Dietz, W.H.** (1992). Long-term morbidity and mortality of overweight adolescents. *New England Journal of Medicine*, **327**, 1350–5.

**Newman, W.P., Freedman, D.S. and Voors, A.W.** (1986). Relation of serum lipoprotein levels and systolic blood pressure to early atherosclerosis: The Bogalusa Heart Study. *New England Journal of Medicine*, **314**, 138–44.

**Newman, W.P. and Strong, J.P.** (1978). Natural history, geographic pathology, and pediatric aspects of atherosclerosis. In W.B. Strong (ed.). *Atherosclerosis: its pediatric aspects*, pp. 15–40. New York: Grune and Stratton,

**Nordgren, H., Freyschuss, U. and Persson, B.** (1994). Blood pressure response to physical exercise in healthy adolescents and adolescents with insulin-dependent diabetes mellitus. *Clinical Science*, **86** (4), 425–32.

**Paffenbarger, R.S., Hyde, R.T., Wing, A.L. and Hsieh, C.** (1986). Physical activity, all-cause mortality, and longevity of college alumni. *New England Journal of Medicine*, **314**, 605–13.

**Paffenbarger, R.S., Hyde, R.T., Wing, A.L., Lee, I.-M., Jung, D.L. and Kampert, J.B.** (1993). The association of changes in physical activity level and other lifestyle characteristics with mortality among men. *New England Journal of Medicine*, **328** (8), 538–45.

**Pangrazi, R.P., Corbin, C.B. and Welk, G.J.** (1996). Physical activity for children and youth. *Journal of Physical Education, Recreation and Dance*, **67** (4), 38–43.

**Pate, R.R., Baranowski, T., Dowda, M. and Trost, S.G.** (1996). Tracking of physical activity in young children. *Medicine and Science in Sports and Exercise*, **28** (1), 92–6.

**Pate, R.R., Pratt, M., Blair, S.N. Haskell, W.L., Macera, C.A., Bouchard, C., Bucher, D., Ettinger, W., Heath, G.W., King, A.C., Kinska, A., Leon, A.S., Marcus, B.H., Morris, J., Paffenbarger, R.S., Patrick, K., Pollock, M.L., Rippe, J.M., Sallis, J. and Wilmore, J.H.** (1995). Physical activity and public health: a recommendation from the Centres for Disease Control and Prevention and the American College of Sports Medicine. *Journal of the American Medical Association*, **273**, 402–407.

**Raitakari, O.T., Porkka, K.V.K., Taimela, S., Telama, R., Rasanen, L. and Vikari, J.S.A.** (1994). Effects of persistent physical activity and inactivity on coronary risk factors in children and young adults. *American Journal of Epidemiology*, **140**, 195–205.

**Reaven, G.M.** (1988). Role of insulin resistance in human disease. *Diabetes*, **37**, 1595–1607.

**Rice, S., Blimkie, C.J., Webber, C.E., Levy, D., Martin, J., Parker, D. and Gordon, C.L.** (1993). Correlates and determinants of bone mineral content and density in healthy adolescent girls. *Canadian Journal of Physiology and Pharmacology*, **71** (12), 923–30.

**Riddoch, C.J. and Boreham, C.A.** (1995). The health-related physical activity of children. *Sports Medicine*, **19** (2), 86–102.

**Riddoch, C.J., Savage, J.M., Murphy, N., Cran, G.W. and Boreham, C.** (1991). Long term health implications of fitness and physical activity patterns. *Archives of Disease in Childhood*, **66**, 1426–33.

**Ring, G.C., Bosch, M. and Chu-Shek, L.** (1970). Effects of exercise on growth, resting metabolism, and body composition of Fischer rats. *Biological Medicine*, **133**, 1162–5.

**Robinson, T.N., Hammer, L.D., Killen, J.D., Kraemer, H.C., Wilson, D.M. and Hayward, C.** (1993). Does television viewing increase obesity and reduce physical activity? Cross-sectional and longitudinal analyses among adolescent girls. *Pediatrics*, **91** (2), 273–80.

**Rowland, T.W.** (1990). *Exercise and children's health*. Champaign: Human Kinetics.

**Rowland, T.W.** (1991). Influence of physical activity and fitness on coronary risk factors in children: how strong an argument? *Pediatric Exercise Science*, **3**, 189–91.

**Rowland, T.W.** (1996). Is there a scientific rationale supporting the value of exercise for the present and future cardio-vascular health of children? The con argument. *Pediatric Exercise Science*, **8**, 303–9.

**Rowland, T.W., Martel, L., Vanderburgh, P., Manos, T. and Charkoudian, N.** (1996). The influence of short-term aerobic training on blood lipids in healthy 10–12 year old children. *International Journal of Sports Medicine*, **17** (7), 487–92.

**Saito, I., Nishino, M, Kawabe, H., *et al.*** (1992). Leisure time physical activity and insulin resistance in young obese students with hypertension. *American Journal of Hypertension*, **5**, 915–18.

**Sallis, J.F., Berry, C.C., Broyles, S.L., McKenzie, T.L. and Nader, P.R.** (1995). Variability and tracking of physical activity over 2 years in young children. *Medicine and Science in Sports and Exercise*, **27** (7), 1042–9.

**Sallis, J.F., McKenzie, T.L. and Alcaraz, J.E.** (1993). Habitual physical activity and health-related physical fitness in fourth-grade children. *American Journal of Diseases in Children*, **147**, 890–6.

**Sallis, J.F. and Patrick, K.** (1994). Physical activity guidelines for adolescents: consensus statement. *Pediatric Exercise Science*, **6**, 302–14.

**Schonfeld-Warden, N. and Warden, C.H.** (1997). Pediatric obesity. An overview of etiology and treatment. *Pediatric Clinics of North America*, **44** (2), 339–61.

**Seefeldt, V. and Vogel, P.** (1987). Children and fitness: a public health perspective. *Research Quarterly for Exercise and Sport*, **58**, 331–3.

**Slemenda, C.W., Reister, T.K., Hui, S.L., Miller, J.Z., Christian, J.C. and Johnston, C.C.** (1994). Influences on skeletal mineralization in children and adolescents: evidence for varying effects of sexual maturation and physical activity. *Journal of Pediatrics*, **125**, 201–7.

**Starnes, J.W. and Bowles, D.K.** (1995). Role of exercise in the cause and prevention of cardiac dysfunction. *Exercise and Sport Sciences Reviews*, **23**, 349–73.

**Stephens, T. and Caspersen, C.J.** (1994). The demography of physical activity. In C. Bouchard, R.J. Shephard, and T. Stephens (eds.), *Physical activity, fitness and health*, pp. 204–13. Champaign: Human Kinetics.

**Strong, W.B.** (1978). Is atherosclerosis a pediatric problem?: an overview. In W.B. Strong (ed.), *Atherosclerosis: its pediatric aspects*, pp. 1–14. New York: Grune and Stratton.

**Strong, W.B., Deckelbaum, R.J., Gidding, S.S., Kavey, R.-E.W., Washington, R., Wilmore, J.H. and Perry, C.L.** (1992). Integrated cardiovascular health promotion in childhood. *Circulation*, **85** (4), 1638–50.

**Suter, E. and Hawes, M.R.** (1993). Relationship of physical activity, body fat, diet and blood lipid profile in youths 10–15 years. *Medicine and Science in Sports and Exercise*, **25**, 748–54.

**Taimela, S., Viikari, J.S., Porkka, K.V. and Dahlen, G.H.** (1994). Lipoprotein (a) levels in children and young adults: the influence of physical activity. The cardiovascular risk in young Finns study. *Acta Paediatrica*, **83** (12), 1258–63.

**Telama, R., Laakso, L. and Yang, X.** (1994). Physical activity and participation in sports of young people in Finland. *Scandinavian Journal of Medicine and Science in Sports*, **4**, 65–74.

**Troiano, R.P., Flegal, K.M., Kuczmarski, R.J., Campbell, S.M. and Johnson, C.L.** (1995). Overweight prevalence and trends for children and adolescents: The National Health and Nutrition Examination Surveys 1963 to 1991. *Archives of Pediatrics and Adolescent Medicine*, **149** (10), 1085–91.

**Twisk, J.W.R., Kemper, H.C.G., Mellenbergh, D.J. and van Mechelen, W.** (1996). Factors influencing tracking of cholesterol and high-density lipoprotein: The Amsterdam Growth and Health Study. *Preventive Medicine*, **25**, 355–64.

**Twisk, J.W.R., Kemper, H.C.G., Mellenbergh, G.J. and van Mechelen, W.** (1996). Relation between the longitudinal development of lipoprotein levels and biological parameters during adolescence and young adulthood in Amsterdam, The Netherlands. *Journal of Epidemiology and Community Health*, **50**, 505–11.

**Twisk, J.W.R., Kemper, H.C.G., Mellenbergh, G.J., van Mechelen, W. and Post, G.B.** (1996). Relation between the longitudinal development of lipoprotein levels and lifestyle parameters during adolescence and young adulthood. *Annals of Epidemiology*, **6**, 246–56.

**Twisk, J.W.R., van Mechelen, W., Kemper, H.C.G. and Post, G.B.** (1997). The relation between long-term exposure to lifestyle during youth and young adulthood and risk factors for cardiovascular disease at adult age. *Journal of Adolescent Health*, **20**, 309–19.

**US Department of Health and Human Services** (1996). *Physical activity and health: a report of the Surgeon General*. Pittsburgh: Department of Health and Human Services, Centres for Disease Control and Prevention, National Centre for Chronic Disease Prevention and Health Promotion.

**Vaccaro, P. and Mahon, A.D.** (1989). The effects of exercise on coronary heart disease risk factors in children. *Sports Medicine*, **8**, 139–53.

Valimaki, M.J., Karkkainen, M., Lamberg-Allardt, C., Laitinen, K., Alhava, E., Heikkinen, J., Impivaara, O., Makela, P., Palmgren, J., Seppanen, R. and Vuori, I. (1994). Exercise, smoking and calcium intake during adolescence and early adulthood as determinants of peak bone mass. *British Medical Journal*, **309**, 230–5.

VandenBergh, M.F., DeMan, S.A., Witteman, J.C., Hofman, A., Trouerbach, W.T. and Grobbee, D.E. (1995). Physical activity, calcium intake and bone mineral content in children in the Netherlands. *Journal of Epidemiology and Community Health*, **49** (3), 299–304.

van Mechelen, W. and Kemper, H.C.G. (1995). Habitual physical activity in longitudinal perspective. In H.C.G. Kemper (ed.), *The Amsterdam growth and health study: a longitudinal analysis of health, fitness and lifestyle*, pp. 135–8. Champaign: Human Kinetics.

van Mechelen, W. (1997). Etiology and prevention of sports injuries in youth. In K. Froberg, O. Lammert, H. Steen Hansen and C.J.R. Blimkie (eds.), *Exercise and fitness – benefits and risks. Children and Exercise XVIII*. Odense: Odense University Press.

Ward, D.S. and Evans, R. (1995). Physical activity, aerobic fitness and obesity in children. *Medicine, Exercise, Nutrition and Health*, **4**, 3–16.

Webber, L.S., Osganian, S.K., Feldman, H.A., Wu, M., Mckenzie, T.L., Nichaman, M., Lytle, L.A., Edmundson, E., Cutler, J., Nader, P.R. and Luepker, R.V. (1996). Cardiovascular risk factors among children after a two and a half year intervention – The CATCH Study. *Preventive Medicine*, **25**, 432–41.

Welk, G.J. (1994). *A comparison of methods for the assessment of physical activity in children*. Unpublished doctoral dissertation. Arizona State University, Tempe, USA.

Welten, D.C., Kemper, H.C.G., Post, G.B., Van Mechelen, W., Twisk, J., Lips, P. and Teule, G.J. (1994). Weight-bearing activity during youth is a more important factor for peak bone mass than calcium intake. *Journal of Bone and Mineral Research*, **9**, 1089–96.

Whincup, P.H., Cook, D.G., Adshead, F., Taylor, S., Papacosta, O., Walker, M. and Wilson, V. (1996). Cardiovascular risk factors in British children from towns with widely differing adult cardiovascular mortality. *British Medical Journal*, **313**, 79.

Wolf, A.M., Gortmaker, S.L., Cheung, L., Gray, H.M., Herzog, D.B. and Colditz, G.A. (1993). Activity, inactivity, and obesity: racial, ethnic, and age differences among schoolgirls. *American Journal of Public Health*, **83**, 1625–7.

World Health Organization (1990). *Prevention in childhood of adult cardiovascular diseases: time for action*. Geneva: World Health Organization.

# Physical activity and its link with mental, social and moral health in young people

Nanette Mutrie[1] and Gaynor Parfitt[2]

[1]Senior Lecturer, Institute of Biomedical and Life Sciences, University of Glasgow;

[2]Lecturer in Exercise Psychology and Sport Psychology, University of Wales, Bangor.

## ▨ Introduction

Mental health for youth has a broad definition and incorporates psychological, social and moral development, the capacity to enter into and sustain satisfying personal relationships and limit distress and maladaptive behaviour to appropriate levels for a child's age and context (NHS Health and Advisory Service, 1995). Thus, in addressing the psychological outcomes of physical activity for this age group it is appropriate to look at the prevention of mental illness and the promotion of good mental health as well as social and moral development. The term physical activity will be used to encompass both health-related and sport-related activity, as it is difficult to distinguish these more specific terms in the literature for this age group.

## ▨ Prevalence of mental health problems

The prevalence of mental health problems among children and adolescents in the UK is estimated at about 20%, with 7–10% having moderate to severe problems that prevent them from functioning normally (Kurtz ,1992). This is similar to the prevalence of mental health problems in the adult population (Scottish Home and Health Department, 1980). The 1988 General Household Survey revealed that the most common long-standing illness for children was respiratory disease, which affected 7% of children aged 0–15 years (Botting and Crawley, 1995). Thus the prevalence of mental health problems cannot be judged as a minor or unimportant area of ill health. There is greater risk of child psychiatric disorders in families suffering socio-economic disadvantage or family discord and in children with chronic illnesses such as diabetes or asthma (Kurtz, 1992). This is clearly a substantial burden in terms of health care. Given the importance of developing the various facets of mental health for this age group, the issues of positive mood, perceptions of well-being and judgements of self-esteem need to be considered in any definition of mental health. If physical activity can be shown to have a link with the promotion of good mental health, as well as in the prevention or treatment of mental health problems, there will need to be increased importance placed on developing and sustaining appropriate activity programmes for youth.

# ▪ Link with physical activity

The literature reviewed here has been categorised into general review articles and specific key studies, including meta-analyses whenever possible. The specific key studies are separated into four areas namely, the prevention and treatment of mental health problems, the promotion of good mental health, cognitive development and social and moral development.

## Search techniques

Literature was searched using Social Citation Index and Embase (which searches medical literature) via BIDS, PsychLit, Firstsearch and Sport Discus. Two decades of work from 1976 to 1997 were searched. Key words included adolescence, youth, teenager, children, mental health, stress, anxiety, depression, moral, social, cognitive, academic, intelligence, deviancy, juvenile delinquency, physical activity, exercise, sport and physical education.

## Review articles

There were six articles or book chapters found that reviewed the link between mental health and physical activity. In order to provide the most up-to-date information this part of the search was restricted to work published since 1990. However, Dishman's (1989) review is included because it is comprehensive and provides a bench mark against which to measure recent progress. Dishman (1989) reviewed all the key areas in exercise and sport psychology for youth and concluded that little is known about this age group. He called for more scientific rigour and in particular more epidemiological studies to show prevalence of activity and inactivity and associated risks and benefits. Furthermore, he suggested that a biosocial paradigm should be adopted in which psychosocial theories and methods are used along with methods from biological sciences to advance understanding of participation rates, determinants and outcomes of sport and physical activity for adolescents. Rowland (1990), in his review, which did not critique the literature in the same depth as Dishman (1989), suggested that the available data on physical activity indicated a positive effect on a wide variety of psychological conditions and supports the use of regular activity as both a therapeutic and preventative measure. Horn and Claytor (1993) were more specific in their conclusions and suggested that participation in a physical activity programme can result in increased self-esteem and internal locus of control, and decreased anxiety and depression. Biddle (1993) concluded that the quantity of data in the area of mental health outcomes from physical activity and exercise for children was low and emphasised the need for well-trained physical educators to provide the kinds of experiences that were most likely to lead to positive benefits. Calfas and Taylor (1994) reviewed cross-sectional and prospective studies and established that:

- ▪ 8 out of 11 studies addressing anxiety/stress had a positive relationship with physical activity.

- ▪ 9 out of 10 studies addressing self-esteem/concept/self-efficacy had a positive relationship with physical activity.

- ▪ 9 out of 11 studies addressing depression had a positive relationship with physical activity.

- ▪ There was little evidence for decreases in hostility/anger with physical activity or improved academic achievement with physical activity.

Calfas and Taylor (1994) also concluded that there was insufficient evidence to draw conclusions about the effectiveness of physical activity as an adjunctive treatment for clinical psychological disorders for this age group. Welsh and Labbe (1994) reviewed studies involving the cognitive and behavioural effects of aerobic conditioning on children (normal and special populations) and concluded that there were no consistent findings. Beneficial changes include increases in self-efficacy in relation to running, increases in creativity, self-esteem, internal locus of control, improved scores on some cognitive functioning variables and improved classroom behaviour.

The reviews in the 1990s suggest that there are positive associations between mental health and physical activity for youth but some reviewers are more cautious in their conclusions than others. All reviewers call for further experimental work in order to verify their conclusions.

## ▨ Empirical research

In the following sections the literature is categorised as follows:

- Prevention and treatment of mental health problems (stress, anxiety, depression, psychiatric disorders).

- Promotion of good mental health (well-being, mood, self-esteem).

- Cognitive development (cognitive performance, academic achievement).

- Social and moral development (pro-social and anti-social behaviour values).

In each area meta-analyses are reported first (if available), then key studies are described. Key studies are generally the most current studies established from the searches and any experimental studies. Studies that were pre-experimental, or had small numbers, were excluded.

## Prevention and treatment of mental health problems

Key studies are described in Table 3.1. Caution is required in drawing conclusions from these studies. Although the meta-analysis suggests there are moderate effects for physical activity on anxiety and depression, which are similar to those found for adults (Mutrie and Biddle, 1995), only five studies were included in the analysis. Both of the experimental studies were hampered by high attrition rates but show promising results. Further experimental studies are required to substantiate the cautious conclusions drawn mainly from correlational data which suggest that physical activity is negatively associated with stress, anxiety and depression. In particular, the use of exercise as an adjunctive treatment in clinically diagnosed mental illness requires attention for this age group. Only one study on this population was found (Brown *et al.*, 1992). It has been suggested that children suffering from chronic diseases (such as diabetes) are at risk of developing mental health problems (Kurtz, 1992). The use of exercise in adult clinical populations is often studied, focusing on the physical health benefits, with the psychological benefits receiving anecdotal rather than empirical support (Mutrie, 1997). For future studies of the role of exercise for children with clinical conditions it is recommended that psychological measures are included.

**Table 3.1.** *Key studies on physical activity and the prevention and treatment of mental health problems in youth*

| Authors | Participants | Design | Treatment groups | Measures | Results |
|---|---|---|---|---|---|
| **Calfas and Taylor (1994)** | Healthy and psychologically 'at risk' adolescents | Meta-analysis of 5 RCT studies | | Depression, anxiety, stress, hostility, anger, intellectual functioning, psychiatric disorders | ES −0.15 for stress anxiety and −0.38 for depression |
| **Brown and Lawton (1986)** | 220 mostly white and high socio-economic status; mean age 14; range 11–17 | Cross-sectional correlational | | Life events survey; seriousness of illness questionnaire; Multiple Affect Adjective Checklist (depression); self-report physical activity | Students' somatic health negatively correlated with increased stress from negative life events, this effect was less in those with higher levels of physical activity |
| **Brown and Siegel (1988)** | 364; grades 7–11 private secondary school; mostly white and high socio-economic status; mean age 13.1 years | prospective observational pre-post | | Life events survey; seriousness of illness questionnaire; self-report of time spent in 14 activities | Stress was associated with a high occurrence of illness primarily among those with low levels of exercise. Among those with high levels of physical exercise stressful life events were not strongly predictive of illness reports |
| **Norris, Carroll and Cochrane (1992)** | 70 boys, 77 girls; mean age 14.3 years; range 13–17; broad socio-economic spectrum | 2 studies; prospective correlational and experimental | 3 training groups 2/week for 10 weeks/25–30 mins: high intensity (70–75%) n=14; mod. intensity (50–60%) n=15; flexibility n=15; control n=16 | Life events questionnaire; seriousness of illness questionnaire; perceived stress scale; Multiple Affect Adjective Checklist As above plus Louisiana step test | Adolescents who report exercising more frequently also reported significantly less stress and depression. Negative low correlation between stress and PA High intensity group reported significantly less stress, anxiety and depression following exercise programme; high attrition |
| **Brown et al., (1992)** | 16 boys, 11 girls psychiatrically institutionalised; mean age 15.6 years. | Experimental, but only 11 completed the 9 weeks due to discharge | Experimental = 3/wk run or aerobics; control = regular PE; conditions achieved by assign classes rather than subjects | Standard fitness tests; POMS; BDI | Experimental group improved vigour and anger POMS scores more than controls; positive treatment effects evident at 41/2 weeks; girls seemed to benefit more than boys. Very small numbers hampered analyses |

RCT: randomised control trial; POMs: profile of mood states; PA: physical activity; ES: effect size; BDI: Beck depression inventory.

No negative effects of physical activity for any psychiatrically at-risk population were found, although those suffering from eating disorders (one group which may be at risk of negative effects from physical activity) were not picked up in any search on this topic. However, there is some concern that involvement in certain sports may increase the risk of some girls developing eating disorders (Dummer *et al.*, 1987). For example, nearly 20% of all elite female athletes in Norway were defined as at risk of eating disorders and 79% of these met the criteria for anorexia nervosa, bulimia nervosa or anorexia athletica (Sundgot-Borgen, 1994). Furthermore, Petrie (1996) reports on differences in the behavioural and psychological indices of eating disorders between non-athletes, lean and non-lean female athletes. Lean female athletes have significantly higher 'drive for thinness' scores. It is unclear whether or not involvement in sports requiring a lean body shape causes or is a catalyst to the development of eating disorders, or if some women are drawn towards such sports as a means of vindicating their eating behaviour. Consequently, in promoting physical activity for the prevention and treatment of mental health problems, we need to be aware that for girls involved in competitive lean sports there may be some risks. However, from a public health perspective, there is no evidence that general involvement in physical activity produces any psychological risks.

## Promotion of good mental health

Key studies in this area are described in Table 3.2, and show a consistent positive relationship between physical activity and well-being. There is no evidence of negative mental health effects of physical activity or sport, although no high risk populations, such as those undertaking high training loads, appear to have been studied. There is, of course, a body of literature which addresses the concept of competitive stress in sports, and children have often been studied. Research shows that competitive sports can cause stress, but this does not appear to have a chronic mental health effect (Dishman, 1989). The meta-analysis by Gruber (1986) supplies convincing evidence of a moderately strong positive effect of activity on self-esteem for normal children and a larger effect for those classified as 'handicapped'. This finding has some support from the small-scale meta-analysis by Calfas and Taylor (1994). None of the experimental studies have a no treatment control group and so no conclusions are possible about whether it is exercise *per se* or peripheral issues (such as the group effect or the leader) that cause the effects which are noted. There is a clear need for further experimental work in this area.

Two studies have been selected for more detailed discussion, as they provide up-to-date UK data using large samples. The first study comes from Steptoe and Butler (1996). They used a cohort of children born in 1970 and who had responded to a follow-up in 1986 (2223 boys, 2838 girls). The authors acknowledge a social class bias in the sample but counter this statistically. A score was obtained on a vigorous activity index depending on participation in a variety of competitive and non-competitive activities; a similar index was created for non-vigorous sport participation, such as darts, billiards and fishing. Two well-validated scales were used to measure emotional well-being. Gender differences were notable in two ways: boys participated in more sports and vigorous recreational activity than girls, and girls reported more emotional distress than

**Table 3.2.** *Key studies on physical activity and the promotion of good mental health in youth*

| Authors | Participants | Design | Treatment groups | Measures | Results |
|---|---|---|---|---|---|
| **Gruber (1986)** | Pre-adolescent children and handicapped individuals (trainable mental retardation, perceptual handicap, emotionally disturbed, economically disadvantaged) under 18 years of age | Meta-analysis of 27 experimental studies with control groups | | Self-concept | ES=0.34 for normal populations; 0.57 for 'handicapped' subjects. The largest effect size was for fitness activities. |
| **Calfas and Taylor (1994)** | Healthy and psychologically 'at risk' adolescents | Meta-analysis of 5 RCT studies | | Self-esteem/concept | ES=0.12, for self-esteem/self-concept. |
| **Hendry, Shucksmith and Cross (1989)** | 5862 (14–20 years of age) | survey postal and supervised | | GHQ: sports participation: high 5+/wk; low 1–4/wk; none | GHQ scores decreased (i.e. improved mental health) as participation increased for both boys and girls; competitive sports types had lower GHQ scores than non-competitive types |
| **Steptoe and Butler (1996)** | 2223 boys, 2838 girls mean age 16.3 years. SD 0.38, all born between 5 April and 11 April 1970 | Cross-sectional Correlational | | GHQ: Malaise inventory; Participation in 10 team and 25 individual sports and recreational activities during the year; participation in non-vigorous activities (e.g. snooker, darts); social class; health status | Activity index was positively associated with emotional well being, independent of sex, social class, health status, and use of hospital services; participation in non-vigorous activities was associated with high psychological and somatic symptoms on the malaise inventory |
| **MacMahon and Gross (1987)** | 98 boys with learning disabilities; mean age 16.3; age range 14–18; 6% African American, 42% Latino, 1% Asian, 51% white | Experimental | 40 minutes 3 times a week for 12 weeks running, basketball Group 1 Heart rate 160; group 2 heart rate 120 | Children's Self Concept Scale; BDI; sub max. cycle test | Group 1 improved fitness and self-concept scores |

**Table 3.2.** *Continued*

| Authors | Participants | Design | Treatment groups | Measures | Results |
|---|---|---|---|---|---|
| **Tuckman and Hinkle (1986)** | *n*=154; 45 4th graders, 53 5th graders, 53 6th graders; proportion of non-white students at each grade ranged from 27–29% (average age 9.3) | Experimental | Treatment = 30 minutes running sessions 3 times a week for 12 weeks; control = regular physical education | 800 m and 50 m run times; skinfolds; Behaviour Rating Scale; perceptual motor ability; creativity; self-concept; planning ability and visual motor co-ordination | No differences were found between groups for self-control in school, self-concept, and perceptual functioning. Running contributed to fitness and creativity but not to general behaviour or perceptual functioning |
| **Gordon and Grant (1997)** | *n*=1634; aged 13.5–14.5 years | Qualitative | | How do you feel today?; open-ended questionnaire responses | About 1/4 of the whole group noted that sport made then feel happy and good about themselves. However, big gender differences noted |

RCT: randomised control trials; SD: Standard deviation; ES: effect size; BDI: Beck depression inventory; GHQ: general health questionnaire.

boys. However, the sport and vigorous activity index was inversely related to psychological symptoms and positively related to well-being independently of sex, social class, health status and use of hospital services. These findings support those of Hendry, Shucksmith and Cross (1989). It is important to remember in correlational designs that positive associations could be caused by lack of well-being (i.e. poor health or disability), preventing physical activity as well as physical activity being linked to increased well-being. However, Steptoe and Butler (1996) re-analysed the data after excluding those who were disabled or who had been absent from school for three months and found that the associations were still significant. These findings, therefore, seem robust and provide data that conform to Dishman's (1989) request for epidemiological and biosocial methods in so far as the responses concerned symptoms as well as activity status.

The second study, which deserves more detailed commentary, is a qualitative study of over 1600 Glaswegian 13- to 14-year-olds (Gordon and Grant, 1997). As part of a city-wide mental health week these children were asked to state three things that made them feel happy and good about themselves. In terms of physical activity the most notable issue was the differences between boys and girls on their view of how sport and exercise affected their mood and self-esteem. While 24% of the group noted that doing sport made them feel happy, a gender analysis showed that 40% of boys and only 10% of girls said this. For boys, sport was the category that had the highest frequency of response, while for girls 'friends' was the most frequently noted (68%) as the factor that made them feel happy. Similarly 42% of boys said that winning/achieving at sport made them

feel good about themselves while only 8.5% of girls noted this. Again this category had the highest response rate for boys; for girls the category with the highest response rate was 'doing well at school' (38%). These gender differences probably reflect different participation rates but it is important to consider that sport and exercise seem to have a more salient role in describing good mental health for boys than for girls in this study.

Both of the above studies provide evidence for positive associations between physical activity and well-being and both point to gender differences. The major issue is lower participation in sport and activity by girls. Experimental work should follow to establish if there is a causal link between activity and well-being for this age group.

## Limitations & Conclusion

Limitations of the studies reviewed in Tables 3.1 and 3.2 are similar to those found in the adult literature (Biddle and Mutrie, 1991). In general there are few experimental studies. Given the lack of such data to back up correlational findings, it is important to remember that positive associations could be caused by lack of well-being preventing physical activity as well as physical activity being linked to increased well-being or decreased anxiety/depression. Studies have focused on different psychological variables and even when the same variables have been used, they may have been measured in different ways. There is also a problem with measuring physical activity, plus an additional problem of differentiating sport, exercise and more general physical activity effects. Finally, most studies are short-term and, given the need to take a developmental perspective with this age group, this presents a serious limitation.

Many researchers with physical education or sport backgrounds look for the positive associations, but all of us who have worked with young people in physical activity and sport know that there is also a chance that poor experiences damage self-esteem, and yet no studies investigating this topic were found. One indication that there is cause for concern is found in the Allied Dunbar National Fitness Survey (Health Education Authority and Sports Council, 1992): one of the most commonly stated barriers to physical activity participation was that adults felt they were not 'the sporty type'.

There is very little information on the intensity of activity required to provide a positive psychological benefit or whether related physical fitness increases are related to psychological change. Moderate intensity activity has been associated with mental health benefits in adults (Moses *et al.*, 1989) and the issue of intensity of activity, fitness effects and psychological outcome requires further investigation in youth.

Longitudinal studies are required for two reasons. Firstly, there is a need to adopt a developmental perspective in dealing with children and youth; effects may well be different at each developmental stage, such as at early childhood and at puberty. The role of parental attitudes and involvement, which is a clear factor in development, could also be traced in such studies. Secondly, longitudinal studies are required to elucidate the possible benefits and risks of involvement in physical activity for youth on adult psychological functioning. Steptoe and Butler (1996) suggested that this could be done with British data from their cohort study initiated in 1970, which they have already used to show a positive association between sport participation and emotional well-being for the cohort during adolescence. Dishman (1995) discussed two prospective studies in the United States that show a protective effect of physical activity on the development of adult depression and this provides encouragement to pursue this theme with a cohort moving from adolescence to adulthood.

In the literature that has focused on adults, it is not clear whether exercise itself or the exercise environment is responsible for the psychological benefits noted, and several mechanisms for the potential psychological benefit from physical activity, such as increased mastery and self-esteem or increased production of neurotransmitters related to mood, have been hypothesised (Biddle and Mutrie, 1991). Developmental issues must be taken into account for youth and further mechanisms could be hypothesised. Researchers must be encouraged to explore these mechanisms.

Given these limitations, conclusions must be cautious, but available data suggest that physical activity is associated with good mental health and low levels of mental health problems in youth. Meta-analytic studies provide most confidence in the conclusion that physical activity programmes can increase self-esteem and decrease anxiety and depression. It is likely that effects are greatest for those with initially unfavourable scores on the variable of interest, for example, self-esteem in educationally trainable mentally retarded children.

## Cognitive and academic development

As psychological development is seen as part of mental health for those under 18 years of age, it is appropriate to mention research into cognitive and academic development. Much work in physical education research has been devoted to establishing if those who engaged in physical education benefit intellectually or academically. Kirkendall (1986) concluded that a modest positive relationship existed between motor performance and intellectual performance and that this relationship was strongest in the early stages of development. Kirkendall (1986) also noted that no direct causal link had been identified. Intervention techniques for learning disabled children has been another topic of investigation, but a meta-analysis of 180 studies (Kavale and Mattson, 1983) showed no positive effect on academic, cognitive or perceptual motor performance from perceptual-motor training on children whose average IQ was 88 at age 8. In an experimental study, McMahon and Gross (1987) found no effect on academic performance for a group of boys with learning disabilities who were given a 20-week vigorous aerobic exercise programme. A more recent narrative review of the use of exercise with learning disabled children (Bluechardt, Weiner and Shephard, 1995) also concluded that exercise programmes had not been successful at improving motor performance and were not unique in improving other psychosocial skills. However, exercise programmes are still important for this group of children for the potential health benefits of physical activity.

Tomporowski and Ellis (1986) provided an excellent critique of the effects of exercise on cognitive function. None of the studies mentioned, however, include youth and no such specific reviews were found by the search strategies we employed. One study (Tuckman and Hinkle, 1986) listed in Table 3.2, however, showed that running had a positive effect on creativity, which could be considered a cognitive process. Tomporowski and Ellis (1986) conclude that the evidence is conflicting and that there is a need for systematic research in this area. There clearly is a need to extend this work to those under 18 years and the guidelines offered by Tomporowski and Ellis (1986) should be followed by any researcher intending to investigate this topic for children and youth. The guidelines include: measuring the physical state of the participant prior to testing; measuring appropriate fitness parameters; noting whether or not the effects are dependent on intensity and duration of exercise; stating when the cognitive test was administered; whether or not they are justifying prior experience and motivation of participants; and discussing the selection of cognitive tasks.

The provision of daily physical education programmes for primary school children attracted some research activity during the 1980s. In general, the programmes aimed to increase fitness and/or develop motor skills. Outcome measures almost always included academic performance as well as physical performance. In three studies (Williams, Hughes and Martin, 1982; Dwyer *et al.*, 1983; Pollatschek and O'Hagan, 1989), which had quasi-experimental designs (i.e. a non-equivalent control group), there were no indications that daily physical education had any beneficial effects on academic performance. However, Shephard (1997:119) reports on three longitudinal studies and concludes that 'academic performance is maintained or even enhanced by an increase in a student's level of habitual physical activity, despite a reduction in curricular or free time for the study of academic material'. Equally, Shephard (1997:123) says that 'daily programs of physical education should not be introduced with the expectation that they will lead to major gains in academic performance'.

Cautious conclusions should be made. There appears to be some evidence to support the notion that physical activity improves academic or cognitive performance in youth, but there are very few good studies. However, spending additional time in physical education at least does not appear to hinder academic performance. The youngest age groups may be the most important in this area. Studies with experimental designs have been short-term and again a developmental approach is required in the next generation of research.

## Social and moral development

Social and moral development can be seen as part of the definition for mental health for this age group. There is almost universal agreement that early play experiences, conducted in a group, can enhance the development of social skills (Sage, 1986). Furthermore, sport experiences are able to provide opportunities for learning about co-operation with team mates and leadership responsibilities. Much as been written about this area of social psychology and there is a well-respected body of literature (Sage, 1986). In the area of social development, physical education lessons, sport coaching classes and exercise classes all present situations in which young people are required to interact with each other and with adults in a way that is different from the standard academic environment. This presents a rich opportunity for social development. However, the empirical evidence for these possibilities is hard to find and the special nature of sport interactions also includes the possibility of abuse of power by adults and has led to guide-

lines being issued to children and coaches on how to keep the sport environment safe (National Coaching Foundation, 1996).

Educators and government agencies have projected the notion that sport develops 'character' and teaches right from wrong. In *Sport, raising the game*, the Department of National Heritage (1995: 7) states that:

> The Government believes that such concepts as fair play, self-discipline, respect for others, learning to live by laws and understanding one's obligations to others in a team are all matters which can be learnt from team games properly taught.

A further example comes from The Scottish Sports Council (1996: 4) who suggest, in a strategy document concerning youth sport, that :

> Playing sports can promote leadership skills, improve physical development and provide young people with a broad range of social skills. These positive experiences can help social interaction and awareness, increase self-esteem and the development of moral values.

Politicians sometimes take these sentiments to extremes as the following quotation from Ian Sproat, Minister for Sport in 1994 (quoted in Spencer, 1994), shows:

> team spirit, discipline, good sportsmanship, and fair play are all extremely important and are only teachable by experiences on the sports field. If we had more organised team games in schools we could have fewer little thugs like those who murdered James Bolger out in the street.

There is, however, another body of literature which suggests that sport could develop anti-social or immoral behaviour (Bredemeier and Shields, 1984). It has been proposed that in certain sports a 'bracketed morality' is encouraged in which the sport appears to operate on a different moral code to that of society in general. This bracketed morality allows certain behaviours in sport to be judged as acceptable (e.g. standing on an opponent's head in rugby) when the same behaviour would be judged as unacceptable outside of sport. Such a scenario retards moral development rather than enhances it. Empirical research on this topic, however, is sparse, perhaps because promoters of programmes of sport and activity do not want to believe this viewpoint. However, one study from the United States supports the suggestion that for school level athletes there is no advantage to moral development from sport participation. Beller and Stoll (1995) found that in a sample of 1330 high school students in the United States, male team sport athletes had a lower level of moral reasoning than male or female non-athletes or female team sport athletes. This study further suggests that the lack of moral development is more of a problem for male sports. Perhaps in youth sports for boys there is more of a conflict between winning and playing fairly or respecting opponents and rules. It is clear that teachers and coaches must teach moral development rather than expecting it to happen as a natural consequence of participation. Sheilds and Bredemeier (1994) have provided some guidance for teachers and coaches on how to achieve this. In the UK, Lee (1997) has also raised the question of whether or not sport and physical education can promote moral development. Lee's own work (Lee, 1993) has suggested that children involved in sport in the UK report a largely positive moral value system in which winning is not seen as the most important value, but he also is aware that such positive outcomes are a result of a complex interaction between good coaching and teaching environments and influences of significant others. Lee (1997: 19) makes a plea for re-emphasising moral teaching in the current climate and concludes that:

> Unfortunately the increasing commercialism within sport and its significance as a source of national pride places pressure on coaches and administrators to achieve competitive success for the few at the cost of more altruistic motives for the many. If sport is to be used successfully as an effective vehicle for moral development it is even more important that those entrusted with the future of youth sport make it explicit that moral values are part of life and are to be upheld both on and off the field.

Another way to explore the relationship of social and moral development with physical activity is to look at delinquent behaviour. However, one problem in this approach is that no accurate identification, definition or measurement of delinquency exists. Most researchers use self-report rather than official measures of delinquency, i.e. contact with official law enforcing agencies. No meta-analytic reviews were located on this topic. Several authors have hypothesised a negative relationship between sports participation and juvenile delinquency (Lutz, 1981; McMahon, 1990). Segrave (1983) suggests that although deviancy amongst athletic groups is generally lower than among non-athletic groups, the effectiveness of sport as an antidote to delinquency is unclear. Segrave (1983) further suggests that the relationship between athletics and delinquency is a function of social class. Three of the four correlational studies (Segrave and Hastad, 1982; Hastad *et al.*, 1984; Segrave, Moreau and Hastad, 1985) listed in Table 3.3 supported the hypothesis that sports participation has a negative association with delinquency. As these three studies used samples in which the majority of participants were involved in sport, the negative association could be explained by delinquents being less inclined towards involvement in organised sport as well as sport decreasing the likelihood of delinquent behaviour. In contrast, a New Zealand longitudinal cohort study (Begg *et al.*, 1996) found the opposite; that high sports participation at 15 years of age was more likely to result in delinquent behaviour at 18 years than low sports participation. The cohort study may well have avoided the selection bias inherent in the previously mentioned correlational studies, and thus may present a truer picture. The randomised control trial study by Trulson (1986) implies that the content of the physical activity may be fundamental to the potential benefit it can have upon delinquent behaviour. The changes in behaviour of a group who trained in the traditional martial art of Tae Kwon Do indicated significant improvements in aggressive behaviour, sociability and self-esteem compared to a 'modern' martial arts training group. In fact, the 'modern' martial arts training group showed an even greater tendency toward delinquency on the Minnesota Multiphasic Personality Inventory than they did at the beginning of the study. The inclusion of the psychological/philosophical aspects and the basic technical skills of the traditional Tae Kwon Do differentiated the training the two groups received. The 'modern' martial arts training group focused on free-sparring and self-defence techniques. These results suggest that physical activities which focus upon fighting (as in the case of the 'modern' martial arts training) would not be recommended as a means of improving moral and social development for this population.

Outdoor adventure type programmes were proposed as a particularly effective mechanism for the re-socialisation of delinquents (Sugden and Yiavnakis, 1982) but no evidence for this hypothesis was located. The one piece of empirical research that is close to this topic displayed some interesting findings. Skogen and Wichstrom (1996) surveyed 10,839 boys and girls aged between 13 and 20 years. The questionnaire divided physical activity into exercise and outdoor adventure activities and sought information on behavioural conduct problems.

Results revealed that amongst boys, crime involvement increased with increased involvement in adventurous activities, but decreased with exercise involvement. The authors suggested that this may be linked to how conformists and non-conformists define outdoor adventurous activities. An example of this may be a camping weekend where conformists go to return to nature, while non-conformists arrive with beer and music for a party. Both groups may define this as outdoor adventure.

In conclusion, there is equivocal evidence about the relationship between involvement in sport and anti-social behaviour. Some evidence which seems to support the idea that sport is negatively related to delinquency may have an inherent selection bias that excludes those with anti-social tendencies. The type of sport activity may be an important consideration in future studies. There is no experimental evidence to support physical activity as an effective treatment for delinquency or to support the hypothesised effectiveness of outdoor adventure type programmes. No UK studies were found.

If the claims that sport provides opportunities for social and moral development are to be upheld we need further evidence, including evidence from the UK. Obvious contradictions to this claim, such as football hooliganism, need to be

**Table 3.3.** *Sport and physical activity in the treatment and development of juvenile delinquency*

| Authors | Subjects | Design | Treatment groups | Measures | Results |
|---|---|---|---|---|---|
| **Munson et al. (1985)** | Youth development centre for males; N=31, 21 were black, 10 were Caucasian; age range 14–18; mean age 17 | Experimental with random assignment to groups | Strength training and leisure counselling (n=12); strength training and informal discussion (n=11); no treatment control group (n=8) Experimental groups met 3/week for 7 weeks for 90 minutes. | Self-esteem inventory; leisure attitude scale; leisure behaviour rating scale; muscular fitness (lift maximal load for a specific number of repeats) | No significant differences between three groups on self-esteem, leisure attitudes or leisure behaviours. No difference between experimental groups for measures of muscular fitness |
| **Munson (1988)** | Behaviourally disordered youth (convicted of arson, rape, robbery and auto theft) without mental retardation or learning difficulties; mean age = 17.2 years; 22 were white, 14 black, 2 Hispanic; all lower socio-economic class; | Experimental with random assignment to groups | Leisure education (n=13) Physical activity (n=14) informal discussion (n=12) 1 hour/week/10 weeks | Self-esteem inventory; leisure diagnostic battery; attitudes; leisure participation and satisfaction; physical activity recall | Multivariate analyses of variance revealed no significant differences among the three groups on self-esteem, leisure functioning, attitudes towards self, leisure and work or leisure participation and satisfaction |
| **Trulson (1986)** | High school males, categorised as juvenile delinquent by MMPI, age range 13–17 years | Experimental with random assignment to groups | Traditional Tae Kwon Do (n=15); 'modern' martial arts (n=11); general physical activity group (n=9). Groups met 1 hour 3 times per week for 6 months | Jackson Personality Inventory, Rosenzweig Picture Frustration Test and MMPI | Traditional TKD displayed normal MMPI, below average aggressiveness, increase in self-esteem and sociability compared to 'modern' martial arts group. 'Modern' martial arts group increased in delinquency characteristics, and aggressiveness. Physical activity group: no significant changes. |
| **Hastad et al. (1984)** | 381 (186 males, 195 females); age range 11–13 years | Correlational | | 145 boys and 133 girls were classified as youth sport participants; self-report questionnaires revealed: socio-economic status; self-image; attachment to school; deviant associates; peer status; personal values; deviant behaviour. | 15% reported no deviant behaviour; majority classified as sports participants; youth sport participants report 9.9% less drug related deviance, 0.7% less school related deviance, 5.4% less non-school related deviance and 9.2% less composite deviancy than non-participants. Socio-economic status, physical self-concept and self-concept are negatively associated with deviancy and sports participation |

**Table 3.3.** *continued*

| Authors | Subjects | Design | Treatment groups | Measures | Results |
|---------|----------|--------|------------------|----------|---------|
| **Malmisur and Schempp (1984)** | 203 male age range 13–16 years | Correlational | | Self-report levels of participation in sports and delinquent behaviours | No differences in sport participation between those classified as delinquent and non-delinquent |
| **Segrave and Hastad (1982)** | 1935 students from 8 high schools; sample was classified by age, gender, social class, race, residential background | Survey, correlational | | Self-report questionnaire; delinquents were classified by type of offence; athletes were classified by type of sport and degree of participation (51% reported no deviant behaviour) | High school athletes less delinquent than non-athletes; high school athletes in major sports showed more delinquent behaviour than those involved in minor sports; for males and low social class groups the greater number of years of participation the less involvement in delinquent behaviour |
| **Segrave, Moreau and Hastad (1985)** | 124 ice hockey players and 46 non-athletes (male high school athletes): age range 15–16 years | Survey, correlational | | Self-report socio-psychological variables; attachment to school, delinquent associates, subterranean values orientations, conventional value orientations, perceptions of limited opportunity, delinquent behaviour (drugs, theft, violence and vandalism) | No significant difference in total delinquency involvement between ice hockey players and non-athletes; ice hockey players reported significantly more involvement in delinquency of a violent nature than non-athletes; among ice hockey players and non-athletes attachment to school, delinquent associates and perceptions of limited opportunity were significantly related to total delinquency |
| **Begg et al. (1996)** | 876 boys and girls in a New Zealand cohort study | Longitudinal cohort study | Interviews at age 15 and 18 years | Leisure time physical activity; self-reported delinquency; aggressive behaviour | No support for sporting activity deterring delinquent behaviour; both boys and girls with high levels of sport activity at age 15 years were more likely to be delinquent at 18 than those with low sport activity |

MMPI: Minnesota Multiphasic Personality Inventory; TKD: Tae Kwon Do.

addressed. We also need to know if there are UK sports that can be associated with 'bracketed morality'. It is important to provide coaches and teachers with guidelines about how to structure sport and physical education experiences in order to maximise opportunities for moral development and minimise moral retardation.

# ◼ **Conclusions**

The literature has made some progress towards Dishman's (1989) goals for research in this area. In particular, we can be more confident of the association between activity and well-being for this age group. We still need experimental work to show if this is a causal link. There is little evidence to support positive outcomes from physical activity on academic performance and cognitive function. Much of the rhetoric about the benefits of physical activity in social and moral development needs further empirical support with non-US data to establish whether or not other cultures show the same trends.

### **What we know**

- Physical activity is associated with good mental health; the strongest evidence is in the area of self-esteem.

- Physical activity is associated with low levels of mental health problems; however, using physical activity as a treatment for clinically diagnosed mental health problems has not been frequently explored for this age group.

- There is little evidence to support the idea that physical activity can promote cognitive or academic enhancement. However, spending additional time in physical education does not interfere with academic performance.

- The potential for physical activity involvement to provide opportunities for social and moral development is widely recognised, however, empirical evidence is scarce and there is some support for the notion that sport (especially male team sports) is associated with low levels of moral reasoning.

- There is equivocal evidence that juvenile delinquency could be negatively related to sport participation.

### **What we need to know**

- Is physical activity an effective treatment (or adjunctive treatment) for psychiatric disorders?

- Is there a psychological benefit from physical activity for youth with chronic diseases, such as diabetes?

- Is there epidemiological evidence to illustrate the longitudinal relationship between activity (or inactivity) and the onset of adult mental health problems?

- In the normal population what is the optimum intensity, duration, frequency and mode of activity to produce positive psychological outcomes?

- What are the mechanisms (causes) of psychological benefit for this age group?

- What are the most appropriate measurement tools for assessing psychological outcomes in youth?

- Is there a relationship between sports participation and juvenile delinquency in the UK?

- Do outdoor adventure type programmes offer an effective treatment for delinquency?

- Do some sports in the UK operate 'bracketed morality' and thus retard moral development?

- What guidelines should teachers and coaches operate to maximise the potential for social and moral development through physical activity and to maximise rather than undermine self-esteem development?

## Acknowledgements

The support of the HEA, the library skills of Claire Carney, the helpful comments from Stuart Biddle, Andrew Steptoe and Martin Lee, and the comments from the HEA 'Young and Active' consensus meeting audience are all gratefully acknowledged.

## References

**Beller, J.M. and Stoll, S.K.** (1995). Moral reasoning of high school students: an empirical study versus personal testimony. *Pediatric Exercise Science*, **7**, 352–63.

**Begg, D.J., Langley, J.D., Moffit, T. and Marshall, S.W.** (1996). Sport and delinquency: an examination of the deterrence hypothesis in a longitudinal study. *British Journal of Sports Medicine*, **30**, 335–41.

**Biddle, S.** (1993). Children, exercise and mental health. *International Journal of Sport Psychology*, **24**, 200–16.

**Biddle, S. and Mutrie, N.** (1991). *Psychology of physical activity and exercise: a health-related perspective*. London: Springer-Verlag.

**Bluechardt, M.H., Wiener, J. and Shephard, R.J.** (1995). Exercise programmes in the treatment of children with learning disabilities. *Sports Medicine*, **19**, 55–72.

**Botting, B. and Crawley, R.** (1995). Trends and patterns in childhood mortality and morbidity. In B. Botting (ed.), *The health of our children*. OPCS Decennial Supplement series 11, pp. 61–81. London: HMSO.

**Bredemeier, B.J. and Shields, D.L.** (1984). Divergence in moral reasoning about sport and everyday life. *Sociology of Sport Journal*, **1**, 348–57.

**Brown, J.D. and Lawton, M.** (1986). Stress and well-being in adolescence: the moderating role of physical exercise. *Journal of Human Stress*, **12**, 125–31.

**Brown, J.D. and Siegel, J.M.** (1988). Exercise as a buffer of life stress: a prospective study of adolescent health. *Health Psychology*, **7**, 341–53.

**Brown, S.W., Welsh, M.C., Labbe, E.E., Vitulli, W.F. and Kulkarni, P.** (1992). Aerobic exercise in the psychological treatment of adolescents. *Perceptual and Motor Skills*, **74**, 555–60.

**Calfas, K.J. and Taylor, C.** (1994). Effects of physical activity on psychological variables in adolescents. *Pediatric Exercise Science*, **6**, 406–23.

**Department of National Heritage** (1995). *Sport, raising the game*. London: Department of National Heritage.

**Dishman, R.K.** (1989). Exercise and sport psychology in youth 6 to 18 years of age. In C.V. Gisolfi and D.R. Lamb (eds.), *Perspectives in exercise science and sports medicine: II. Youth exercise and sport*, pp. 47–97. Indianapolis: Benchmark Press.

**Dishman, R.K.** (1995). Physical activity and public health: mental health. *Quest*, **47**, 362–85.

**Dummer, G.M., Rosen, L.W., Heusner, W.W., Roberts, P.J. and Counsilman, J.E.** (1987). Pathogenic weight-control behaviours of young competitive swimmers. *The Physician and Sports Medicine*, **15** (5), 75–84.

**Dwyer, T., Coonan, W.E., Leitch, D.R., Hetzel, B.S. and Baghurst, R.A.** (1983). An investigation of the effects of daily physical activity on the health of primary school students in South Australia. *International Journal of Epidemiology*, **12**, 308–13.

**Gordon, J. and Grant, G.** (eds.). (1997). *How we feel*. London: Jessica Kingsley Publishers.

**Gruber, J.J.** (1986). Physical activity and self-esteem development in children: a meta-analysis. In G. Stull and H. Eckert (eds.), *Effects of physical activity on children*, pp. 330–48. Champaign: Human Kinetics.

**Health Education Authority and Sports Council** (1992). *Allied Dunbar National Fitness Survey: main findings*. London: Health Education Authority.

**Hastad, D.N., Segrave, J.O., Pangrazi, R. and Petersen, G.** (1984). Youth sport participation and deviant behavior. *Sociology of Sport Journal*, **1**, 366–73.

**Hendry, L.B., Shucksmith, J. and Cross, J.** (1989). Young people's mental well-being in relation to leisure. In Health Promotion Research Trust (ed.), *Fit for life*, pp. 129–53. Cambridge: Health Promotion Research Trust.

**Horn, T.S. and Claytor, R.P.** (1993). Developmental aspects of exercise psychology. In P. Seraganian (ed.), *Exercise psychology*, pp. 299–38. New York: John Wiley & Sons.

**Kavale, K. and Mattson, D.P.** (1983). 'One jumped off the balance beam': Meta-analysis of perceptual motor training. *Journal of Learning Disabilities*, **16** (3), 165–73.

**Kirkendall, D.R.** (1986). Effects of physical activity on intellectual development and academic performance. *American Academy of Physical Education Papers*, **19**, 49–63.

**Kurtz, Z.** (ed.) (1992). *With health in mind*. London: Action for Sick Children.

**Lee, M.J.** (1993). Moral development and children's sporting values. In J. Whitehead (ed.), *Developmental issues in children's sport and physical education*, pp. 30–42. Bedford: Institute for the Study of Children in Sport.

**Lee, M.J.** (1997). Moral well-being: the role of physical education and sport. In N. Armstrong, B.J. Kirby and J. Welsman (eds.), *Children and exercise XIX: promoting health and well-being*, pp. 542–62. London: E. and F.N. Spon.

**Lutz, D.F.** (1981). Juvenile delinquency and recreation. *Journal of Physical Education, Recreation and Dance*, **52** (7), 81–2.

**MacMahon, J. R.** (1990). The psychological benefits of exercise and the treatment of delinquent adolescents. *Sports Medicine*, **9**, 344–351.

**MacMahon, J.R. and Gross, R.T.** (1987). Physical and psychological effects of aerobic exercise in boys with learning disabilities. *Developmental and Behavioural Pediatrics*, **8**, 274–7.

**Malmisur, M.C. and Schempp, P.G.** (1984). Sport participation: its influence on juvenile delinquency. *International Journal of Physical Education*, **21**, 14–16.

**Moses, J., Steptoe, A., Mathews, A. and Edwards, S.** (1989). The effects of exercise training on mental well-being in the normal population: a controlled trial. *Journal of Psychosomatic Research*, **33**, 47–61.

**Munson, W.W.** (1988). Effects of leisure education versus physical activity or informal discussion on behaviorally disordered youth offenders. *Adapted Physical Activity Quarterly*, **5**, 305–17.

**Munson, W.W., Baker, S.B. and Lundegren, H.M.** (1985). Strength training and leisure counselling as treatments for institutionalized juvenile delinquents. *Adapted Physical Activity Quarterly*, **2**, 65–75.

**Mutrie, N.** (1997). The therapeutic effects of exercise on the self. In K.R. Fox (ed.), *The physical self: from motivation to well-being* pp. 506–60. Champaign: Human Kinetics.

**Mutrie, N. and Biddle, S.J.H.** (1995). Effects of exercise on non-clinical populations. In S.J.H. Biddle (ed.), *European perspectives on exercise and sport psychology*, pp. 50–70. Champaign: Human Kinetics.

**National Coaching Foundation.** (1996). *Sport should be fun and you should feel safe*. Poster. Leeds: NCF Publications.

**NHS Health and Advisory Service.** (1995). *Child and adolescent mental health services*. London: HMSO.

**Norris, R., Carroll, D. and Cochrane, R.** (1992). The effects of physical activity and exercise training on psychological stress and well-being in an adolescent population. *Journal of Psychosomatic Research*, **36**, 55–65.

**Petrie, T.A.** (1996). Differences between male and female college lean athletes, non-lean athletes, and non-athletes on behavioural and psychological indices of eating disorder. *Journal of Applied Sport Psychology*, **8**, 218–30.

**Pollatschek, J.L. and O'Hagan, F.J.** (1989). An investigation of the psychophysical influences of a quality daily physical education programme. *Health Education Research: Theory and Practice*, **4**, 342–50.

**Rowland, T. W.** (1990). *Exercise and children's health.* Champaign: Human Kinetics.

**Sage, G.** (1986). Social development. In V. Seefeldt (ed.), *Physical activity and well-being,* pp. 343–71. Reston, VA: American Alliance for Health, Physical Education and Dance.

**Scottish Home and Health Department.** (1980). *Mental Health in Focus.* Edinburgh: HMSO.

**Segrave, J.O.** (1983). Sport and juvenile delinquency. *Exercise and Sport Sciences Reviews,* **11**, 181–209.

**Segrave, J. and Hastad, D.N.** (1982). Delinquent behavior and interscholastic athletic participation. *Journal of Sport Behavior,* **5**, 96–111.

**Segrave, J. Moreau, C. and Hastad, D.N.** (1985). An investigation into the relationship between ice hockey participation and delinquency. *Sociology of Sport Journal,* **2**, 281–98.

**Shephard, R.J.** (1997). Curricular physical activity and academic performance. *Pediatric Exercise Science,* **9**, 113–26.

**Shields, D.L.L. and Bredemeier, B.J.L.** (1994). *Character development and physical activity.* Champaign: Human Kinetics.

**Skogen, K. and Wichstrom, L.** (1996). Delinquency in the wilderness: patterns of outdoor recreation activities and conduct problems in the general adolescent population. *Leisure Studies,* **15**, 151–69.

**Spencer, D.** (1994). Minister out of step with aerobics. *Times Educational Supplement,* 4 February, p. 16.

**Steptoe, A. and Butler, N.** (1996). Sports participation and emotional well-being in adolescents. *Lancet,* **347**, 1789–92.

**Sugden, J. and Yiannakis, A.** (1982). Sport and juvenile delinquency: a theoretical base. *Journal of Sport and Social Issues,* **6** (1), 22–30.

**Sundgot-Borgen, J.** (1994). Risk and trigger factors for the development of eating disorders in female elite athletes. *Medicine and Science in Sports and Exercise,* **26**, 414–19.

**The Scottish Sports Council.** (1996). *A youth sport strategy for Scotland.* Edinburgh: The Scottish Sports Council.

**Tomporowski, P.D. and Ellis, N.R.** (1986). Effects of exercise on cognitive processes: a review. *Psychological Bulletin,* **99**, 338–46.

**Tuckman, B.W. and Hinkle, J.S.** (1986). An experimental study of the physical and psychological effects of aerobic exercise on schoolchildren. *Health Psychology,* **5**, 197–207.

**Trulson, M.E.** (1986). Martial arts training: a novel 'cure' for juvenile delinquency. *Human Relations,* **39**, 1131–40.

**Welsh, M.C. and Labbe, E.** (1994). Children and aerobic exercise: a review of cognitive and behavioral effects. *Journal of Experimental Child Psychology,* **58**, 405–17.

**Williams, L.R.T., Hughes, J.R. and Martin, C.** (1982). Effects of daily physical education on children's attitudes toward physical activity. *New Zealand Journal of Health, Physical Education and Recreation,* **15**, 31–5.

# Are young people fit and active?

Neil Armstrong[1] and Willem Van Mechelen[2]

[1]Professor of Health and Exercise Science,
University of Exeter;

[2]Associate Professor of Social Medicine,
Vrije, Amsterdam, Netherlands.

Although physical fitness and physical activity are often used interchangeably, they are not synonymous, and before proceeding the terms require clarification. Physical fitness is a complex phenomenon that is difficult to define(Bouchard *et al.*, 1990) but is widely accepted as 'a set of attributes that people have or achieve and that relates to the ability to perform physical activity' (Caspersen, Powell and Christenson, 1985). Thus defined, physical fitness includes such components as cardiorespiratory endurance, skeletal muscular strength, skeletal muscular power, speed, flexibility, agility, balance, reaction time and body composition.

Traditionally, physical fitness has been linked with performance in sports and physical education and in adults in specialised occupations such as the fire service, police force and military services. Health-related fitness, as opposed to performance-related fitness, comprises by definition those aspects of physical fitness that are related to health – cardiorespiratory fitness, muscular strength and endurance, body composition and flexibility. The physical fitness component that has been most frequently studied in adults for an association to health is cardiorespiratory fitness, also referred to as cardiovascular (endurance) fitness or aerobic (power) fitness. Similarly, the aerobic fitness of young people has been extensively documented since Robinson's (1938) classical studies of boys in Chicago.

Research into the health benefits of muscular fitness and flexibility in adults has primarily focused on the aetiology of lower back pain and on its relationship with functional freedom, independence and overall health in the ageing population (Oja and Tuxworth, 1995). Until recently such research has been lacking in children (Kemper and Van Mechelen, 1996).

The assessment of physical fitness is a highly developed measurement area, in both adults and children. The different components of physical fitness can be measured by means of various laboratory and field tests. EUROFIT is one example of a field test battery for children (Kemper and Van Mechelen, 1996) and for adults (Oja and Tuxworth, 1995). However, according to Astrand and Rodahl (1987), field tests (or components thereof) are not really suitable for the assessment of single, basic physiological functions. Given the considerations mentioned above and acknowledging the importance of other components of physical fitness, this review will focus on laboratory measures of aerobic fitness.

Physical activity is defined as a complex set of behaviours that encompass any bodily movement produced by skeletal muscles that results in energy expenditure (Caspersen *et al.*, 1985). Physical activity is therefore a component of total energy expenditure, which also includes resting metabolism, the thermic effect of food and growth (Baranowski *et al.*, 1992).

## Method of review

Relevant studies for review were located through computer searches of Medline, Sport Discus and personal databases complemented with an extensive search of bibliographies of accessed studies.

## ▨ Aerobic fitness

Peak oxygen uptake (peak $\dot{V}O_2$) the highest oxygen uptake elicited during an exercise test to exhaustion, is widely recognised as the best single index of young people's aerobic fitness (Armstrong and Welsman, 1994; Armstrong, Welsman and Winsley, 1996). The measurement of young people's peak $\dot{V}O_2$ has been addressed in a number of recent reviews (Rowland, 1993; Welsman and Armstrong, 1996; Armstrong and Welsman, 1997) and interested readers are referred to these sources for detailed analyses of the topic.

### Peak $\dot{V}O_2$ and age

The extant literature contains a substantial amount of cross-sectional data on the peak $\dot{V}O_2$ of untrained children and several longitudinal studies have been reported. No information appears to be available on randomly selected groups of young people and selection bias cannot be ruled out. As a result, very inactive or overweight children and adolescents may have been excluded from the literature.

Armstrong and Welsman (1994) represented graphically published data representing 4000 treadmill peak $\dot{V}O_2$ determinations in relation to chronological age (Figure 4.1) and this figure clearly illustrates a progressive, linear increase in boys' peak $\dot{V}O_2$ with age. Longitudinal studies, over different age ranges, have also provided a consistent picture of a gradual rise in boys' peak $\dot{V}O_2$ from 8 through 18 years (Cunningham, Paterson, Blimkie and Donner, 1984; Mirwald and Bailey, 1986; Rutenfranz, *et al.*, 1981). Table 1 describes the published longitudinal studies from which relevant data can be extracted.

Girls demonstrate a similar but less consistent trend (Figure 4.1). From age 8 to 13 years, girls' peak $\dot{V}O_2$ appears to increase with chronological age but several cross-sectional studies have indicated a levelling off or even a fall in peak $\dot{V}O_2$ from 13 years of age (e.g. Nagawa and Ishiko, 1970; Yoshizawa, 1972; Chatterjee *et al.*, 1979). Longitudinal studies of Norwegian and German girls, although limited by small sample sizes, indicate that peak $\dot{V}O_2$ reaches its highest value at 13.3 and 14.7 years respectively (Rutenfranz *et al.*, 1981). However, the Amsterdam Growth Study (Van Mechelen and Kemper, 1995) reported girls' peak $\dot{V}O_2$ to increase from 13 to 16 years before levelling off in adult life.

As most physical activity involves moving body mass from one place to another, to compare the peak $\dot{V}O_2$ of young people who differ in body mass, peak $\dot{V}O_2$ is conventionally expressed in relation to mass as millilitres of oxygen per kilogram body mass per minute (i.e. $mL \cdot kg^{-1} \cdot min^{-1}$)[1].

---

[1] We have argued elsewhere that expressing peak $\dot{V}O_2$ in ratio with body mass may be inappropriate but the theoretical and statistical principles involved are beyond the scope of this review (Welsman and Armstrong, 1996; Welsman *et al.*, 1996; Armstrong and Welsman, 1997).

**Figure 4.1.** *Peak V̇o₂ by age. (Redrawn from Armstrong and Welsman 1994, Exercise and Sport Sciences Reviews, **22**, 435-76. Reprinted with permission)*

When peak V̇o₂ is expressed in ratio with body mass, a different picture emerges from that apparent when absolute values (L·min⁻¹) are used. Figure 4.2 represents 6000 peak V̇o₂ data points and illustrates that boys' mass-related peak V̇o₂ remains remarkably stable, with values approximating 50 mL·kg⁻¹·min⁻¹ whereas girls' values show a tendency to fall with increasing age, from about 45 to 39 mL·kg⁻¹·min⁻¹ (Armstrong and Welsman, 1994). Individual longitudinal studies generally confirm the stability of boys' mass-related peak V̇o₂ with age (Rutenfranz *et al.*, 1981; Mirwald and Bailey, 1986; Van Mechelen and Kemper, 1995), although there are reports of both an increase (Spryranova, Parizkova and Bunc, 1987) and a decrease (Rutenfranz *et al.*, 1981) in mass-related peak V̇o₂ between 12 and 14 years of age. Longitudinal studies of girls' mass-related

peak V̇o₂ show unequivocally a progressive decline with age (Rutenfranz *et al.*, 1981; Mirwald and Bailey, 1986; Van Mechelen and Kemper, 1995). Boys demonstrate higher mass-related peak V̇o₂ than girls from 8 through 18 years, the sex difference being reinforced by the greater accumulation of body fat by girls during puberty (Malina and Bouchard, 1991; Armstrong and Welsman, 1994).

### Are young people fit?

There is no scientific evidence to suggest that young people's aerobic fitness has declined over the last 50 years and an analysis of data reported since the pioneering work of Robinson (1938) reveals a remarkable consistency over time in children's and adolescents' peak V̇o₂ whether expressed in L·min⁻¹ or mL·kg⁻¹·min⁻¹

**Table 4.1.** *Longitudinal studies or aerobic fitness*

| Citation | Country | Age (years) | N | Mode | Peak V̇O₂ L·min⁻¹ | Peak V̇O₂ mL·kg⁻¹·min⁻¹ |
|---|---|---|---|---|---|---|
| **Boys** | | | | | | |
| Rutenfranz *et al.* (1981) | Germany | 12.7 | 28 | CE | 2.33 ± 0.32 | 57. 4 ± 7.1 |
| | | 13.7 | 27 | CE | 2.50 ± 0.46 | 54.1 ± 5.6 |
| | | 14.7 | 26 | CE | 2.83 ± 0.49 | 52.1 ± 4.2 |
| | | 15.8 | 27 | CE | 3.05 ± 0.54 | 51.8 ± 3.6 |
| | | 16.7 | 23 | CE | 3.00 ± 0.34 | 47.1 ± 3.6 |
| | | 17.8 | 26 | CE | 3.11 ± 0.48 | 47.5 ± 4.4 |
| Rutenfranz *et al.* (1981) | Norway | 8.4 | 28 | CE | 1.44 ± 0.19 | 52.7 ± 3.9 |
| | | 9.4 | 29 | CE | 1.59 ± 0.24 | 51.4 ± 5.2 |
| | | 10.4 | 31 | CE | 2.03 ± 0.30 | 60.0 ± 6.5 |
| | | 11.4 | 29 | CE | 2.07 ± 0.30 | 56.9 ± 6.1 |
| | | 12.3 | 30 | CE | 2.31 ± 0.34 | 58.0 ± 8.0 |
| | | 13.3 | 29 | CE | 2.70 ± 0.51 | 61.4 ± 6.7 |
| | | 14.5 | 27 | CE | 2.82 ± 0.41 | 56.6 ± 5.0 |
| | | 15.3 | 27 | CE | 3.14 ± 0.38 | 56.0 ± 4.4 |
| Cunningham *et al.* (1981) | Canada | 10.8 | 62 | CE | 1.72 ± 0.38 | 48.8 ± 8.8 |
| | | 11.8 | 62 | CE | 1.90 ± 0.28 | 49.0 ± 7.0 |
| | | 12.8 | 62 | CE | 2.16 ± 0.40 | 49.6 ± 7.6 |
| | | 13.8 | 62 | CE | 2.58 ± 0.55 | 51.9 ± 7.4 |
| | | 14.8 | 62 | CE | 2.88 ± 0.51 | 51.3 ± 7.6 |
| Mirwald and Bailey (1986) | Canada | 8 | 75 | TM | 1.42 ± 0.21 | 55.6 ± 6.4 |
| | | 9 | 75 | TM | 1.60 ± 0.20 | 56.1 ± 5.3 |
| | | 10 | 75 | TM | 1.77 ± 0.22 | 56.3 ± 5.1 |
| | | 11 | 75 | TM | 1.93 ± 0.25 | 56.3 ± 5.1 |
| | | 12 | 75 | TM | 2.12 ± 0.29 | 56.1 ± 5.1 |
| | | 13 | 75 | TM | 2.35 ± 0.38 | 55.6 ± 5.3 |
| | | 14 | 75 | TM | 2.66 ± 0.46 | 55.0 ± 5.8 |
| | | 15 | 75 | TM | 2.98 ± 0.48 | 54.4 ± 5.6 |
| | | 16 | 75 | TM | 3.22 ± 0.45 | 53.6 ± 5.2 |
| Amsterdam Growth and Health Study (unpublished data) | The Netherlands | 13 | 83 | TM | 2.66 ± 0.39 | 59.4 ± 5.5 |
| | | 14 | 80 | TM | 3.07 ± 0.48 | 59.4 ± 6.3 |
| | | 15 | 84 | TM | 3.37 ± 0.43 | 58.5 ± 4.7 |
| | | 16 | 79 | TM | 3.68 ± 0.52 | 58.7 ± 5.2 |
| **Girls** | | | | | | |
| Rutenfranz *et al.* (1981) | Germany | 12.7 | 24 | CE | 2.19 ± 0.30 | 47.9 ± 7.4 |
| | | 13.7 | 24 | CE | 2.20 ± 0.22 | 43.8 ± 6.6 |
| | | 14.7 | 22 | CE | 2.26 ± 0.26 | 41.8 ± 6.3 |
| | | 15.7 | 22 | CE | 2.18 ± 0.29 | 39.1 ± 6.8 |
| | | 16.7 | 17 | CE | 1.97 ± 0.31 | 33.4 ± 4.9 |
| | | 17.8 | 19 | CE | 2.06 ± 0.33 | 35.0 ± 5.1 |
| Rutenfranz *et al.* (1981) | Norway | 8.2 | 33 | CE | 1.25 ± 0.20 | 47.4 ± 7.0 |
| | | 9.3 | 33 | CE | 1.48 ± 0.19 | 48.5 ± 6.6 |
| | | 10.3 | 34 | CE | 1.79 ± 0.23 | 52.4 ± 6.4 |
| | | 11.2 | 34 | CE | 1.88 ± 0.22 | 50.1 ± 5.9 |
| | | 12.2 | 34 | CE | 2.26 ± 0.32 | 53.6 ± 6.8 |
| | | 13.3 | 33 | CE | 2.48 ± 0.46 | 51.8 ± 9.2 |
| | | 14.2 | 32 | CE | 2.35 ± 0.26 | 44.7 ± 6.6 |
| | | 15.2 | 30 | CE | 2.44 ± 0.30 | 43.6 ± 6.0 |
| Mirwald and Bailey (1986) | Canada | 8 | 22 | TM | 1.27 ± 0.14 | 50.6 ± 6.0 |
| | | 9 | 22 | TM | 1.39 ± 0.15 | 49.8 ± 5.8 |
| | | 10 | 22 | TM | 1.53 ± 0.20 | 49.2 ± 6.4 |
| | | 11 | 22 | TM | 1.72 ± 0.28 | 48.7 ± 7.2 |
| | | 12 | 22 | TM | 1.97 ± 0.36 | 48.2 ± 7.3 |
| | | 13 | 22 | TM | 2.20 ± 0.39 | 47.3 ± 7.1 |
| Amsterdam Growth and Health Study (unpublished data) | The Netherlands | 13 | 97 | TM | 2.45 ± 0.31 | 51.2 ± 6.1 |
| | | 14 | 97 | TM | 2.60 ± 0.35 | 50.1 ± 5.3 |
| | | 15 | 96 | TM | 2.58 ± 0.34 | 47.2 ± 4.7 |
| | | 16 | 96 | TM | 2.65 ± 0.33 | 46.7 ± 4.1 |

Values are mean ± standard deviation. Mode: CE is cycle ergometer; TM is treadmill.

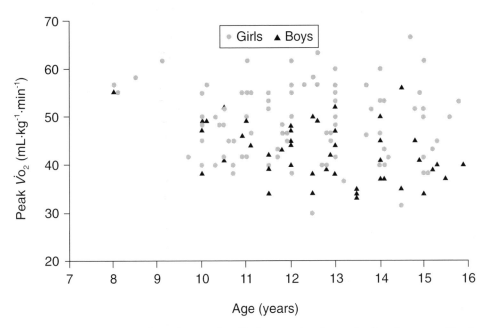

**Figure 4.2.** *Mass-related treadmill determined peak V̇o₂ by age. (Redrawn from Armstrong and Welsman 1994. Exercise and Sports Sciences Reviews, **22**, 435-76. Reprinted with permission)*

(Krahenbuhl, Skinner and Kohrt, 1985; Armstrong and Welsman, 1994).

There is no consensus about levels of optimal aerobic fitness for children and adolescents and the concept is confounded with the problems associated with the interpretation of young people's peak V̇o₂ in relation to body size and maturity. Nevertheless, an expert group drawn from the European Group of Pediatric Work Physiology suggested that it may be possible to express a lower limit of peak V̇o₂ that, in the absence of other health-related problems, may represent a 'health risk' (Bell *et al.*, 1986). They proposed 35 mL·kg⁻¹·min⁻¹ for boys and 30 mL·kg⁻¹·min⁻¹ for girls. They also suggested levels greater than 40 mL·kg⁻¹·min⁻¹ for boys and 35 mL·kg⁻¹·min⁻¹ for girls may be used as 'health indicators'. No empirical evidence was provided in support of the proposals.

Few studies have reported their results in sufficient detail to estimate the number of young people falling below these levels of peak V̇o₂ but a recent study of a representative sample of prepubertal children reported that all children had values above the 'health risk' threshold. All girls (N = 53) demonstrated a level of aerobic fitness above their 'health indicator' threshold and only two boys, from a sample of 111, had values below 40 mL·kg⁻¹·min⁻¹ (Armstrong *et al.*, 1995). Over 2500 young people have had their peak V̇o₂ determined in the Children's Health and Exercise Research Centre during the period 1987–97 and a re-analysis of the data in the context of the threshold put forward by Bell *et al.* (1986) has revealed that less than 2% of the values have fallen below the proposed 'health risk' thresholds. Furthermore, scrutiny of Figure 4.1 reveals that the mean values of all treadmill studies located lie above the 'health risk' threshold by Bell *et al.* (1986). There is little evidence to suggest that low levels of aerobic fitness are common among young people.

In summary, the assessment and interpretation of young people's aerobic fitness is complex. Boys' peak $\dot{V}O_2$ (L·min⁻¹) progressively increases from childhood through puberty and into adult life, whereas girls' peak $\dot{V}O_2$ appears to level off in mid-teens. When expressed in ratio with body mass (mL·kg⁻¹·min⁻¹) a different picture emerges with boys' values remaining stable from 8 to 18 years and girls' values falling with increasing age. It remains to be proven that either young people's aerobic fitness has declined over time or that they have low levels of aerobic fitness.

# ■ Physical activity

## Measurement issues

The assessment of the habitual physical activity of young people is one of the most difficult tasks in epidemiological research (Saris, 1985; Baranowski and Simons-Morton, 1991). The technique used must be socially acceptable, it should not burden the child with cumbersome equipment and it should minimally influence the person's normal physical activity pattern. Ideally the intensity, frequency and duration of activities should be monitored and, if a true picture of habitual physical activity is required, some account should be taken of any day-to-day variation. A minimum monitoring period of three days has been recommended (Bar-Or, 1983).

More than 30 different methods of assessing physical activity have been identified (LaPorte *et al.*, 1985), but the reliability, objectivity and validity of many of

these methods have not been established with children and adolescents (Melanson and Freedson, 1996; Armstrong and Welsman, 1997). The issue is further confounded by the lack of a universally accepted 'gold standard' analogous to peak $\dot{V}O_2$ in aerobic fitness assessment. The available techniques can be grouped into four categories: self-report and proxy report; observation; motion sensor monitoring; and physiological analyses.

## Self-report and proxy report

Self-report methods include retrospective questionnaires, interview-administered recall and activity diaries. With young children, proxy reports by parents and/or teachers have been employed. Sallis (1991: 215) has pointed out that actual behaviour is not directly assessed by self-reports and the data obtained are,

> memories of the behaviour of interest that have decayed, been filtered through perceptions and biases, and have been tainted by competing memories, social desirability and misunderstanding of instructions.

Considerable demands are placed on the young person's abilities to recall specific events from the past (Baranowski *et al.*, 1984) and several writers have expressed concern over self-report methods of estimating children's physical activity (e.g. Livingstone, 1994; Simons-Morton, Taylor and Huang, 1994). Self-report data have been used to estimate young people's energy expenditure, usually on the basis of extrapolating data obtained from adults to children. This may underestimate true energy costs by about 20% in 10-year-olds, decreasing to about 5% by the age of 16 years (Sallis, Buono and Freedson, 1991; Pate, 1993).

Teachers and parents can only provide secondary information, especially when it concerns activities outside school or home, and proxy reports therefore tend to lack validity (Saris, 1986; Ching and Dietz, 1995). Diaries may be superior to retrospective questionnaires (Baranowski *et al.*, 1984) but keeping a diary may in itself influence physical activity (Salonen and Lakka, 1987) and the quality of completed physical activity diaries has been reported to be inconsistent with young people (Saris, 1985).

## Observation

Observation allows for different dimensions of activity to be simultaneously recorded and the better systems are sensitive to brief periods of activity, which is important when monitoring children (Melanson and Freedson, 1996). Recent advances in data storage and analysis have promoted this method of assessing physical activity (McKenzie, 1991). Several instruments have been developed (Klesges *et al.*, 1984; Puhl *et al.*, 1990) but none appears to have been validated for use with older children and adolescents (McKenzie, 1991). Observation studies are labour intensive and the extent to which observers influence behaviour of the young person (subject reactivity) has not been determined (O'Hara *et al.*, 1989). Few observational studies have monitored large numbers of children over extended periods of time (Baranowski *et al.*, 1993; DuRant *et al.*, 1993) but detailed observation of small samples over limited time periods has provided valuable information about young people's physical activity patterns (Bailey *et al.*, 1995).

## Motion sensors

The simplest form of motion sensor is the pedometer, which was used widely in early studies of children's physical activity (Saris, 1985; 1986). Pedometers function on the principle of a delicately balanced arm which turns a series of gears when it is displaced by a jolt in the vertical plane. The impact of a foot strike therefore transmits an impulse to the balance arm and an estimate of distance travelled can be obtained by calibrating the pedometer to stride length. Pedometers have been gradually replaced by more sophisticated movement counters, such as actometers (Schulman and Reisman, 1959) and Large Scale Integrated (LSI) activity monitors (LaPorte *et al.*, 1982).

Actometers are modified wrist watches in which the rotor is directly connected to the hands. In principle, the actometer records both movements and their intensity – the stronger the movement the faster the rotor will turn. LSIs are activity monitors that can be placed on various parts of the body and in which a tilt of more than 3° results in the closure of a mercury switch and the registration of a movement. Every 16 closures is registered as a count. LSIs are less susceptible to intra- and inter-instrument variability than pedometers and actometers but they are not sensitive to the short burst, intense activity often observed in children (Klesges *et al.*, 1985). Careful and extensive field validation of pedometers, actometers and LSIs with young people has not been carried out (Freedson, 1991).

Electronic motion sensors, known as accelerometers, which measure both frequency and intensity of movement in the vertical plane have largely replaced movement counters in physical activity research (Danner, *et al.*, 1991; Janz, Witt and Mahoney, 1995). The most popular instrument is the Caltrac accelerometer in which vertical accelerations result in twisting of an internal ceramic piezoelectric transducer. The amount of twisting is proportional to the size of the acceleration. Accelerations are only measured in the vertical plane, and the Caltrac is not sensitive to activities that include bending or twisting movements or activity involving the arms. The Caltrac is about the size of a pocket calculator and can be enclosed in a locked pouch secured to the waist. The validity of the Caltrac has been studied in young people and although its use has been supported it has been suggested that sporadic activity patterns may not be adequately represented by a simple unidimensional device (Sallis *et al.*, 1990; Bray *et al.*, 1992; Ellison *et al.*, 1992).

The Tritrac-R3D, which is based on the same accelerometry principles as the Caltrac but is capable of assessing activity in three dimensions rather than one, has been recently developed to correct some of the limitations of the Caltrac. Early trials have been promising but the instrument requires further evaluation before being accepted as a valid means of measuring young people's physical activity (Freedson *et al.*, 1997; Welk and Corbin, 1995; Eston, Rowland and Ingledew, 1997).

Both Caltrac and Tritrac-R3D can be programmed to estimate energy expenditure but the methodology makes a number of unsubstantiated assumptions. For example, the equations that predict energy expenditure were developed from adult data. For research purposes it is advisable to use activity 'counts' as the criterion measure (Freedson, 1991; Pate, 1993).

## Physiological analyses

Energy expenditure can be directly measured by determining oxygen uptake ($\dot{V}o_2$) if it is assumed that daily physical activity is almost entirely aerobic. The recent application of the technique of using stable isotopes (doubly-labelled water) to estimate $\dot{V}o_2$ has overcome the restrictions of wearing a face mask and provided an unobtrusive and non-invasive means of measuring energy expenditure. The doubly-labelled water technique measures the disappearance rate of a labelled isotope ($^2H_2^{18}O$) from urine samples to measure carbon dioxide $\dot{V}co_2$ production over several days. Using an estimated respiratory exchange ratio $\dot{V}co_2/\dot{V}o_2$ and standard calorimetric equations, $\dot{V}o_2$, and therefore energy expenditure, can be calculated (Prentice, 1990; Speakman, Nair and Goran, 1993).

The use of stable isotopes to estimate energy expenditure provides a powerful tool. The method appears to be accurate to within 5% relative to data derived by indirect calorimetry for those living in metabolic chambers (Saris, 1992). However, the data obtained only provide a measure of total energy expenditure over the study period and no information is provided on the individual's physical activity pattern.

A number of self-contained, computerised telemetry systems have been developed for the unobtrusive measurement of heart rate over several days. They are socially acceptable, they permit freedom of movement, they are not immediately noticeable and therefore should not unduly influence children's normal physical activity patterns. The Polar Vantage NV is the instrument of choice and heart rate monitoring has been extensively tested and found to be reliable and valid with young people (Tsanakas *et al.*, 1986; Treiber *et al.*, 1989).

The interpretation of heart rate is quite complex, as it not only reflects the metabolism of the individual but also the transient emotional state, the prevailing climatic conditions and the specific muscle groups that perform the activity. Heart rate monitoring does, however, offer an attractive, objective method of estimating physical activity in real-life situations (Melanson and Freedson, 1996; Armstrong and Welsman, 1997).

Several investigators have reported the totalised time or percentage time heart rates were above certain criteria during the period studied (Seliger *et al.*, 1974; Gilliam *et al.*, 1981). Others have argued that in addition to noting total time in specific heart rate bands the number and length of sustained periods above threshold levels may offer a more informative picture of physical activity patterns (Armstrong *et al.*, 1990; Janz *et al.*, 1992).

Because of the ease of measuring heart rate in field conditions, several investigators have used the linear relationship between heart rate and $\dot{V}o_2$ to estimate energy expenditure (Cunningham *et al.*, 1984; Riddoch *et al.*, 1991b). There are several problems with this technique, notably that steady state exercise in a laboratory is somewhat different from the intermittent physical activity experienced in real-life situations. A careful study using a whole body calorimeter clearly illustrated the limitations of the heart rate/$\dot{V}o_2$ relationship and demonstrated that, as the average 24-hour heart rate is low and outside the range of the heart rate/$\dot{V}o_2$ linear relationship, the use of heart rates accurately to estimate daily energy expenditure is not tenable (Dauncey and James, 1979). In addition, heart rate may be more affected than $\dot{V}o_2$ by different modes of activity (static v. dynamic), activity with different muscle groups (arms v. legs), the ambient temperature, fatigue, emotional stress and state of training. Heart rates also tend to return to resting levels more slowly than $\dot{V}o_2$ following activity. Estimates of individual youngsters' energy expenditure on the

basis of heart rates must therefore be interpreted very cautiously.

## Comparison of methods of assessing physical activity

Physical activity is a behaviour but it can only occur as a result of skeletal muscle activity that is supported by energy expenditure. Physical activity is therefore interrelated with energy expenditure, but it may cause an elevation in metabolic rate that persists long after cessation of observable movement. Different techniques may therefore be measuring different dimensions of physical activity and this could, at least in part, account for the often weak relationships between different measurement techniques used on the same children and youth.

Low to moderate relationships have been reported between self-report measures and observational techniques (Baranowski *et al.*, 1984; Wallace, McKenzie and Nader, 1985), heart rate monitoring (Biddle, Mitchell and Armstrong, 1991; Riddoch *et al.*, 1991a), and with monitoring using motion sensors (Klesges, Haddock and Eck, 1990; Sallis, 1993). Similarly, only low to moderate relationships have been observed between Caltrac scores and both observation (Mukeshi *et al.*, 1990; Noland *et al.*, 1990) and heart rate monitoring (Ballor *et al.*, 1989; Sallis *et al.*, 1991). Comparison of heart rate monitoring with doubly-labelled water has resulted in a close estimation of total energy expenditure in one study (Livingstone *et al.*, 1992) and a 12% overestimation of energy expenditure in another (Emons *et al.*, 1992).

In summary, the assessment of young people's habitual physical activity is extremely complex and a clear understanding of current methodology is required to interpret adequately the extant literature. To obtain a true picture of habitual physical activity, a minimum period of three days monitoring has been recommended. Heart rate monitoring, observation and motion sensor monitoring are generally considered to be the most objective measures of activity (Melanson and Freedson, 1996; Armstrong and Welsman, 1997) but all methods have deficiencies. Heart rate can provide an indication of the intensity, frequency and duration of activity but may be influenced by factors independent of exercise. Most motion sensors do not discriminate physical activity patterns but some recent sensors (e.g. Tritrac-R3D) have internal real-time clocks which allow this facility. Both heart rate and motion sensor monitoring have low levels of subject reactivity whereas observational methods may cause individuals to alter their normal activity patterns. Observation, however, provides information on the type of physical activity performed. Self-report is problematic because of the demands placed on young people's ability to recall specific events. Doubly-labelled water provides an accurate measure of total energy expenditure over several days but provides no information on physical activity patterns.

Ideally a combination of different techniques should be used. For example, simultaneous use of doubly-labelled water, heart rate monitoring and structured observation would yield information on total energy expenditure, patterns of relative physiological load (intensity) on the cardiopulmonary system, and frequency, duration and type of physical activity experienced. Unfortunately, the choice of method is likely to be dictated largely by logistic and financial considerations.

# ◼ Habitual physical activity

Large scale national surveys of self-reports of young people's physical activity have been carried out in the United States (Ross and Gilbert, 1985), Canada (Shephard, 1986), Northern Ireland (Riddoch, 1990) and Wales (Heartbeat Wales, 1986). Many smaller studies have been reported, and data from North America and Europe are extensive (see Pate, Long and Heath, 1994; Armstrong, 1995; Riddoch and Boreham, 1995). Methodological difficulties preclude direct comparison between studies but it is possible to examine age and sex-related trends within and across studies.

Sallis (1993) analysed a selection of self-report studies, including national surveys, and observed that most studies indicated a decline in physical activity from age 10 to 16 years. He reported that boys were about 14% more active than girls, with a range of 4 to 30%. The annual mean decrease in physical activity was 1.8% (range 1.3 to 2.0%) in boys and 2.6% (range 1.2 to 5.0%) in girls.

A multi-national study of 11 European countries illustrates self-report trends in physical activity (King and Coles, 1992). Representative samples of three age groups, 11, 12, and 13 years, were recruited and the children were asked how often per week they exercised outside school hours to the point that they got out of breath or sweated. Sample sizes were substantial, ranging from 2984 in Austria to 6498 in Hungary. Figure 4.3 gives the percentages of boys and girls who exercised once a week or less by age and participating country. The decrease in exercise participation with age, especially for girls, is readily apparent and generally consistent across countries. Fewer girls

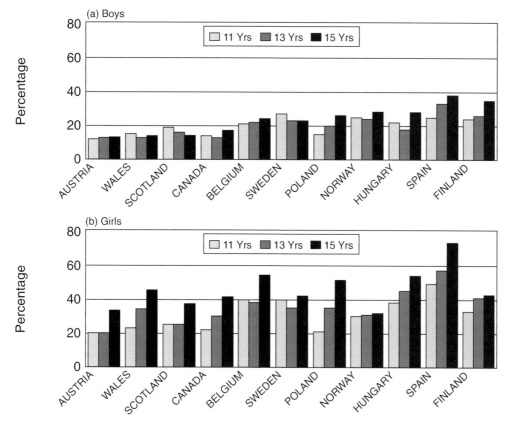

**Figure 4.3.** *Percentage of young people who exercise less than once a week outside school: (a) boys; (b) girls. (Figures drawn from data reported by King and Coles, 1992 and reprinted from Armstrong and Welsman, 1997 Young People and Physical Activity: Oxford University Press, by permission of Oxford University Press.)*

than boys exercised at least once a week at all ages studied.

Sallis (1993) revealed similar patterns in data from studies that used objective physical activity measures, with boys observed to be 12 to 30% more physically active than girls, and the mean sex difference being approximately 23%. The decline in physical activity with age, however, was reported to be almost twice as steep when assessed objectively compared to self-report. Boys' mean annual decline in physical activity, from 6 to 17 years, was reported as 2.7%, with a range of 1.6

to 3.8%, whereas the corresponding figures for girls were 7.4% and 2.5 to 17.0% (Sallis, 1993).

The results of all located studies which have used objective methods to monitor physical activity over sustained time periods are summarised in Table 4.2. As one day of monitoring is not adequate to characterise a child's habitual physical activity (Bar-Or, 1983; Sallis, McKenzie and Alcaraz, 1993) only studies that monitored activity for two or more days are included.

**Table 4.2.** *Studies of habitual physical activity*

| Citation | Subjects | Physical activity measure | Outcomes |
|---|---|---|---|
| **Verschuur et al. (1984)** | 215 girls, 195 boys; age: 13–14 years; The Netherlands | 2 day HR monitoring<br>3 day pedometer monitoring | 30 min·d⁻¹ (boys) and 37 min·d⁻¹ (girls) spent with HR >150 beats·min⁻¹. The activity scores derived from pedometry showed boys to spend significantly more time 'on heavy activities' than girls, boys median 99 min, girls 1 min. |
| **Atomi et al. (1986)** | 11 boys; age: 10.4 years; Japan | 3 day HR monitoring | 34 min·d⁻¹ spent with HR > 60% max $\dot{V}O_2$ and 130 min·d⁻¹ spent with HR > 120 beats·min⁻¹ |
| **Baranowski et al. (1987)** | 14 girls, 10 boys; age: 7–10 years; United States | 2 day observation | No 20 min events of rapid trunk movement occurred, therefore 'movement' below includes both slow and fast movement<br>20 min of movement with no stop: day 1, 3 children; day 2, 2 children<br>20 min of movement with 1 stop: day 1, 8 children; day 2, 9 children<br>14 min of movement with no stop: day 1, 11 children, day 2, 11 children<br>14 min of movement with 1 stop: day 1, 15 children, day 2, 14 children |
| **Armstrong et al. (1990a)** | 163 girls, 103 boys; age: 11–16 years; England | 4 day HR monitoring | Boys had HR >139 beats·min⁻¹ for sig. greater percentage of time than girls (6.2% v. 4.3%) during 3 weekdays and a Saturday, boys (n = 92) 5.6% v. girls (n = 120) 2.6%. A sig. negative correlation with age was found with girls (weekday r= -0.27, Saturday r= -0.21) but not with boys. 51.5% of girls and 35.9% of boys did not exhibit a single 10 min sustained period with HR >139 beats·min⁻¹ over 3 weekdays. On Saturday the corresponding figures were 70.7% of boys and 93.3% of girls. |
| **Armstrong and Bray (1990)** | 11 girls, 13 boys; age: 10–11 years; England | 6 day HR monitoring | Children spent 8.8% of time with HR >139 beats·min⁻¹ and 3.6% of time with HR >159 beats·min⁻¹. 33.4% of children did not exhibit a single 10 min sustained period with HR >139 beats·min⁻¹ and 62.5% did not exhibit a single 10 min sustained period with HR >159 beats·min⁻¹. No sig. differences were detected between boys and girls |
| **Armstrong and Bray (1991)** | 65 girls, 67 boys; age: 10.7 years; England | 4 day HR monitoring | No sig. sex differences in time spent with HR >139 beats·min⁻¹ during 3 weekdays (boys 9.4% v. girls 8.2%) or a Saturday (boys (n = 16) 5.2% v. girls (n = 23) 6.0%). Boys spent sig. more time with HR >159 beats·min⁻¹ during weekdays (4.5% v. 3.5%) but not during Saturdays (1.8% v. 1.8%). 25% of girls and 19% of boys did not exhibit a single 10 min sustained period with HR >139 beats·min⁻¹ during weekdays. On Saturday the corresponding figures were 75% of boys and 65% of girls |

**Table 4.2.** *continued*

| Citation | Subjects | Physical activity measure | Outcomes |
| --- | --- | --- | --- |
| **Biddle et al. (1991)** | 20 girls, 26 boys; age: 12.2 years; England | 3 day HR monitoring | No sig. sex differences in time spent with HR >139 beats·min⁻¹ during 3 weekdays but boys spent significantly more time with their HR >159 beats·min⁻¹ (2.7% v. 1.9%). 45.9% of boys and 34.3% girls did not sustain a single 10 min period with HR >139 beats·min⁻¹. The corresponding figures for 10 min periods with HR >159 beats·min⁻¹ were 64.9% of boys and 91.4% of girls. |
| **Riddoch et al. (1991)** | 22 girls, 23 boys; age: 11–16 years; Ireland | 2–4 day HR monitoring | No sig. sex difference in daily time spent with HR >50% peak $\dot{V}O_2$ (boys, 24 min; girls, 17 min). Boys spent sig. more time than girls with HR >70% peak $\dot{V}O_2$ (8 min v. 4 min). Younger boys engaged in sig. more total activity than older boys and in more vigorous activity than younger girls. A sig. negative correlation (r=−0.48) was found between age and total activity in boys but not in girls. |
| **Du Rant et al. (1993)** | 98 girls, 82 boys; age: 3–7 years; United States | 1–4 day observation | Boys had significantly higher mean levels of activity than girls. The average physical activity level over the whole period of monitoring equated to 'stationary-with movement' i.e. with an expected HR of 100–119 beats·min⁻¹. The percentage of time that had some activity with an expected HR >139 beats·min⁻¹ was reported as 'only between 4.8% and 13.7% of the time within each hour of the day were ever spent at these levels'. |
| **McManus and Armstrong (1995)** | 100 girls, 100 boys; age: 11.1 years; England | 3 day HR monitoring | Boys spent sig. more time than girls with HR >139 beats·min⁻¹ (9.1% v. 7.3%) and HR >159 beats·min⁻¹ (4.3% v. 3.0%). 22% of boys and 30% of girls did not sustain a single 10 min period with HR >139 beats·min⁻¹ and 49% of boys and 57% of girls did not sustain a single 10 min period with HR >159 beats·min⁻¹ |
| **Gilbey and Gilbey (1995)** | 64 girls, 50 boys; age: 9.9 years; Singapore | 4 day HR monitoring | Boys spent 47 min during weekdays and 42 min (n = 43) during Saturday with HR > 140 beats·min⁻¹, 15 min during weekdays and 13 min during Saturday was spent with HR >160 beats·min⁻¹. Girls spent 30 min during weekdays and 33 min (n = 53) during Saturday with HR >140 beats·min⁻¹, 10 min during both weekdays and Saturdays were spent with HR >160 beats·min⁻¹. 20% of boys and 51.5% of girls did not sustain a single 10 min period with HR >140 beats·min⁻¹ over 3 weekdays. The corresponding figs for Saturday were 46.5% of boys and 69.8% of girls. 86% of boys and 92.2% of girls did not sustain a 10 min period with HR >160 beats·min⁻¹ over 3 weekdays. The corresponding figures for Saturday were 95.4% of boys and 86.8% of girls. |

**Table 4.2.** *continued*

| Citation | Subjects | Physical activity measure | Outcomes |
|---|---|---|---|
| **Janz et al. (1995)** | 15 girls, 15 boys; age: 7–15 years; United States | 6 day accelerometer monitoring | Boys had significantly higher values than girls for average movement count and daily frequency of vigorous physical activity. Age was not significantly correlated to any activity variables. |
| **McManus and Armstrong (1997)** | 14 girls, 21 boys; age: 9 years; Hong Kong | 3 day HR monitoring | Girls were significantly less active than boys. 33% of boys and 86% of girls did not exhibit a single 10 min sustained period with HR >139 beats·min$^{-1}$. 76% of the boys and 100% of the girls failed to exhibit a single 10 min sustained period with HR >159 beats·min$^{-1}$ |
| **Sleap and Warburton (1996)** | 93 girls, 86 boys; age: 5–11 years; England | 3 day observation (mean total time 418 min per child) | Children were engaged in moderate to vigorous physical activity (MVPA) for 29.3% of total time observed. 21% of children recorded at least one sustained 20 min period of MVPA while 30% registered at least one sustained 15 min period of MVPA. 95% of children engaged in at least one 5 min period of MVPA. No differences were observed between boys and girls. |
| **Sallo and Silla (1997)** | 29 girls, 25 boys; age: 7 years; Estonia | 4 day HR monitoring | The children spent 7.9% of monitored time with HR >139 beats·min$^{-1}$. No sex differences were detected. 55% of girls and 64% of boys did not exhibit a 10 min sustained period with HR >139 beats·min$^{-1}$ |
| **Welsman and Armstrong (1997)** | 31 girls, 26 boys; age: 6–9 years; England | 3 day HR monitoring | Boys spent significantly more time than girls with HR >139 beats·min$^{-1}$ (11.1 v. 8.7%) and HR >159 beats·min$^{-1}$ (4.7% v. 3.3%). 23% of boys and 31% of girls did not exhibit a 10 min sustained period with HR >139 beats·min$^{-1}$, corresponding figures for HR >159 beats·min$^{-1}$ were 69% of boys and 83% of girls. Time with HR >139 and 159 beats·min$^{-1}$ declined significantly with age in both boys and girls |

HR: heart rate

Observational studies have focused on young children. For example Baranowski and co-workers (1987) observed 24 children aged 7 to 10 years for an average of 9.83 hours on each of two days. Initially Baranowski *et al.* (1987) wanted to detect events of aerobic physical activity defined as '20 minutes in which rapid trunk movement through space was maintained without stopping'. In 472 hours of child observation they did not detect one single event and so had to devise less stringent criteria of aerobic activity that included both slow and fast movement through space. They reported that about half of the children exhibited 14 minutes of movement with not more than one stop on each day. The average amount of aerobic activity was 32 minutes per day.

In a subsequent study, the same group (Du Rant *et al.*, 1993) observed 180 children aged 3 to 7 years for up to 12 hours per day, four days per week for three years. They reported that the average level of physical activity over the whole period of monitoring was 'stationary-with-movement', equivalent to standing/colouring or standing/ball activity with an expected heart rate of 100–119 beats·min$^{-1}$. Boys were observed to have a significantly higher mean level of physical activity than girls.

In three studies, Sleap and Warburton (1992, 1994, 1996) observed 93 girls and 86 boys, aged 5 to 11 years, during school break times, lunch times and physical education lessons. Further observations were undertaken on one weekday evening and one 4-hour period on either a weekend or during a school vacation. The average observation time per child was 418 minutes. They reported that children were engaged in what they defined as moderate to vigorous physical activity for 29.3% of the time they were observed. However, this value must be interpreted in the context that classroom lessons were not observed and the children were likely to have been inactive at these times. No significant differences in physical activity were observed between boys and girls.

Janz *et al.* (1995) used accelerometry to monitor the physical activity patterns of 15 girls and 15 boys, aged 7 to 15 years, over six days. Boys demonstrated significantly higher values than girls for both average movement count and daily frequency of vigorous physical activity. Age was not significantly correlated to any activity variables in this relatively small sample of young people.

Verschuur, Kemper and Besseling (1984) studied 400 Dutch youngsters, aged 13 to 14 years, using heart rate monitoring over two days and pedometry over the same two days plus a weekend day. The pedometry scores indicated that boys spent significantly more time than girls on 'heavy activities' whereas the heart rate data revealed that the boys spent 30 ± 17 minutes per day and the girls spent 37 ± 24 minutes per day with their heart rates above 150 beats·min$^{-1}$. Atomi *et al.* (1986) monitored 11 Japanese boys aged 10 years for three days and reported that 18.1% of the time was spent with heart rates above 120 beat·min$^{-1}$ and 4.7% of the time was spent with heart rates at a level greater than 60% of $\dot{V}O_2$ max.

In a series of studies, Armstrong and colleagues (Armstrong *et al.*, 1990a; Armstrong and Bray, 1990, 1991; Biddle *et al.*, 1991; Welsman and Armstrong, 1992; McManus and Armstrong, 1995) monitored the heart rates of 743 children aged 10 to 16 years from South West England over three normal schooldays (summarised in Armstrong and Welsman, 1997). In order to interpret their data they exercised 40 young people at various speeds on a horizontal treadmill and noted that brisk walking at 6 km·h$^{-1}$

elicited a mean steady state heart rate of 146 beats·min⁻¹ and jogging at 8 km·h⁻¹ elicited a steady state heart rate of 164 beats·min⁻¹ (Armstrong *et al.*, 1990b). They therefore defined moderate physical activity (equivalent to brisk walking) as generating a heart rate above 139 beats·min⁻¹ and vigorous physical activity (equivalent to jogging) as generating a heart rate above 159 beats·min⁻¹.

These data have been re-analysed on the basis of primary schoolchildren, aged 10 to 11 years (mean 10.9 years), and secondary schoolchildren, aged 11 to 16 years (mean 13.1 years). The primary schoolboys ($n=167$) spent a significantly greater percentage of time with their heart rate above 139 beats·min⁻¹ (9.2%) than both primary schoolgirls ($n=165$, 7.7%) and secondary schoolchildren (boys $n=168$, 6.3%; girls $n=243$, 4.7%). The younger girls spent significantly longer above the threshold than the older girls. Estimated physical activity was negatively correlated with age in girls ($r=-0.27$) but not significantly related to age in boys, although the trend indicated a steady decline.

On a Saturday 252 of the secondary schoolchildren and 114 of the primary schoolchildren also had their heart rates monitored. The secondary schoolgirls ($n=137$) spent significantly less time (2.8%) with their heart rates above 139 beats·min⁻¹ than secondary schoolboys ($n=115$, 5.5%), primary schoolboys ($n=56$, 5.5%) and primary schoolgirls ($n=58$, 6.0%). No other significant differences were detected although again girls' physical activity was negatively correlated ($r=-0.21$) with age.

Because of the limitations of simply reporting percentages of time above a threshold value and to provide a clearer picture of young people's physical activity patterns Armstrong and colleagues (Armstrong *et al.*, 1990a; Armstrong and Bray, 1990, 1991; Biddle *et al.*, 1991; Welsman and Armstrong 1992; McManus and Armstrong, 1995) also determined the number of 5, 10 and 20 minute periods with heart rate sustained above 139 and 159 beats·min⁻¹. Five minute periods with heart rate above 139 beats·min⁻¹ were experienced (equivalent to) daily by 82% of boys and 63% of girls, but 38% of boys and 50% of girls did not experience a single sustained 10 minute period with their heart rate above 139 beats·min⁻¹ over three days of monitoring. Seventy-six percent of boys and 84% of girls did not experience a single sustained 20-minute period with their heart rate above 159 beats·min⁻¹. Three percent of boys were reported to experience three 20-minute periods with their heart rate above 159 beats·min⁻¹. Of the 408 girls monitored for three weekdays and 195 girls monitored on a Saturday, not a single girl experienced the equivalent of a daily 20-minute period of vigorous physical activity.

Riddoch *et al.* (1991a) monitored the heart rates of 14 children aged 11 to 16 years for four days, 18 for three days and 13 for two days and averaged each child's recordings to give the mean amount of time per day spent at or above heart rates equivalent to 50 and 70% of peak $\dot{V}O_2$. They reported no significant difference between boys and girls in time spent with heart rate greater than 50% of peak $\dot{V}O_2$ but boys spent significantly more time than girls with their heart rate greater than 70% of peak $\dot{V}O_2$. Younger boys engaged in more vigorous physical activity than younger girls and a significant negative correlation ($r=-0.48$) was found between age and total activity in boys but not in girls.

Three- or four-day heart rate monitoring studies of young children have been reported from Singapore (Gilbey and

Gilbey, 1995), Hong Kong (McManus and Armstrong, 1997), Estonia (Sallo and Silla, 1997) and England (Welsman and Armstrong, 1997). All studies used the same methodology and analytical techniques as Armstrong *et al.* (1990a).

The 9-year-old Singaporean children spent about 37 minutes per day with their heart rate above 140 beats·min⁻¹ during both weekdays and Saturdays. Few children were reported to be active for sustained periods of time on a daily basis and 20% of the boys and 51.5% of the girls did not experience a single sustained 10-minute period with their heart rate above 140 beats·min⁻¹ over three days of weekday monitoring. On a Saturday the corresponding figures were 46.5% of boys and 69.8% of girls. However, 82% of boys and 56.2% of girls experienced the equivalent of a daily 5-minute period of moderate physical activity and 6% of boys and 1.6% of girls demonstrated a daily 10-minute period of vigorous physical activity. The similarly aged Hong Kong children were less active than those from Singapore. One-third of the boys and 86% of the girls did not exhibit a single 10-minute period of moderate physical activity during three days of monitoring. Girls were significantly less active than boys and whereas 47.6% of the boys experienced a daily 5-minute period of moderate physical activity only 2.1% of the girls did so.

Sallo and Silla (1997) monitored 54 Estonian children aged 7 years for three days and reported that they spent 7.9% of time with their heart rate above 139 beats·min⁻¹. No significant difference was detected between weekend and weekday activity when 22 of the children were monitored on a Saturday. Fifty five per cent of girls and 64% of boys did not experience a single 10 minute sustained period with their heart rate above 139 beats·min⁻¹ but on average one period of 5

to 9 minutes with heart rate above 139 beats·min⁻¹ was experienced by each child. No significant sex differences in physical activity were detected.

Welsman and Armstrong (1997) studied 57 similarly aged English children who appear to have been more active than the Estonians. Boys were reported to spend significantly more time than girls with their heart rate above 139 beats·min⁻¹ (11.1 v. 8.7%) and the time spent with heart rate above this threshold declined significantly with age in both boys and girls. Twenty three percent of boys and 31% of girls did not sustain a 10-minute period with their heart rate above 139 beats·min⁻¹ over 3 days of monitoring. However, the equivalent of a daily 5-minute period of moderate physical activity was experienced by 88.5% of boys and 82.8% of girls.

In summary, although many of the studies which used objective measures of physical activity have reported data on relatively small and often unrepresentative samples, the results are generally consistent and congruent with findings from studies that have employed self-reports of physical activity. Most, but not all studies, have reported boys to be more physically active than girls and some studies have identified this differences even among young children.

Boys appear to engage in vigorous, sustained physical activities more often than girls, but sustained periods of physical activity do not appear to be characteristic of young people's physical activity patterns. Studies that have focused on sustained periods of physical activity have reported even 10-minute periods of moderate physical activity to be sparse and some young people seldom, if ever, experience physical activity of this type. In this context, a recent observational study is of interest (Bailey *et al.*, 1995).

Bailey *et al.* (1995) analysed the level and tempo of physical activity of 6- to 10-year-olds over nine 4-hour observation blocks, encompassing the period from 0800 to 2000 and involving three observation periods within each time block, 0800 to 1200, 1200 to 1600 and 1600 to 2000. Two-thirds of observations occurred on school days, one-third occurred on weekend days or holidays, and no more than one observation period per day was performed on the same child. Although the study only included eight boys and seven girls, it is of interest because of the high resolution with which physical activities were observed. The children spent most of their time engaged in activities of low intensity and over a hypothetical 12-hour day they spent a mean of 22.3 minutes in high intensity activities. The results indicated that children engage in very short bouts of intense physical activity interspersed with varying intervals of activity of low or moderate intensity. No period of intense activity lasting 10 consecutive minutes was recorded, and 95% of intense periods of physical activity lasted less than 15 seconds. The median duration of an activity at any level (low, medium or high) was 6 seconds and the median duration of an intense activity was 3 seconds.

Cross-sectional studies of 800 children aged 5 to 16 years from the same catchment area by Armstrong and colleagues (Armstrong *et al.*, 1990a; Armstrong and Bray, 1990, 1991; Biddle *et al.*, 1991; Welsman and Armstrong, 1992, 1997; Armstrong and Welsman, 1997) support the findings of Sallis (1993) and suggest a decline in physical activity with age which is more marked in girls. The definitive longitudinal study of physical activity patterns from childhood, through adolescence and into young adulthood has, however, yet to be performed.

The Amsterdam Growth Study (Kemper, 1985) used self-report, pedometry and two-day heart rate monitoring to estimate physical activity, and provided valuable data on adolescents aged 13 to 18 years. The data obtained in the first year of the study are described in Table 4.2 (Verschuur *et al.*, 1984). Subsequent annual measurements indicated a gradual decrease in habitual physical activity with increasing age in both boys and girls (Verschuur and Kemper, 1985). Differences in activity patterns between the sexes were reported with boys spending more time than girls on 'heavy' activities and girls spending more time than boys on 'light' activities. No sex differences in 'medium-heavy' activities were detected. These findings are consistent with those described in Table 4.2.

## Are young people active?

The monitoring of young people's physical activity has a relatively short history and it is not possible to use objective data to determine whether there has been a general decline in physical activity over time. However, an analysis of energy intake data provided by Durnin (1992) is of interest in this context. Durnin (1992) pooled data collected from the 1930s to the 1980s and demonstrated a progressive decline in the energy intake of young people in the UK. As an example, Figure 4.4 illustrates data from 14- and 15-year-olds. The body mass of both boys and girls was almost identical within each gender for all four time frames and the methods used were the same on each occasion. The very marked reduction in energy intake without a change in body mass must reflect a diminished energy expenditure. It therefore appears that young people, at least in the United Kingdom, have become more sedentary over the last 50 years.

Whether young people are classified as 'active' or 'inactive' depends upon the criteria used. Until recently, widely recognised recommendations for young people's activity levels were not available but two Consensus Conferences have provided useful guidelines.

In 1993 an International Consensus Conference on Physical Activity Guidelines for Adolescents was convened 'to develop empirically based guidelines that can be used by clinicians in their counselling, as well as by policy makers with responsibility for youth health promotion' (Sallis, Patrick and Long, 1994: 299). A systematic review of the scientific paediatric literature (Alpert and Wilmore, 1994; Armstrong and Simons-Morton, 1994; Bailey and Martin, 1994; Bar-Or and Baranowski, 1994; Calfas and Taylor, 1994; Macera and Wooten, 1994; Morrow and Freedson, 1994; Pate *et al.*, 1994) was presented at the conference and the following recommendations emerged:

■ All adolescents should be physically active daily, or nearly every day, as part of play, games, sports, work, transportation, recreation, physical education or planned exercise, in the context of family, school, and community activities.

■ Adolescents should engage in three or more sessions per week of activities that last 20 minutes or more at a time and that require moderate to vigorous levels of exertion.

Moderate to vigorous activities were defined as those that require at least as much effort as brisk or fast walking (Sallis and Patrick, 1994).

A more recent Consensus Conference (NIH Consensus Development Panel on Physical Activity and Cardiovascular Health, 1996) extended the physical activity recommendations for adults of the Centers for Disease Control and Prevention and the American College of Sports Medicine (Pate *et al.*, 1995: 243) to children and recommended that 'all

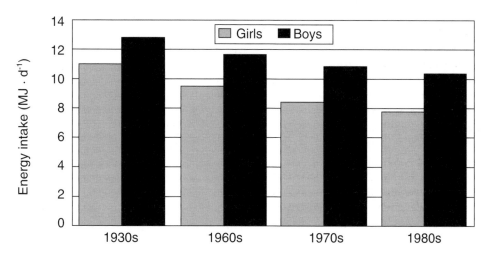

**Figure 4.4.** *Energy intakes of 14- to 15-year-olds in the United Kingdom. (Figures drawn from data reported by Durnin (1992) and reprinted from Armstrong and Welsman, (1997) Young People and Physical Activity: Oxford University Press, by permission of Oxford University Press).*

children and adults should set a long-term goal to accumulate at least 30 minutes or more of moderate-intensity physical activity on most, or preferably all, days of the week'.

Table 4.2 suggests that most children and adolescents appear to satisfy the recommendations of accumulating 30 minutes daily of moderate intensity physical activity. Pate *et al.* (1994) estimated that over 80% of adolescents (11 to 21 years) met this criterion. On the basis of the first guideline of the 1993 International Consensus Conference and the recommendation of the NIH Consensus Conference (NIH Consensus Development Panel on Physical Activity and Cardiovascular Health, 1996) one would have to conclude that most young people are active.

However, if the second guideline of the 1993 International Consensus Conference has to be met before young people can be classified as active, a different picture emerges. Pate *et al.* (1994) speculated that about 50% of adolescents met this recommendation but Table 4.2 suggests that this may be an optimistic estimation. Studies that have monitored sustained periods of physical activity have reported that 20-minute periods of moderate to vigorous exertion are rarely experienced by adolescents. Even 10-minute periods of moderate exertion are seldom, if ever, experienced by significant numbers of young people. Sustained periods of physical activity are not characteristic of young children's activity patterns. So, on the basis of the second guideline one would have to conclude that most young people are not active. It may, of course, be misleading to generalise about young people's level of physical activity. Regardless of the criteria used, the literature reveals some children and adolescents to be very active whereas others are inactive.

In summary, physical activity is a complex behaviour with different dimensions, and the accurate evaluation of young people's physical activity patterns is extremely difficult. In spite of the variation in methods the available data are remarkably consistent. Boys appear to be more active than girls from an early age, and although both males and females reduce their physical activity as they move from childhood, through adolescence and into adult life, the rate of decline is greater in girls. Some children and adolescents undoubtedly lead sedentary lifestyles but other young people appear to be active.

## ■ What we know

### Fitness

■ Optimal levels of aerobic fitness for young people remain to be established but there is no evidence to suggest that low levels of aerobic fitness are common among children and adolescents.

■ Boys' peak $\dot{V}O_2$ increases from childhood through puberty and into adult life, whereas girls' peak $\dot{V}O_2$ appears to reach its maximum in mid-teens. How much of the increase in aerobic fitness is due to improved function of the cardiopulmonary and muscular systems and how much is due to increased size remains to be proven.

■ Boys' peak $\dot{V}O_2$ is generally higher than girls' throughout childhood and adolescence. During puberty the sex difference has been attributed to boys' greater muscle mass and haemoglobin concentration, but the explanation for sex differences in prepubertal children is unknown.

## Physical activity

- Accurate information on the epidemiology of young people's physical activity is limited by the lack of valid, practical and affordable objective measurement techniques that can be used with large representative samples.

- Longitudinal studies of physical activity from early childhood to young adult life are non-existent and most cross-sectional data have been collected during school terms rather than during holiday periods.

- Available data indicate that between the ages of 5 and 17 years boys are more physically active than girls of the same age.

- During childhood and adolescence both boys and girls reduce their physical activity as they grow older but the rate of decline is higher in girls.

- Young people's physical activity patterns appear to be sporadic. Sustained periods of moderate to vigorous physical activity are seldom experienced by many youngsters. Health benefits accruing from very short bursts of activity remain to be elucidated.

- Whether young people are classified as generally active or inactive depends upon the criteria applied. Most children and adolescents satisfy the recommendation of accumulating 30 minutes of daily moderate-intensity activity but few youngsters appear regularly to sustain 20 minute periods of moderate to vigorous exertion as recommended by the 1993 International Consensus Conference.

- Some young people are undoubtedly very active whereas others lead sedentary lifestyles.

- The optimum level of physical activity for the promotion of young people's health and well-being remains to be proven and further research is required.

## ■ References

**Alpert, B.S. and Wilmore, J.H.** (1994). Physical activity and blood pressure in adolescents. *Pediatric Exercise Science*, **6**, 361–80.

**Armstrong, N.** (1995). Children's cardiopulmonary fitness and physical activity patterns – the European scene. In C.J.R. Blimkie and O. Bar–Or (eds.), *New horizons in pediatric exercise science*. pp. 177–89 Champaign: Human Kinetics.

**Armstrong, N., Balding, J., Gentle, P. and Kirby, B.** (1990a). Patterns of physical activity among 11 to 16 year old British children. *British Medical Journal*, **301**, 203–5.

**Armstrong, N., Balding, J., Gentle, P. and Kirby, B.** (1990b). Estimation of coronary risk factors in British schoolchildren: a preliminary report. *British Journal of Sports Medicine*, **24**, 61–6.

**Armstrong, N., Balding, J., Gentle, P., Williams, J. and Kirby, B.** (1990). Peak oxygen uptake and physical activity in 11 to 16 year olds. *Pediatric Exercise Science*, **2**, 349–58.

**Armstrong, N. and Bray, S.** (1990). Primary schoolchildren's physical activity patterns during autumn and summer. *Bulletin of Physical Education*, **26**, 23–6.

**Armstrong, N. and Bray, S.** (1991). Physical activity patterns defined by continuous heart rate monitoring. *Archives of Disease in Childhood*, **66**, 245–7.

**Armstrong, N., Kirby, B.J., McManus, A.M. and Welsman, J.R.** (1995). Aerobic fitness of pre-pubescent children. *Annals of Human Biology*, **22**, 427–41.

**Armstrong, N. and Simons-Morton, B.** (1994). Physical activity and blood lipids in adolescents. *Pediatric Exercise Science*, **6**, 381–405.

**Armstrong, N. and Welsman, J.R.** (1994). Assessment and interpretation of aerobic fitness in children and adolescents. *Exercise and Sport Sciences Reviews*, **22**, 435–76.

**Armstrong, N. and Welsman, J.R.** (1997). *Young people and physical activity*. Oxford: Oxford University Press.

**Armstrong, N., Welsman, J. and Winsley, R.** (1996). Is peak $\dot{V}O_2$ a maximal index of children's aerobic fitness? *International Journal of Sports Medicine*, **17**, 356–9.

**Astrand, P.O. and Rodahl, K.** (1987). *Textbook of work physiology*. New York McGraw Hill.

**Atomi, Y., Iwaoka, K., Hatta, H., Miyashita, M. and Yamamoto, Y.** (1986). Daily physical activity levels in preadolescent boys related to $\dot{V}O_2$ max and lactate threshold. *European Journal of Applied Physiology*, **55**, 156–61.

**Bailey, D.A. and Martin, A.D.** (1994). Physical activity and skeletal health in adolescents. *Pediatric Exercise Science*, **6**, 330–47.

**Bailey, R.C., Olson, J., Pepper, S.L., Porszasz, J., Barstow, T.T. and Cooper, D.M.** (1995). The level and tempo of children's physical activities: an observational study. *Medicine and Science in Sports and Exercise*, **27**, 1033–41.

**Ballor, D.L., Burke, L.M., Knudson, D.V., Olson, J.R. and Montoye, H.J.** (1989). Comparison of three methods of estimating energy expenditure: caltrac, heart rate, and video analysis. *Research Quarterly for Exercise and Sport*, **60**, 362–8.

**Baranowski, T., Bouchard, C., Bar–Or, O., Bricker, T., Heath, G. and Kimm, S.Y.S.** (1992). Assessment, prevalence, and cardiovascular benefits of physical activity and fitness in youth. *Medicine and Science in Sports and Exercise*, **24**: S237–47.

**Baranowski, T., Dworkin, R.J., Cieslik, C., Hooks, P., Clearman, D.R., Ray, L., Dunn, K.J. and Nader, P.R.** (1984). Reliability and validity of self report of aerobic activity: Family Health Report. *Research Quarterly for Exercise and Sport*, **55**, 309–17.

**Baranowski, T. and Simons–Morton, B.G.** (1991). Dietary and physical activity assessment in school-aged children: measurement issues. *Journal of School Health*, **61**, 195–7.

**Baranowski, T., Thompson, W.O., DuRant, R.H., Baranowski, J. and Puhl, J.** (1993). Observations on physical activity in physical locations: age, gender, ethnicity and month effects. *Research Quarterly for Exercise and Sport*, **64**, 127–33.

**Baranowski, T., Tsong, Y., Hooks, P., Cieslik, C. and Nader, P.R.** (1987). Aerobic physical activity among third to sixth grade children. *Journal of Developmental and Behavioural Pediatrics*, **8**, 203–6.

**Bar–Or, O.** (1983). *Pediatric sports medicine for the practitioner*. New York, Springer–Verlag.

**Bar–Or, O. and Baranowski, T.** (1994). Physical activity, adiposity, and obesity among adolescents. *Pediatric Exercise Science*, **6**, 348–60.

**Bell, R.D., Macek, M., Rutenfranz, J. and Saris, W.H.M.** (1986). Health indicators and risk factors of cardiovascular diseases during childhood and adolescence. In J. Rutenfranz, R. Mocellin and F. Klimt (eds.), *Children and Exercise*, XII, pp. 19–27. Champaign: Human Kinetics.

**Biddle, S., Mitchell, J. and Armstrong, N.** (1991). The assessment of physical activity in children: a comparison of continuous heart rate monitoring, self-report and interview techniques. *British Journal of Physical Education Research Supplement*, **10**, 4–8.

**Bouchard, C., Shephard, R.J., Stephens, T., Sutton, J.R. and McPerson, B.D.** (1990). Exercise, fitness and health: the consensus statement. In C. Bouchard, R.J. Shephard, T. Stephens, J.R. Sutton and B.D. McPherson (eds.), *Exercise, fitness and health*. pp. 4–28. Champaign: Human Kinetics.

**Bray, M.S., Morrow, J.R., Pivarnik, J.M. and Bricker, J.T.** (1992). Caltrac validity for estimating caloric expenditure with children. *Pediatric Exercise Science*, **4**, 166–79.

**Calfas, K.J. and Taylor, W.C.** (1994). Effects of physical activity on psychological variables in adolescents. *Pediatric Exercise Science*, **6**, 406–23.

**Caspersen, C.J., Powell, K. and Christenson, G.** (1985). Physical activity, exercise and physical fitness: definitions and distinctions of health-related research. *Public Health Reports*, **100**, 126–131.

**Chatterjee, S., Banerjee, P.K., Chatterjee, P. and Maitra, S.R.** (1979). Aerobic capacity of young girls. *Indian Journal of Medical Research*, **69**, 327–33.

**Ching, P.L.Y.H. and Dietz, W.H.** (1995). Reliability and validity of activity measures in preadolescent girls. *Pediatric Exercise Science*, **7**, 389–99.

**Cunningham, D.A., Paterson, D.H., Blimkie, C.J.R. and Donner, A.P.** (1984). Development of cardiorespiratory function in circumpubertal boys: a longitudinal study. *Journal of Applied Physiology*, **56**, 302–7.

**Danner, F., Noland, M., McFadden, M., DeWalt, K. and Kotchen, J.M.** (1991). Description of the physical activity of young children using movement sensor and observation methods. *Pediatric Exercise Science*, **3**, 11–20.

**Dauncey, M.J. and James, W.P.T.** (1979). Assessment of the heart rate method for determining energy expenditure in man, using a whole body calorimeter. *British Journal of Nutrition*, **42**, 1–13.

**Du Rant, R.H., Baranowski, T., Rohdes, T., Gutin, B., Thompson, W.O., Carroll, R., Puhl, J. and Greaves, K.A.** (1993). Association among serum lipid and lipoprotein concentrations and physical activity. Physical fitness and body composition in young children. *Journal of Pediatrics*, **123**, 185–92.

**Durnin, J.V.G.A.** (1992). Physical activity levels past and present. In N. Norgan (ed.), *Physical activity and health*, pp. 20–27. Cambridge: Cambridge University Press.

**Ellison, R.C., Freedson, P.S., Zevallos, J.C., White, M.J., Marmor, J.K., Garrahie, E.J. and Moore, L.L.** (1992). Feasibility and costs of monitoring physical activity in young children using the Caltrac accelerometer. *Pediatric Exercise Science*, **4**, 136–41.

**Emons, H.J.G., Groenenboom, D.C., Westerterp, K.R. and Saris, W.H.M.** (1992). Comparison of heart rate monitoring combined with indirect calorimetry and the doubly labelled water ($^2H_2{}^{18}O$) method for the measurement of energy expenditure in children. *European Journal of Applied Physiology*, **65**, 99–103.

**Eston, R.G., Rowland, A.V. and Ingledew, D.K.** (1997). Validation of the Tritrac-R3D activity monitor during typical children's activities. In N. Armstrong, B.J. Kirby and J.R. Welsman (eds.), *Children and exercise*, XIX, pp. 132–8. London: Spon.

**Freedson, P.S.** (1991). Electronic motion sensors and heart rate as measures of physical activity in children. *Journal of School Health*, **61**, 220–23.

**Freedson, P.S., Sirard, J., Debold, N., Pate, R., Dowda, M. and Sallis, J.** (1997). Validity of two physical activity monitors in children and adolescents. In N. Armstrong, B.J. Kirby and J.R. Welsman (eds.), *Children and exercise*, XIX, pp. 127–31. London: Spon.

**Gilbey, H. and Gilbey, M.** (1995). The physical activity of Singapore primary school children as estimated by heart rate monitoring. *Pediatric Exercise Science*, **7**, 26–35.

**Gilliam, T.B., Freedson, P.S., Geenen, D.L. and Shahraray, B.** (1981). Physical activity patterns determined by heart rate monitoring in 6–7 year old children. *Medicine and Science in Sports and Exercise*, **13**, 65–7.

**Heartbeat Wales** (1986). *Welsh Youth Health Survey 1986*, Heartbeat Report No. 5. Cardiff: Heartbeat Wales.

**Janz, K.F., Golden, J.C., Hansen, J.R. and Mahoney, L.T.** (1992). Heart rate monitoring of physical activity in children and adolescents: the Muscatine study. *Pediatrics*, **89**, 256–61.

**Janz, K.F., Witt, J. and Mahoney, L.T.** (1995). The stability of children's physical activity as measured by accelerometry and self-report. *Medicine and Science in Sports and Exercise*, **27**, 1326–32.

**Kemper, H.C.G.** (1985). Growth, health and fitness of teenagers. *Medicine and Sport Science*, **20**, 1–202.

**Kemper, H.C.G. and Van Mechelen, W.** (1996). Physical fitness testing of children: a European perspective. *Pediatric Exercise Science*, **8**, 201–14.

**King, A.J.C. and Coles, B.** (1992). *The Health of Canada's Youth*. Canada: Ministry of Health and Welfare.

**Klesges, R.C., Coates, T.J., Moldenhauer–Klesges, L.M., Holzer, B., Gustavson, J. and Barnes, J.** (1984). The FATS: an observational system for assessing physical activity in children and associated parent behaviour. *Behavioural Assessment*, **6**, 333–45.

**Klesges, R.C., Haddock, C.K. and Eck, L.H.** (1990). A multimethod approach to the measurement of childhood physical activity and its relationship to blood pressure and body weight. *Journal of Pediatrics*, **116**, 888–93.

**Klesges, R.C., Klesges, L.M., Swenson, A.M. and Pheley, A.M.** (1985). A validation of two motion sensors in the prediction of child and adult physical activity levels. *American Journal of Epidemiology*, **122**, 400–10.

**Krahenbuhl, G.S., Skinner, J.S. and Kohrt, W.M.** (1985). Developmental aspects of maximal aerobic power in children. *Exercise and Sport Sciences Reviews*, **13**, 503–38.

**LaPorte, R.E., Cauley, J.A., Kinsey, C.M., Corbett, W., Robertson, R., Black-Saunder, R., Kuller, C.H. and Falkel, J.** (1982). The epidemiology of physical activity in children, college students, middle-aged men, menopausal females, and monkeys. *Journal of Chronic Diseases*, **35**, 787–95.

**LaPorte, R.E., Dearwater, S., Cauley, J.A., Slemenda, C. and Cook, T.** (1985). Physical activity or cardiovascular fitness: which is more important for health? *The Physician and Sports Medicine*, **13**, 145–50.

**Livingstone, M.B.E.** (1994). Energy expenditure and physical activity in relation to fitness in children. *Proceedings of the Nutrition Society*, **53**, 207–21.

**Livingstone, M.B.E., Coward, A.W., Prentice, A.M., Davies, P.S.W., Strain, J.J., McKenna, P.G., Mahoney, C.A., White, J.A., Stewart, C.M. and Kerr, M.-J.J.** (1992). Daily energy expenditure in free-living children: comparison of heart rate monitoring with the doubly-labelled water ($^2$H$_2$$^{18}$O) method. *American Journal of Clinical Nutrition*, **56**, 343–52.

**Macera, C.A. and Wooten, W.** (1994). Epidemiology of sports and recreation injuries among adolescents. *Pediatric Exercise Science*, **6**, 424–33.

**Malina, R.M. and Bouchard, C.** (1991). *Growth, maturation and physical activity*. Champaign: Human Kinetics.

**McKenzie, T.L.** (1991). Observational measures of children's physical activity. *Journal of School Health*, **61**, 224–7.

**McManus, A. and Armstrong, N.** (1995). Patterns of physical activity among primary schoolchildren. In F.J. Ring (ed.), *Children in sport*, pp. 17–23. Bath: Bath University Press.

**McManus, A. and Armstrong, N.** (1997). The physical activity patterns of boys and girls. In D.J. McFarlane (ed.), *Gender Issues in Sport and Exercise* pp. 36–9. Hong Kong: Hong Kong University Press.

**Melanson, E.L. and Freedson, P.S.** (1996). Physical activity assessment: a review of methods. *Critical Reviews in Food Science and Nutrition*, **36**, 385–96.

**Mirwald, R.L. and Bailey, D.A.** (1986). *Maximal aerobic power*. London, Ontario: Sports Dynamics.

**Morrow, J.R. and Freedson, P.S.** (1994). Relationship between habitual physical activity and aerobic fitness in adolescents. *Pediatric Exercise Science*, **6**, 315–29.

**Mukeshi, M., Gutin, B., Anderson, W., Zybert, P. and Basch, C.** (1990). Validation of the Caltrac movement sensor using direct observation in young children. *Pediatric Exercise Science*, **2**, 249–54.

**Nagawa, A. and Ishiko, T.** (1970). Assessment of aerobic capacity with special reference to sex and age of junior and senior high school students in Japan. *Japanese Journal of Physiology*, **20**, 118–29.

**NIH Consensus Development Panel on Physical Activity and Cardiovascular Health** (1996). Physical activity and cardiovascular health. *Journal of the American Medical Association*, **276**, 241–6.

**Noland, M., Danner, F., Dewalt, K., McFadden, M. and Kotchen, J.M.** (1990). The measurement of physical activity in young children. *Research Quarterly for Exercise and Sport*, **61**, 146–53.

**O'Hara, N.M., Baranowski, T., Simons–Morton, B.G., Wilson, B.S. and Parcel, G.S.** (1989). Validity of the observation of children's physical activity. *Research Quarterly for Exercise and Sport*, **60**, 42–7.

**Oja, P. and Tuxworth, B.** (eds.) (1995). *Eurofit for adults: assessment of health-related fitness*. Tampere, Finland: Council of Europe/CDDS and UKK Institute for Health Promotion Research.

**Pate, R.R.** (1993). Physical activity assessment in children and adolescents. *Critical Reviews in Food Science and Nutrition*, **33**, 321–6.

**Pate, R.R., Long, B.J. and Heath, G.** (1994). Descriptive epidemiology of physical activity in adolescents. *Pediatric Exercise Science*, **6**, 434–47.

**Pate, R.R., Pratt, M., Blair, S.N., Haskell, W.L., Macera, C.A., Bouchard, C., Buchner, D., Ettinger, W., Heath, G.W., King, A.C., Kriska, A., Leon, A.S., Marcus, B.H., Morris, J., Paffenbarger, R.S., Patrick, K., Pollock, M.L., Rippe, J.M., Sallis, J. and Wilmore, J.H.** (1995). Physical activity and public health. *Journal of the American Medical Association*, **273**, 402–7.

**Prentice, A.M.** (1990). *The doubly-labelled water method for measuring energy expenditure: technical recommendations for use in humans. A consensus report by the IDECG Working Group.* Vienna: International Atomic Energy Agency.

**Puhl, J., Greaves, K., Hoyt, M. and Baranowski, T.** (1990). Children's activity rating scale (CARS): description and calibration. *Research Quarterly for Exercise and Sport*, **61**, 26–36.

**Riddoch, C.** (1990). *Northern Ireland Health and Fitness Survey.* Belfast: Sports Council for Northern Ireland and Department of Health and Social Services.

**Riddoch, C.J. and Boreham, C.A.G.** (1995). The health-related physical activity of children. *Sports Medicine*, **19**, 86–102.

**Riddoch, C., Mahoney, C., Murphy, N., Boreham, C. and Cran, G.** (1991a). The physical activity patterns of Northern Irish schoolchildren ages 11 to 16 years. *Pediatric Exercise Science*, **3**, 300–9.

**Riddoch, C., Savage, J.M., Murphy, N., Cran, G.W. and Boreham, C.** (1991b). Long-term health implications of fitness and physical activity patterns. *Archives of Disease in Childhood*, **66**, 1426–33.

**Robinson, S.** (1938). Experimental studies of physical fitness in relation to age. *Arbeitsphysiologie*, **10**, 251–323.

**Ross, J.G. and Gilbert, G.G.** (1985). The National Children and Youth Fitness Study. A summary of findings. *Journal of Physical Education, Recreation, and Dance*, **56**, 45–50.

**Rowland, T.W.** (1993). Aerobic exercise testing protocols. In T.W. Rowland (ed.), *Pediatric laboratory exercise testing*, pp. 19–41. Champaign: Human Kinetics.

**Rutenfranz, J., Andersen, K.L., Seliger, V., Klimmer, F., Berndt, I. and Ruppel, M.** (1981). Maximum aerobic power and body composition during the puberty growth period: similarities and differences between children of two European countries. *European Journal of Pediatrics*, **136**, 123–33.

**Sallis, J.F.** (1991). Self-report measures of children's physical activity. *Journal of School Health*, **61**, 215–19.

**Sallis, J.F.** (1993). Epidemiology of physical activity and fitness in children and adolescents. *Critical Reviews in Food Science and Nutrition*, **33**, 403–8.

**Sallis, J.F., Buono, M.J. and Freedson, P.S.** (1991). Bias in estimating caloric expenditure from physical activity in children. *Sports Medicine*, **11**, 203–9.

**Sallis, J.F., Buono, M.J., Roby, J.J., Carlsen, D. and Nelson, J.A.** (1990). The Caltrac accelerometer as a physical activity monitor for school-age children. *Medicine and Science in Sports and Exercise*, **22**, 698–703.

**Sallis, J.F., McKenzie, T.L. and Alcaraz, J.E.** (1993). Habitual physical activity and health-related physical fitness in fourth-grade children. *American Journal of Diseases of Children*, **147**, 890–95.

**Sallis, J.F. and Patrick, K.** (1994). Physical activity guidelines for adolescents: a consensus statement. *Pediatric Exercise Science*, **6**, 302–14.

**Sallis, J.F., Patrick, K. and Long, B.J.** (1994). Overview of the International Consensus Conference on Physical Activity Guidelines for Adolescents. *Pediatric Exercise Science*, **6**, 299–302.

**Sallo, M. and Silla, R.** (1997). Physical activity with moderate to vigorous intensity in pre-school and first grade schoolchildren. *Pediatric Exercise Science*, **9**, 44–54.

**Salonen, J.T. and Lakka, T.** (1987). Assessment of physical activity in population studies – validity and consistency of the methods in the Kupoio ischemic heart disease risk factor study. *Scandinavian Journal of Sports Science*, **9**, 89–95.

**Saris, W.H.M.** (1985). The assessment and evaluation of daily physical activity in children: a review. *Acta Paediatrica Scandinavica*, **318**, 37–48.

**Saris, W.H.M.** (1986). Habitual physical activity in children: methodology and findings in health and disease. *Medicine and Science in Sports and Exercise*, **18**, 253–63.

**Saris, W.H.M.** (1992). New developments in the assessment of physical activity in children. In J. Coudert and E. Van Praagh (eds.), *Pediatric work physiology*. pp. 107–14. Paris: Masson.

**Schulman, J.L. and Reisman, J.M.** (1959). An objective measure of hyperactivity. *American Journal of Mental Deficiency*, **64**, 455–6.

**Seliger, V.S., Trefny, S., Bartenkova, S. and Pauer, M.** (1974). The habitual physical activity and fitness of 12 year old boys. *Acta Paediatrica Belgica*, **28**, 54–9.

**Shephard, R.J.** (1986). The Canada Fitness Survey: some international comparisons. *Journal of Sports Medicine and Physical Fitness*, **26**, 292–300.

**Simons–Morton, B.G., Taylor, W.C. and Huang, I.W.** (1994). Validity of the physical activity interview and caltrac with pre-adolescent children. *Research Quarterly for Exercise and Sport*, **65**, 84–8.

**Sleap, M. and Warburton, P.** (1992). Physical activity levels of 5–11 year old children in England determined by continuous observation. *Research Quarterly for Exercise and Sport*, **63**, 238–45.

**Sleap, M. and Warburton, P.** (1994). Physical activity levels of preadolescent children in England. *British Journal of Physical Education Research Supplement*, **14**, 2–6.

**Sleap, M. and Warburton, P.** (1996). Physical activity levels of 5–11-year-old children in England: cumulative evidence from three direct observation studies. *International Journal of Sports Medicine*, **17**, 248–53.

**Speakman, J.R., Nair, K.S. and Goran, M.I.** (1993). Revised equations for calculating $CO_2$ production from doubly labeled water in humans. *American Journal of Physiology*, **264**, E912–E917.

**Spryranova, S., Parizkova, J. and Bunc, V.** (1987). Relationships between body dimensions and resting and working oxygen consumption in boys aged 11 to 18 years. *European Journal of Applied Physiology*, **56**, 725–36.

**Treiber, F.A., Musante, L., Hartdagan, S., Davis, H., Levy, J. and Strong, W.B.** (1989). Validation of a heart rate monitor for children in laboratory and field settings. *Medicine and Science in Sports and Exercise*, **21**, 338–42.

**Tsanakas, J.N., Bannister, O.M., Boon, A.W. and Milner, R.D.G.** (1986). The 'Sport Tester', a device for monitoring the free running test. *Archives of Disease in Childhood*, **61**, 912–14.

**Van Mechelen, W. and Kemper, H.C.G.** (1995). Body growth, body composition, and physical fitness. In H.C.G. Kemper (ed.), *The Amsterdam growth study*, pp. 52–85. Champaign: Human Kinetics.

**Verschuur, R. and Kemper, H.C.G.** (1985). The pattern of daily physical activity. *Medicine and Sport Science*, **20**, 169–86.

**Verschuur, R., Kemper, H.C.G. and Besseling, C.W.M.** (1984). Habitual physical activity and health in 13 and 14 year old teenagers. In J. Ilmarinen and I. Valimaki (eds.), *Children and sport*, pp. 255–61. New York, Springer-Verlag.

**Wallace, J.P., McKenzie, T.L. and Nader, P.R.** (1985). Observed vs recalled exercise behaviour, a validation of a 7-day exercise recall for boys 11–13 years old. *Research Quarterly for Exercise and Sport*, **56**, 161–5.

**Welk, G.J. and Corbin, C.B.** (1995). The validity of the Tritrac-R3D activity monitor for the assessment of physical activity in children. *Research Quarterly for Exercise and Sport*, **66**, 202–9.

**Welsman, J.R. and Armstrong, N.** (1992). Daily physical activity and blood lactate indices of aerobic fitness. *British Journal of Sports Medicine*, **26**, 228–32.

**Welsman, J.R. and Armstrong, N.** (1996). The measurement and interpretation of aerobic fitness in children: current issues. *Journal of the Royal Society of Medicine*, **89**, 281–5.

**Welsman, J.R. and Armstrong, N.** (1997). Physical activity patterns of 5–11 year old children. In N. Armstrong, B.J. Kirby and J.R. Welsman (eds.), *Children and exercise,* XIX, pp. 139–44. London: Spon.

**Welsman, J.R., Armstrong, N., Kirby, B.J., Nevill, A.M. and Winter, E.M.** (1996). Scaling peak $\dot{V}O_2$ for differences in body size. *Medicine and Science in Sports and Exercise,* **28**, 259–65.

**Yoshizawa, S.** (1972). A comparative study of aerobic work capacity in urban and rural adolescents. *Journal of Human Ergology,* **1**, 45–65.

# Behavioural factors associated with physical activity in young people

Ilse De Bourdeaudhuij

*Researcher, Department of Psychology,
University of Ghent, Belgium*

The main aim of this chapter is to review the scientific literature on the determinants of physical activity in young people aged between 5 and 18 years. More specifically, the focus is on determinants that reside or originate in the individual. Environmental factors are beyond the scope of this review and are dealt with by Wold and Hendry (Chapter 6). A further aim is to report up-to-date knowledge and to give guidelines for future research. The computer searches included PsychLIT and MEDLINE. Manual searches were also made using the reference lists from relevant articles. In order to give a recent 'state of the art' review 1990 was chosen as a starting point. Some important studies published before 1990 (e.g. Godin and Shephard, 1986) were also included.

Research on behavioural determinants of physical activity in young people originating from a public health perspective is relatively new (Sallis *et al.*, 1992). In the past, such physical activity research focused primarily on adults, based on the assumption that adults were the population especially at risk of ill health from physical inactivity. Children and adolescents were considered to be exercising enough. However, recently more attention has been given to the importance of studying physical activity in children and adolescents, including determinants. The main reasons for this recent focus are:

- Not all children exercise enough for health (Armstrong *et al.*, 1990; Davies, 1992; Kemper, 1994).

- The awareness that diseases related to sedentariness in adults, such as obesity, cardiovascular problems, osteoporosis and some kinds of cancer, originate in childhood (Frerichs *et al.*, 1979; Sallis *et al.*, 1992).

- The increase in prevalence of childhood obesity, due to a likely imbalance between energy expenditure and energy intake (Craig, Goldberg and Dietz, 1996).

- The widespread assumption that health-enhancing physical activity patterns in adults are established in youth (Blair *et al.*, 1988; Simons-Morton *et al.*, 1990; Stucky-Ropp and Dilorenzo, 1993).

Until now, too few studies were available on children in order for the whole picture on the determinants of physical activity (Dishman, 1991) to be obtained. A better understanding of the determinants of physical activity in youth is essential in developing appropriate activity promotion interventions resulting in long-term increases in physical activity levels in this population. It should be noted, however, that because of the cross-sectional nature of most studies, the term 'determinant' mostly indicates only a reliable association or correlation (Dishman, Sallis and Orenstein, 1985; Dishman, 1991; Sallis *et al.*, 1992), and the methods used in most studies do not allow any inference of causality.

# ■ Motivation in physical activity today: the cognitive perspective

The study of motivation in exercise, physical activity and sport is at present dominated by cognitively based theories (Brustad, 1992; Godin, 1994; Kimiecik and Harris, 1996). These theories or models are generally developed in the context of health or achievement behaviours. They show individual differences in the way cognitive appraisal processes influence health-related behaviour. The way in which children and adolescents perceive themselves in relation to physical activity also influences their subsequent behaviour. Youth sport psychology researchers have largely emphasised the role of cognitions, particularly self-perception characteristics and achievement goal orientations, as determinants of sport and exercise (Duda, 1987, 1989; Brustad, 1992; Duda and Nicholls, 1992).

# ■ The 'Theoretical' Approach

To facilitate the understanding of factors influencing health behaviour various models have been developed. The major cognitive approaches used to predict health behaviour, and later applied to exercise, are: the Theory of Planned Behaviour (Ajzen and Madden, 1986), which is an extension of the Theory of Reasoned Action (Ajzen and Fishbein, 1980), and the Social Cognitive Theory (Bandura, 1986); and for youth sport research: the Competence Motivation Theory (Harter, 1978, 1981) and the Theory of Achievement Motivation and Goal Orientations (Nicholls, 1984). Most theories incorporate the role of self-related cognitions as well as environmental or socialisation influences. The different theories, together with their application to physical activity research of children and adolescents, with a special focus on research done in the 1990s are discussed in the following section.

## Theories and their application to physical activity research

### *Theories of Reasoned Action and of Planned Behaviour*

According to the Theory of Reasoned Action, the intention to perform physical activity serves as an immediate determinant of the action. Intentions, in turn, are presumed to be influenced by two components: the person's attitude toward performing physical activity and the perceived social pressure, referred to as subjective norm (Ajzen and Fishbein, 1980). Attitudes are a function of the individual's salient behavioural beliefs, such as expected positive or negative outcomes. Multiplying the evaluation (i.e. value or importance) of each expected outcome by the strength of the belief that performing the behaviour will lead to each outcome, results in the attitude of a person. The subjective norm is predicted by multiplying the strength of the normative beliefs of others by the motivation to comply with such individuals. In the Theory of Planned Behaviour, a behavioural control construct is added to the Theory of Reasoned Action to control for goal-directed behaviour that is not completely under volitional control. This perceived behavioural control construct is defined in both narrow and broad terms in the physical activity literature. The narrow perspective asked people how strongly they believe that the particular behaviour is under their control. Other researchers follow a broad definition (e.g. Craig *et al.*, 1996), including such internal factors as skills, ability, knowledge, perseverance, planning, as well as external factors or barriers, such as lack of time, resistance of significant others and competing activities.

In general, there is support for the theories of Reasoned Action and of Planned Behaviour in their application to physical activity using adults or students as a research population (Dzewaltowski, 1989; Dzewaltowski, Noble and Shaw, 1990).

Studies looking at children and adolescents and physical activity are scarce. Godin and Shephard (1986) were the first to investigate the Theory of Reasoned Action in children 12 to 14 years of age. They found support for the attitude but less so for the subjective norm component. They also found direct and independent influence of external variables on exercise intention. The Theory of Reasoned Action, however, is not able to explain the variance in exercise intention in children.

Recently, Wankel and co-workers (1994) with a large, nationally representative sample, studied predictors of physical activity across age. For adolescents (19 years and under), the intention to be active was related to perceived behavioural control and attitudes, and to a lesser extent to subjective norm. They concluded that due to the behavioural control construct, the Theory of Planned Behaviour could account for a greater percentage of the variance in intention than the Theory of Reasoned Action. Papaioannou and Theodorakis (1996) tried to predict the intention to participate in physical education lessons for high school students (14 to 17 years old) and found that perceived behavioural control and attitudes had direct effects on intention. Craig *et al.* (1996) investigated the applicability of the Theory of Planned Behaviour in children (11 years old) and adolescents (14 years old), and found that perceived behavioural control significantly predicted children's intention to participate in vigorous activity. Using a broad definition of the behavioural control concept, they argue that enabling children to experience a sense of competence and fun or excitement in physical activity can increase their perceived behavioural control and activity levels. Recently, Hausenblas, Carron and Mack (1997) conducted a meta-analysis, investigating the application of the theories of Reasoned Action and of Planned Behaviour to exercise. Largest effect sizes on intention and behaviour were found for perceived behavioural control and attitudes, whereas subjective norm had only a moderate affect.

A major limitation of the research on the theories of Reasoned Action and of Planned Behaviour is that intention is often used as a surrogate for behaviour, based on the assumption that a strong relationship between both constructs exists. However, many studies focusing on different types of health behaviour have found weak relationships between behaviour and intentions. When applied to physical activity, research has also come to contradictory conclusions (see below). This problem must be kept in mind when interpreting the findings and their relevance for health promotion.

To conclude, it can be argued that perceived behavioural control and attitudes towards physical activity, and to a lesser extent social norm, are related to the physical activity or the intentions for children and adolescents. Enhancing positive attitudes, such as by stressing the positive outcomes of physical activity, together with enhancing a strong belief that the behaviour is under their control, while considering internal and external factors, might be a promising strategy.

### The Social Cognitive Theory

Bandura's (1986) Social Cognitive Theory is a model in which environmental, personal and behavioural factors reciprocally interact to predict personal control and self-direction (Taylor, Baranowski and Sallis, 1994). In this theory, self-efficacy is one of the most important and most studied personal mechanisms of behaviour change. It is defined as a person's judgement of their ability to perform a particular behaviour. Perceived efficacy is believed to affect both the initiation and the persistence of behaviour. Other central motivators of behaviour highlighted by Bandura are outcome expectations and personal goals together with behavioural feedback. An outcome expectation is defined as the judgement of what the performance of a task will produce, in other words, the expectations about the consequences of a given behaviour. The

goal is the standard the individual wants to attain. Based on self-evaluation or feedback one becomes either satisfied or dissatisfied. Dissatisfaction will motivate the individual to perform physical activity to attain his or her goals. In the past most studies failed to include the goal construct as an element of the Social Cognitive Theory. Moreover this goal construct is very similar to intention in the theories of Reasoned Action and of Planned Behaviour (Yordy and Lent, 1993).

Research looking into the usefulness of the Social Cognitive Theory in determining physical activity has mostly been concerned with the relationship between self-efficacy and exercise behaviour. A number of studies have supported this relationship in adults (King *et al.*, 1992; Godin, 1994). Dzewaltowski and colleagues (Dzewaltowski, 1989; Dzewaltowski *et al.*, 1990) investigating the Social Cognitive Theory, including environmental, personal and behavioural factors, found, in general, that these constructs were good predictors of participation in physical activity.

Research concerning the relationship between one or more personal constructs from the Social Cognitive Theory and physical activity in children and adolescents is scarce. Reynolds *et al.* (1990) investigated psychosocial predictors of physical activity, including self-efficacy, using a longitudinal design with adolescents (aged 14 to 16 years old). They found that high levels of self-efficacy were related to higher levels of activity for both males and females. Self-efficacy contributed 24–28% of the variance in physical activity.

Zakarian *et al.* (1994) found a significant relationship between self-efficacy and physical activity among adolescents (aged 15 to 17 years old) from low socioeconomic backgrounds. Self-efficacy was one of the variables explaining a relatively large proportion of the variance in vigorous exercise, accounting for 15–22% of the variance. As a consequence, they both state that going through a series of successful exercise experiences will motivate adolescents.

Research into elementary school children is more ambiguous. Stucky-Ropp and Dilorenzo (1993) found that child self-efficacy did not emerge as an important predictor of exercise behaviour in 11-year-old children. In contrast, in a recent prospective study of 11- to 12-year-old children, Trost *et al.* (1997) did find a relationship between self-efficacy and physical activity. They included physical activity self-efficacy using three dimensions – the child's confidence in their ability to seek support (ask parent to take them to sport), to overcome barriers (while having a lot of homework), and to handle competing activities (watching TV or playing video games). A major finding was the significant relationship between self-efficacy in overcoming barriers and future physical activity behaviour. They argue that assisting children in overcoming barriers to physical activity could be a good strategy to encourage participation. These seemingly contradictory findings may, as the authors themselves argue, be due to a deficiency in the definition and measurement of self-efficacy in the study of Stucky-Ropp and Dilorenzo (1993). Their assessment of self-efficacy did not sufficiently comply with the self-efficacy construct defined by Bandura (1986). Trost *et al.* (1997) included a second component to the Social Cognitive Theory – measuring the beliefs about the consequences of being physically active, which can be considered as the attitude component of the Theory of Reasoned Action, or as the outcome expectations component of the Social Cognitive Theory. These

beliefs about consequences (good health, fun, etc.) were correlated significantly with intention in the study of Saunders *et al.* (1997) and also with behaviour in the study of Trost *et al.* (1997).

To conclude, a clear relationship was found between self-efficacy and physical activity for children and adolescents when self-efficacy was defined properly. Further, a more specific definition and measurement of self-efficacy (self-efficacy in overcoming barriers) is more useful in future exercise promotion programmes. In general, enhancing children and adolescents' perceived competence in relation to physical activity could be useful. However, as the method to realise this is helping children to go through a series of successful exercise experiences, this might not be so obvious for sedentary children and adolescents not engaged in any physical activity. More specifically, helping youngsters to deal with overcoming the barriers would also be a good strategy to enhance physical activity in youth.

### *The Transtheoretical Model*

This model (see Prochaska and DiClemente, 1983), initially constructed to explain changes made by people who stop smoking, has also been proposed as useful for understanding the adoption and maintenance of exercise behaviour (Sonstroem, 1988; Armstrong *et al.*, 1993). In the Transtheoretical Model it is argued that people progress through the stages of change during the process of changing their behaviour. The stages have been labelled precontemplation, contemplation, preparation, action and maintenance. In the precontemplation stage, individuals do not intend to change their behaviour. In the contemplation stage, people seriously intend to change in the next six months. In the preparation stage, individuals intend to take action in the near future (within a few weeks) or are already changing their behaviour at an inconsistent level. Action is the stage in which behaviour changes have occured recently (within the past six months). In the maintenance stage, people have made changes more than six months previously or until the risk no longer exists of relapse to the old behaviour. The result of the progression through the stages is the stable adoption of new healthy behaviour (Prochaska and Marcus, 1994). The Transtheoretical Model is more a model giving guidelines for intervention than it is a model for studying behavioural determinants *per se*. A major contribution of the model, however, is its matching of determinants of health behaviour with the readiness of the individual to change, or in other words, its taking into account of stage differences.

In recent years a mismatch has been shown between the action-oriented physical activity programmes offered and the condition of the very sedentary population (mostly in precontemplation) (e.g. Prochaska and Marcus, 1994). Consequently, the Transtheoretical Model has become influential in adult physical activity. Many researchers (see Booth *et al.*, 1993; Marcus *et al.*, 1994; Cardinal, 1995) have found evidence supporting the use of this model for the understanding of adoption and maintenance of exercise in adults. Two central determinants useful in the application of the Transtheoretical Model to physical activity are self-efficacy and the decision-balance between perceived benefits and barriers (pros and cons). Marcus *et al.* (1994) showed that an individual's level of physical activity could be predicted by knowing their stage of readiness for exercise, their perception of the costs and benefits and their self-efficacy.

Until now the utility of the Transtheoretical Model applied to youth physical activity has not been studied extensively. Some problems may be expected, such as the higher levels of physical activity in youth resulting in fewer people in the precontemplation and contemplation stages. In addition, the processes of change may be different for adults and young people. Moreover, it is not clear whether the decision-making model is relevant for children. This concept might stress cognitive considerations and rational choices too much, not taking environmental factors sufficiently into account. Children are also engaged in some compulsory physical education at school, making it difficult to fit them into the concepts of the Transtheoretical Model. However, because of the promising results using this model in adult populations, the investigation of its application to physical activity in children and adolescents, and how the model might be adapted for youth, should be encouraged.

### The Competence Motivation Theory and the Theory of Achievement Motivation and Goal Orientations

As the Competence Motivation Theory and the Theory of Achievement Motivation focus on competence and control in an achievement area, the theory is especially useful for research into competition sports and athletes, and to a lesser extent for research into health-related physical activity in youth. However, some aspects of these theories can also be linked to motives for participation and drop-out in sports or physical activity. Also, given that many young people may choose sport as their prefered mode of physical activity, these perspectives are appropriate for further consideration.

Competence Motivation Theory (Harter 1978, 1981) and the Theory of Achievement Motivation (Nicholls, 1984, 1989; Dweck, 1986; Duda, 1987; 1986; Ames, 1992) both emphasise that perceived competence has an important influence on motivation. Moreover, they both take a developmental perspective. According to Nicholls, children from ages 2 to 12 years, pass through several developmental stages, resulting in continuous further differentiation of the concept of ability from those of task difficulty and effort. Harter also stresses the different stages that children go through in their development of perceived competence. This developmental perspective is important, as in most research on children, cognitive models are use in which children are considered to be 'little adults' without taking their level of cognitive development into account.

Research concerning the relationship between perceived competence and physical activity or sport has shown that children who perceive more competence in physical activity develop an intrinsic motivational orientation and are more likely to engage in future challenging behaviour (Duda, 1982, 1987; Roberts, 1984; Klint and Weiss, 1987).

Nicholls has argued that there are two major achievement goals that involve different conceptions of competence. For some individuals, success is norm-referenced, which means that the demonstration of competence is dependent upon performing better than others. These goal orientations are labelled ego (Nicholls, 1984) or performance (Dweck, 1986; Ames, 1992) goals. For others, success is self-referenced, which means that competence is experienced as a consequence of personal improvement. These goal orientations are labelled task (Nicholls, 1984), learning (Dweck, 1986) or mastery (Ames, 1992) goals. In general empirical studies demonstrate a positive relationship between a task goal orientation and perceived competence. Feelings of competence leads to greater intrinsic interest, which in turn leads to greater effort, within the context of some self-determination (Markland and Hardy, 1997). No consistent relationships could be found for ego orientation and percieved competence (Duda *et al.*, 1992, 1995; Seifriz, Duda and Chi, 1992; Treasure and Roberts, 1994). If sport participants are high in task and ego goal orientation they demonstrate adaptive motivated behaviour, which suggests that task rather than ego goal orientation is more important in children's evaluations of competence, ability and effort (Duda, 1988; Fox *et al.*, 1994; Williams and Gill, 1995).

Results of the recent research on the Theory of Achievement Motivation has interesting implications for motivating children and adolescents to engage in sport and physical activity. There is a consensus that a task orientation, singly or in combination with an ego orientation, is likely to facilitate adaptive cognitive and affective patterns in the context of competitive sport (Treasure and Roberts, 1994). Fortunately, an achievement goal orientation is not only a disposition, it is influenced by significant others, especially parents (Roberts, Treasure and Hall, 1994; Biddle and Goudas, 1996), it is changeable over time and it can be reconstructed by interventions or environmental influences (Ames, 1992; Nicholls, 1989; Treasure and Roberts, 1994). As Papaioannou (1995) and Papaioannou and Theodorakis (1996) argue, by emphasising a mastery orientation in physical education classes and decreasing social comparison, it is possible to decrease youngsters' ego orientation, and to increase motivation of all students.

To conclude, task-oriented individuals, singly or in combination with an ego orientation, are hypothesised to be more likely to adopt and adhere to physical activity. Task orientation should be encouraged in children and adolescents by structuring environments and feedback from significant others in such a way that social comparison and competition is de-emphasised, and personal goal-setting, personal improvement, mastery and learning is emphasized.

A more general implication of both theories is the importance of the communication of competence-related beliefs and expectations to children and adolescents by parents, teachers and coaches. Youngsters perceiving more physical and social competence may be more likely to engage in physical activity.

It can be argued that not only perceived physical competence, but also perceived social competence may be an important motivator in youth physical activity. Enhancing both forms of perceived competence and choosing activities and sport contexts for children and adolescents that link up with their predominant perceived competence levels should be of benefit. In addition, studies are needed that directly test the ability of these theories to explain physical activity in young people.

## Problems and shortcomings of social-cognitive based theories

Some researchers and practitioners (e.g. Liska, 1984; Fazio, 1990; Bagozzi and Warshaw, 1992) have highlighted problems and shortcomings of the social-cognitive based theories explaining health behaviours. Firstly, they stress the uncertain relationship between intention and behaviour. Nowadays, many researchers study the behavioural determinants in relation to intention, leaving the relation-

ship with behaviour unknown. However, with regard to physical activity, ambiguous results were found concerning the relationship between intention to be active and the level of activity itself. Some authors argue that intention is a strong predictor of subsequent exercise behaviour (Godin *et al.*, 1987; Dzewaltowski *et al.*, 1990; Greenockle, Lee and Lomax, 1990; Theodorakis *et al.*, 1991). Others, however, have reported behavioural intention as accounting for less than 10% of the variance in physical activity (Wurtele and Maddux, 1987; Dzewaltowski, 1989). Only moderate correlations between intention and behaviour (Godin and Shephard, 1986), or only significant relationships between some determinants and intention, and not actual activity (Biddle and Goudas, 1996) have been reported. Moreover, Warshaw and Davis (1985) suggested that expectation might be a better predictor of behaviour than intention, especially for behaviours that are not completely volitional. In their meta-analysis, Hausenblas *et al.* (1997) did find a large effect size for intention on exercise behaviour. Comparing the expectation-behaviour and the intention-behaviour relationships, they found a larger effect size for the former.

Secondly, a number of researchers have questioned the completeness of these research models because of the emphasis on mainly individual cognitive influences. The primacy of rational decision-making about health, ignoring emotional processes, is questioned (Logue and Smith, 1986; Rozin and Vollmecke, 1986; Tuorila, 1990), while the importance of contextual characteristics is emphasised (Sallis and Nader, 1988; Miller, 1990). These studies suggest that health behaviour is influenced more by the general social context that underlies daily routines than by the specific motivation for being healthy (Godin and Shephard, 1986; Hansell and Mechanic, 1990). It is argued that in order to broaden the total picture, social contexts as well as emotional components need to be included.

Thirdly, the accuracy of the definition of certain constructs used in the models and theories can be questioned (Sallis *et al.*, 1992). Researchers and theorists alternately use a narrow or broad, specific or general, strict or loose definition and operationalisation of the same construct (e.g. self-efficacy, attitude or belief, control, competence, goal) leading to confusion and ambiguous results.

Fourthly, the focus on cognitions in studying young children is a problem because of their cognitive development. Few models emphasise a developmental perspective and, if they do (e.g. the Competence Motivation Theory and the Theory of Achievement Motivation), very little research is available showing relevant data relating cognitive development to physical activity motivation.

Finally, physical activity, exercise and sport, are more complex than other health behaviours, such as smoking and alcohol use, because of the possible differences in participation (e.g. sedentary, adoption, drop-out, sport, competition, organised or recreation physical activity, transportation), there are many different models and theories used to study these levels of participation (e.g. recreative v. competition sports), and this results in pieces of knowledge only applicable to sections of populations.

### The need for integration of constructs and theories

All the theories described so far emphasise cognitive mechanisms underlying the self-regulation of behaviour. Usually, researchers test one or more theories applied to physical activity. Until now, few researchers have compared the constructs of different theories in exercise research. However, some theorists demonstrate similarities in constructs. Ajzen (1991) argued that the 'perceived behaviour control' construct of the Theory of Planned Behaviour is similar to 'self-efficacy' in the Social Cognitive Theory, referring to the judgements people make of their perceived competence in performing the behaviour. Moreover similarities can be found between self-efficacy and the perceived competence construct in the Theory of Achievement Motivation and the Competence Motivation Theory.

To date, it is clear that the main theories are less distinct than they appear to be. The time has come for the different theories and models to be better integrated, to result in a more dynamic and powerful understanding of the determinants of physical activity and exercise (Kimiecik, 1992). Such an integrated approach could provide a general framework for exercise researchers, making sure that the relative importance and strength of different determinants in their influence on youth physical activity can be detected (Sallis *et al.*, 1992).

### ■ The 'A-Theoretical' Approach

The studies described so far involve mainly testing one or more specific theory of determinants of physical activity or sport in children and adolescents. However, a second group of researchers have tried to explain physical activity by including the most relevant constructs of the theories mentioned above, together with other constructs that are not related to a specific theory but have proven their usefulness in previous empirical research (Sallis *et al.*, 1989). These studies, mostly referred to in literature as the 'a-theoretical' approach, is not completely a-theoretical, but rather pragmatic and relevant. The main constructs of the social-cognitive theories are frequently included together with other variables such as perceived barriers and benefits, demographic characteristics, enjoyment, family and peer influence. Moreover, this approach is considered to be more promising in explaining variance in physical activity in sedentary individuals and drop-outs from a public health perspective. This 'a-theoretical' approach does not include an integration of construct or models, resulting in a general theory, but rather a collection of the most relevant constructs. In the past, most of these studies were conducted using adult populations, with few studies done using children and adolescents.

Zakarian *et al.* (1994) conducted a study to test a more comprehensive model of determinants, including psychological, social and environmental variables in a sample of low educational status 15- to 17-year-old adolescents. Important correlates of physical activity in their research were self-efficacy, perceived barriers and benefits, and friend and family support. The relationship with other health behaviours or indexes (smoking, alcohol use, Body Mass Index) was not always in the expected direction. Environmental variables, such as availability of facilities and hours of television viewing, were not related to exercise.

Stucky-Ropp and Dilorenzo (1993) investigated determinants of exercise in 11-year-old children, with a specific focus on socialisation variables. Enjoyment of physical activity was the most salient predictor of exercise behaviour for both boys and girls. Furthermore, perceived barriers to exercise and family support contributed significantly. As noted before, Stucky-Ropp and Dilorenzo (1993) did not find an influence for self-efficacy, probably due to assessment problems.

Trost *et al.* (1997) executed a prospective study of the determinants of physical activity in children, aged 11–12 years, to infer causal relationships between outcome beliefs, social influence, and three self-efficacy measures. Gender, self-efficacy in overcoming barriers, participation in community sports and beliefs regarding physical activity outcomes were found to be important predictors of physical activity behaviour. In our own study (De Bourdeaudhuij, Van Oost, and Mommerency, 1993) of adolescents and young adults (aged 16–25 years old), perceived barriers and benefits, self-efficacy and social support from friends accounted for most of the variance in vigorous physical activity, with enjoyment and social interaction being the most important benefits. Lack of interest and lack of self-discipline were the most important barriers. Few relationships were found between determinants and activities of low and moderate intensity.

In general, the models employed in the 'a-theoretical' studies mostly explain 15–20% of the variance in physical activity, which is similar to comparable surveys in an adult population. However, the majority of the variance has still to be explained. Future research into other variables explaining an additional proportion of this variance is needed. Moreover, the picture concerning determinants of moderate and low intensity physical activity is even less clear.

Looking at the results, the 'theoretical' and 'a-theoretical' approaches come to comparable conclusions. A major difference, however, is that in the 'a-theoretical' approach more determinants are integrated in one study, which has the advantage of being able to investigate their relative position and strength in explaining physical activity. From a health promotion perspective, the 'a-theoretical' approach could be considered on the one hand as more complete and integral and on the other hand more flexible and dynamic and thus more useful and promising. However, a major problem for both the theoretical and atheoretical approach is the measurement of dependent and independent variables. There is no one good measure of physical activity in children and adolescents that satisfies the criteria of validity and reliability to be used in many research contexts. Together with the problems already mentioned and the use of the behavioural (cognition–emotion–action) constructs, many of the interpretation and comparison problems have still to be overcome.

## ■ The role of enjoyment

Investigating perceived benefits or motives in all age groups usually shows high correlations between measures of enjoyment or fun and physical activity. Much of the research on enjoyment has focused on participation motivation in youth sport (Kimiecik and Harris, 1996). The degree to which children enjoy sport seems to be a strong predictor of adoption, adherence or drop-out (Gould, Feltz and Weiss, 1985; Wankel and Kreisel, 1985). However the concept of enjoyment is not completely clear. Few studies have tried to determine the factors underlying or influencing enjoyment. In a recent paper, Kimiecik and Harris (1996) addressed these problems and clarified the definitions of enjoyment with the pur-

pose of presenting implications for future enjoyment research. They argue that in most research, enjoyment is defined as a positive affective response to physical activity reflecting feelings and perceptions such as pleasure, liking and fun (Scanlan and Lewthwaite, 1986; Scanlan, Stein and Ravizza, 1989; Scanlan *et al.*, 1993). As a result of their analyses they suggest conceptualising enjoyment as 'flow'. In this view enjoyment is related to the physical activity itself, which means that executing this specific activity is the source of the enjoyment, characterised by an optimal psychological flow state that is associated with performing the activity for its own sake, stressing the intrinsic motivational factors. Previous findings also highlighted the relationship between task orientation in physical achievement situations and positive affect or enjoyment in children (Vlachopoulos, Biddle and Fox, 1996). In a reaction to the work of Kimiecik and Harris (1996), Wankel (1997: 105) states, 'I choose to use the term enjoyment in a broad, inclusive, positive affect sense that may relate to diverse aspects of the sport or exercise experience. I believe that the positive feelings – whether they come from the challenge of the activity, the social relationships, the nature of the activity, or something about the surrounding environment can have a positive motivational influence for continued involvement'.

Other researchers (Maehr and Braskamp, 1986; Tappe, Duda and Menges-Ehrnwald, 1990; Ashford, Biddle and Goudas 1993) have also argued that in most cases enjoyment will be a state or outcome associated with participating in physical activity for another particular reason. Ashford *et al.* (1993) found that socio-psychological well-being was the primary source of enjoyment for adult recreational exercisers. However, as much of the variance in enjoyment was left unexplained, they suggest that enjoyment is specific to sub-group factors and will vary along sports, locations, age, culture and socio-demographic characteristics.

From a public health perspective of physical activity in youth, this second thesis might be especially important. It is clear that defining enjoyment as a flow experience, stressing intrinsic motivation, is more related to sport and exercise experiences and thus to children and adolescents who have already incorporated physical activity into everyday life. In this context, it is likely that enjoyment is not only related to intrinsic motivation, but also exercise climate, task and/or ego orientation, perceived control and autonomy.

If our purpose is to encourage youngsters to adopt enough physical activity based on a health promotion perspective, the links between enjoyment and other motives, such as being with friends and family, making new friends, staying in good shape and feeling fitter, are also important. Few studies have addressed these relationships. In our own research on determinants of physical activity in adolescents (De Bourdeaudhuij *et al.*, 1993), enjoyment and social motives were closely related.

It is also possible to conceptualize enjoyment from an operant point of view as being related to the reinforcing nature of the activity. Epstein and co-workers (1991) have applied behavioural economic theory to physical activity and sedentary behaviours. They argue that obese children choose sendentary activities because they find them more reinforcing than vigorous activities. Replacing sedentary activities with vigorous activities may result in the reduction of the usual amount of reinforcement and in an increase in unpleasant experiences. Based

on several experiments they found that children chose sedentary activities over vigorous activities even when vigorous and sedentary activities were given similar liking ratings (Epstein *et al.*, 1991). The results also showed that future research is needed to identify alternative vigorous activities that can effectively compete with sedentary activities among obese individuals.

To conclude, from a health promotion point of view, further research is required here so that physical activity interventions in youth can also target enjoyment and result in an increase in regular physical activity in youngsters.

## Demographic differences in determinants

So far, demographic differences in determinants of physical activity in youth have not been considered. Many researchers have shown important sex differences in cognitive and affective determinants of physical activity. Research in the context of the Competence Motivation Theory and the Theory of Achievement Motivation has found that boys were higher in perceived competence than girls (Eccles and Harrold, 1991; Brustad, 1992; Duda *et al.*, 1995; Williams and Gill, 1996). These differences are considered to begin at age 11 years (Weiss, McAuley, Ebbeck and Wiese, 1990; Craig *et al.*, 1996). The effect of this difference in girls is because of their lower perceived competence, being less interested in physical activity and sports. Some authors argue that adults (such as parents and teachers) are most important in mediating children's perceived competence (Brustad, 1992). Lirgg (1991) conducted a meta-analysis of recent studies of gender differences in self-confidence in physical activity. She demonstrated possible bias in prior research, such as using male oriented tasks and problematic confidence measures, and came to the conclusion that the difference in confidence is certainly present, but it is probably not as large as usually assumed.

Sallis *et al.* (1996) found that girls perceived more barriers to physical activity than boys, although no differences were found in beliefs about its benefits. The same results were found by Kendzierski and Johnson (1993) in their study of older adolescents, which looked at the reasons and excuses for not exercising. Females consistently scored higher on barriers (reasons and excuses) in comparison with males. In our own research, girls reported fewer benefits and more barriers associated with physical activity than boys (De Bourdeaudhuij *et al.*, 1993). It could be argued that rationally evaluating the perceived benefits and barriers, or costs, of being physically active results in adoption and adherence for males, but drop-out and sedentariness for females.

Godin and Shephard (1986) report differences in the nature of benefits between boys and girls. Boys especially liked to have fun, whereas girls looked for the benefit of looking better. In our research this was confirmed with girls reporting more benefits related to physical appearance, and boys more benefits related to competition, health, enjoyment and social interaction (De Bourdeaudhuij *et al.*, 1993). Covey and Feltz (1991) showed relationships between physical activity and self-image, gender role identity and self-perceived attractiveness in female adolescents, arguing the existence of a gender specific importance of self-presentation and identity in physical activity.

Trost *et al.* (1997) found gender differences in the nature of the barriers perceived. Activity in girls was predicted most by such barriers as tiredness and homework obligations, whereas for boys only the item concerning outdoor weather conditions was predictive. They argued for a gender-specific basis for addressing barriers to physical activity in children. Girls should be encouraged to participate in non-competitive activities, while boys should be educated about benefits and provided with positive beliefs about physical activity.

Trost *et al.* (1996) argued that although several determinants differed on gender, only differences in self-efficacy and participation in community sports contributed significantly to explaining gender differences in physical activity. This means that not all gender differences in determinants are responsible for differences in physical activity between boys and girls.

Few studies have investigated the possible differences in determinants of physical activity between youngsters of different socio-economic status. So far, only Sallis *et al.* (1996) has compared ethnicity and socio-economic status on determinants of physical activity in the United States. They concluded that no broad differences could be found.

# ■ The influences of socialisation

The social factors of behavioural determinants of physical activity in youth have so far not been considered. However, as our focus is on children and adolescents, some comment is needed about the relationship between socialisation and behavioural determinants of physical activity in youth.

In general, social influences, such as modelling, support, encouragement of family and friends are considered to contribute significantly, along with other behavioural determinants, to the explanation of variance in physical activity in youth. Findings of significant familial resemblance in activity habits (Sallis and Nader, 1988), together with a large body of research showing correlates between social influences and activity (see Brustad, 1992) support this view. It seems most logical that social and environmental influences are very important in young children and become less important when social-cognitive factors become more dominant in adolescents.

However, besides the direct relationship between social factors and physical activity other researchers stress, there exists an important indirect relationship in which social factors influence physical activity mediated through behavioural, social cognitive determinants (Bandura, 1986; Duda, 1987; Biddle and Goudas, 1996). Brustad (1992) pleads for the integration of these socialisation influences, particularly parental behaviours, into the study of children's sport motivation. More knowledge about the influence of family, peer or school socialisation patterns upon children's self-efficacy, goal orientation, perceived competence, achievement motivation, beliefs and attitudes, norms and perceived control, is needed.

## ■ **What we know**

■ The Theories of Reasoned Action and of Planned Behaviour are relevant frameworks for studying determinants of physical activity in youth. Perceived behavioural control and attitudes towards physical activity have been found to be correlates of physical activity in youth. However, most studies have shown associations between these constructs and intentions to be physically active rather than the physical activity itself.

■ The Social Cognitive Theory, and especially its most studied concept of self-efficacy, is a determinant of physical activity in children and adolescents. General, as well as more specific, measures of perceived competence in relation to physical activity are also relevant. Empirical support has been found for the relationship between self-efficacy and physical activity in youth.

■ The Transtheoretical Model, which is becoming influential in adult physical activity, has only once been used to study physical activity in children and adolescent physical activity.

■ The Competence Motivation Theory and the Theory of Achievement Motivation were found to be successful in explaining exercise in an achievement situation, more specifically youth sports or physical education classes. Firstly, both theories stress the importance of perceived competence in determining sport motivation and secondly, the advantage of a task goal orientation, singly or in combination with an ego goal orientation, was shown. However, as both theories emphasise skill development and achievement rather than participation, only some aspects of both theories, which are comparable with the self-efficacy construct, are useful from a health promotion perspective.

■ The 'a-theoretical' approach, in which theoretical as well as empirically relevant constructs are included to explain as much variance as possible in physical activity in youth, appear to be promising from a public health perspective. Most empirical support is found for self-efficacy, attitudes or beliefs, family or friend support, and perceived benefits and barriers. Less or no support is found for convenience of facilities, knowledge, family modelling and neighbourhood characteristics.

- In children and adolescents enjoyment or fun is an important 'benefit' or 'motive' for adopting and adhering to physical activity. Sometimes enjoyment can be considered as an optimal psychological state associated with performing of the activity for its own sake, whereas for others enjoying oneself through physical activity is the result of participation for other reasons. Empirical support for the importance of enjoyment as a determinant of physical activity has been found. The precise meaning or nature of enjoyment in youth, however, is not clear.

- In line with gender differences in physical activity itself, with males being significantly more physically active at all ages in comparison with females, major differences also exist between males and females concerning determinants of physical activity. Females have lower levels of perceived competence, they perceive more barriers or costs of physical activity, they perceive or expect less benefits in general and less fun and enjoyment in particular. These gender differences are well documented but this does not necessarily mean that they can account for major gender differences in physical activity.

# What we need to know

- What determinants can be identified through representative and prospective population studies in youth?

- The integration of constructs and theories into unified theories.

- What are the determinants of physical activity of low and moderate intensity in youth?

- What are the main socialisation influences on behavioural determinants of physical activity in youth?

- What are the key developmental changes in determinants of physical activity?

- What are the main differences in determinants for specific subpopulations of youth?

# References

**Ajzen, I.** (1991). The theory of planned behavior. Special issue: theories of cognitive self-regulation. *Organizational Behavior and Human Decision Processes*, **50**, 179–211.

**Ajzen, I. and Fishbein, M.** (1980). *Understanding attitudes and predicting social behavior*. Englewood Cliffs: Prentice-Hall.

**Ajzen, I. and Madden, T.J.** (1986). Prediction of goal-directed behavior: attitudes, intentions and perceived behavioral control. *Journal of Experimental Social Psychology*, **22**, 453–74.

**Ames, C.** (1992). Classrooms: goals, structures and student motivation. *Journal of Educational Psychology*, **84**, 261–71.

**Armstrong, N., Balding, J., Gentle, P. and Kirby, B.** (1990). Patterns of physical activity among 11- to 16-year-old British children. *British Medical Journal*, **301**, 203–5.

**Armstrong, C., Sallis, J., Hovell, M. and Hofstetter, C.** (1993). Stages of change, self-efficacy and the adoption of vigorous exercise: a prospective analysis. *Journal of Sport and Exercise Psychology*, **15**, 390–402.

**Ashford, B., Biddle, S. and Goudas, M.** (1993). Participation in community sports centres: motives and predictors of enjoyment. *Journal of Sports Sciences*, **11**, 249–56.

**Bagozzi, R.P. and Warshaw, P.R.** (1992). An examination of the etiology of the attitude–behaviour relation for goal-directed behaviours. *Multivariate Behavioural Research*, **27**, 601–43.

**Bandura, A.** (1986). *Social foundations of thought and action: a social cognitive theory*. Englewood Cliffs: Prentice Hall.

**Biddle, S. and Goudas, M.** (1996). Analysis of children's physical activity and its association with adult encouragement and social cognitive variables. *Journal of School Health*, **66** (2), 75–8.

**Blair, S., Clark, D., Cureton, K. and Powell, K.** (1988). Exercise and fitness in childhood: implications for a lifetime of health. In C. Gisolfi and D. Lamb (eds.), *Perspectives in exercise science and sports medicine: youth, exercise and sport*, pp. 401–30. Indianapolis: Benchmark Press.

**Booth, M., Macaskill, P., Owen, N., Oldenburg, B., Marcus, B. and Bauman, A.** (1993). Population prevalence and correlates of stages of change in physical activity. *Health Education Quarterly*, **20**, 431–40.

**Brustad, R.** (1992). Integrating socialization influences into the study of children's motivation in sport. *Journal of Sport and Exercise Psychology*, **14**, 59–77.

**Cardinal, B.** (1995). The stages of exercise scale and stages of exercise behavior in female adults. *Journal of Sports Medicine and Physical Fitness*, **35**, 87–92.

**Covey, L. and Feltz, D.** (1991). Physical activity and adolescent female psychological development. *Journal of Youth and Adolescence*, **20** (4), 463–74.

**Craig, S., Goldberg, J. and Dietz, W.** (1996). Psychosocial correlates of physical activity among fifth and eighth graders. *Preventive Medicine*, **25**, 506–13.

**Davies, P.** (1992). Developments in the assessment of physical activity. In N. Norgan (ed.), *Physical activity and health*, pp. 45–56. Cambridge: Cambridge University Press.

**De Bourdeaudhuij, I., Van Oost, P. and Mommerency, G.** (1993). *Psychological determinants of physical activity in adolescents and young adults*. Unpublished manuscript, University of Ghent, Belgium.

**Dishman, R.K.** (1991). Increasing and maintaining exercise and physical activity. *Behavior Therapy*, **22**, 345–78.

**Dishman, R.K., Sallis, J.F. and Orenstein, D.R.** (1985). The determinants of physical activity and exercise. *Public Health Reports*, **100**, 158–71.

**Duda, J.** (1982). Toward a phenomenology of children in sport: new directions in sport psychology research. In L.L. Gedvilas (ed.), *NAPEHE Proceedings*, pp. 38–47. Champaign: Human Kinetics.

**Duda, J.** (1987). Toward a developmental theory of children's motivation in sport. *Journal of Sport and Exercise Psychology*, **9**, 130–45.

**Duda, J.** (1988). The relationship between goal perspectives, persistence and behavioural intensity among male and female recreational sport participants. *Leisure Sciences*, **10** (2), 95–106.

**Duda, J.** (1989). Goal perspective, participation and persistence in sport. *International Journal of Sport Psychology*, **20**, 42–56.

**Duda, J., Chi, L., Newton, M. and Walling, M.** (1995). Task and ego orientation and intrinsic motivation in sport. *International Journal of Sport Psychology*, **26**, 40–63.

**Duda, J., Fox, K., Biddle, S. and Armstrong, N.** (1992). Children's achievement goals and beliefs about success in sport. *British Journal of Educational Psychology*, **62**, 313–23.

**Duda, J. and Nicholls, J.** (1992). Dimensions of achievement motivation in schoolwork and sport. *Journal of Educational Psychology*, **84**, 290–99.

**Dweck, C.** (1986). Motivational processes affecting learning. *American Psychologist*, **41**, 1040–48.

**Dzewaltowski, D.** (1989). Toward a model of exercise motivation. *Journal of Sport and Exercise Psychology*, **11**, 251–69.

**Dzewaltowski, D., Noble, J. and Shaw, J.** (1990). Physical activity participation: social cognitive theory versus the theory of reasoned action and planned behavior. *Journal of Sport and Exercise Psychology*, **12**, 388–405.

**Eccles, J. and Harold, R.** (1991). Gender differences in sport involvement: applying the Eccles expectancy-value model. *Journal of Applied Sport Psychology*, **3**, 7–35.

**Epstein, L., Smith, J., Vara, L. and Rodefer, J.** (1991). Behavioral economic analysis of activity choice in obese children. *Health Psychology*, **10**, 311–16.

**Fazio, R.H.** (1990). Multiple processes by which attitudes guide behaviour: the mode model as an integrative framework. *Advances in Experimental Social Psychology*, **23**, 75–105.

**Fox, K., Goudas, M., Biddle, S., Duda, J. and Armstrong, N.** (1994). Children's task and ego goal profiles in sport. *British Journal of Educational Psychology*, **64**, 253–61.

**Frerichs, R., Webber, L., Voors, A., Srinivasan, S. and Berenson, G.** (1979). Cardiovascular disease risk factor variables in children at two successive years: the Bogalusa Heart Study. *Journal of Chronic Disease*, **32**, 251–62.

**Godin, G.** (1994). Theories of reasoned action and planned behavior: usefulness for exercise promotion. *Medicine and Science in Sports and Exercise*, **26**, 1391–4.

**Godin, G. and Shephard, R.** (1986). Psychosocial factors influencing intentions to exercise of young students from grades 7 to 9. *Research Quarterly for Exercise and Sport*, **57**, 41–52.

**Godin, G., Valois, P., Shephard, R. and Desharnais, R.** (1987). Prediction of leisure time exercise behavior: a path analysis (LISREL) model. *Journal of Behavioral Medicine*, **10**, 145–58.

**Gould, D., Feltz, D. and Weiss, M.** (1985). Motives for participating in competitive youth swimming. *International Journal of Sport Psycholgy*, **16**, 126–40.

**Greenockle, K., Lee, A. and Lomax, R.** (1990). The relationship between selected student characteristics and activity patterns in a required high school physical education class. *Research Quarterly for Exercise and Sport*, **61**, 59–69.

**Hansell, S. and Mechanic, D.** (1990). Parent and peer effect on adolescent health behavior. In K. Hurrelman and F. Lösel (eds.), *Health hazards in adolescence*, pp. 43–65. Berlin: Walter de Gruyter.

**Harter, S.** (1978). Effectance motivation reconsidered: toward a developmental model. *Human Development*, **21**, 34–64.

**Harter, S.** (1981). A model of intrinsic mastery motivation in children: individual differences and developmental change. In A. Collins (ed.), *Minnesota symposium on child psychology*, pp. 215–55. Hillsdale: Erlbaum.

**Hausenblas, H., Carron, A. and Mack, D.** (1997). Application of the Theory of Reasoned Action and Planned Behavior to exercise behavior: a meta-analysis. *Journal of Sport and Exercise Psychology*, **19**, 36–51.

**Kemper, H.** (1994) The natural history of physical activity and aerobic fitness in teenagers. In R.K. Dishman (ed.) *Advances in exercise adherence*, pp. 293–318. Champaign: Human Kinetics.

**Kendzierski, D. and Johnson, W.** (1993). Excuses, excuses, excuses: a cognitive behavioral approach to exercise implementation. *Journal of Sport and Exercise Psychology*, **15**, 207–19.

**Kimiecik, J. and Harris, A.** (1996). What is enjoyment? A conceptual/definitional analysis with implications for sport and exercise psychology. *Journal of Sport and Exercise Psychology*, **18**, 247–63.

**Kimiecik, J.** (1992). Predicting vigorous physical activity of corporate employees: comparing the Theories of Reasoned Action and Planned Behavior. *Journal of Sport and Exercise Psychology*, **14**, 192–206.

**King, A., Blair, S., Bild, D., Dishman, R., Dubbert, P., Marcus, B., Oldridge, N., Paffenbarger, R., Powell, K. and Yeager, K.** (1992). Determinants of physical activity and interventions in adults. *Medicine and Science in Sports and Exercise*, **24**, S221–S236.

**Klint, K. and Weiss, M.** (1987). Perceived competence and motives for participating in youth sports: a test of Harter's Competence Motivation Theory. *Journal of Sport and Exercise Psychology*, **9**, 55–65.

**Lirgg, C.** (1991). Gender differences in self-confidence in physical activity: a meta-analysis of recent studies. *Journal of Sport and Exercise Psychology*, **8**, 294–310.

**Liska, A.E.** (1984). A critical examination of the causal structure of the Fishbein/Ajzen attitude-behaviour model. *Social Psychology Quarterly*, **47**, 61–74.

**Logue, D. and Smith, M.** (1986). Predictors of food preferences in adult humans. *Appetite*, **7**, 109–25.

**Maehr, M. and Braskamp, L.** (1986). *The motivation factor: a theory of personal investment*. Lexington: Lexington Press.

**Marcus, B., Eaton, C., Rossi, J. and Harlow, L.** (1994). Self-efficacy, decision-making and stages of change: an integrative model of physical exercise. *Journal of Applied Social Psychology*, **24**, 489–508.

**Markland, D. and Hardy, L.** (1997). On the factorial and construct validity of the intrinsic motivation inventory: conceptual and operational concerns. *Research Quarterly for Exercise and Sport*, **68**, 20–32.

**Miller, L.** (1990). Intimacy and liking: mutual influence and the role of unique relationships. *Journal of Personality and Social Psychology*, **59**, 50–60.

**Nicholls, J.** (1984). Achievement motivation: conceptions of ability, subjective experience, task choice and performance. *Psychological Review*, **91**, 328–46.

**Nicholls, J.** (1989). *The competitive ethos and democratic education*. Cambridge: Harvard University Press.

**Papaioannou, A.** (1995). Differential perceptual and motivational patterns when different goals are adopted. *Journal of Sport and Exercise Psychology*, **17**, 18–34.

**Papaioannou, A. and Theodorakis, Y.** (1996). A test of three models for the prediction of intention for participation in physical education lessons. *International Journal of Sport Psychology*, **27**, 383–99.

**Prochaska, J. and DiClemente, C.** (1983). Stages and processes of self-change of smoking: toward an integrative model of change. *Journal of Consulting and Clinical Psychology*, **51**, 390–95.

**Prochaska, J. and Marcus, B.** (1994). The transtheoretical model: applications to exercise. In R. Dishman (ed.), *Advances in exercise adherence*, pp. 161–80. Champaign: Human Kinetics.

**Reynolds, K., Killen, J., Bryson, S., Maron, D., Taylor, C., Maccoby, N. and Farquhar, J.** (1990). Psychosocial predictors of physical activity in adolescents. *Preventive Medicine*, **19**, 541–51.

**Roberts, G.C.** (1984). Toward a new theory of motivation in sport: the role of perceived ability. In J. Silva and R. Weinberg (eds.), *Psychological foundations of sport*, pp. 214–28. Champaign: Human Kinetics.

**Roberts, G., Treasure, D. and Hall, H.** (1994). Parental goal orientations and beliefs about the competitive sport experience of their child. *Journal of Applied Social Psychology*, **24**, 631–45.

**Rozin, P. and Vollmecke T.** (1986). Food likes and dislikes. *Annual Review on Nutrition*, **6**, 433–56.

**Sallis, J., Hovell, M., Hofstetter, C., Faucher, P., Elder, J., Blanchard, J., Caspersen, C., Powell, K. and Christenson, G.** (1989). A multivariate study of determinants of vigorous exercise in a community sample. *Preventive Medicine*, **18**, 20–34.

**Sallis, J. and Nader, P.** (1988). Family determinants of health behaviors. In D. Gochman (ed.), *Health behavior: emerging research perspectives*, pp. 107–24. New York: Plenum Press.

**Sallis, J., Simons-Morton, B., Stone, E., Corbin, C., Epstein, L., Faucette, N., Iannotti, R., Killen, J., Klesges, R., Petray, C., Rowland, T. and Taylor, W.** (1992). Determinants of physical activity and interventions in youth. *Medicine and Science in Sports and Exercise*, **24**, S248–57.

**Sallis, J., Zakarian, J., Hovell, M. and Hofstetter, R.** (1996). Ethnic, socioeconomic and sex differences in physical activity among adolescents. *Journal of Clinical Epidemiology*, **49** (2), 125–34.

**Saunders, R., Pate, R., Felton, G., Dowda, M., Weinrich, M., Ward, D., Parsons, M. and Baranowski, T.** (1997). Development of questionnaires to measure psychosocial influence on children physical activity. *Preventive Medicine*, **26**, 241–7.

**Scanlan, T. and Lewthwaite, R.** (1986). Social psychological aspects of competition for male youth sport participants. IV. Predictors of enjoyment. *Journal of Sport Psychology*, **8**, 25–35.

**Scanlan, T., Simons, J., Carpenter, P., Schmidt, G.** (1993). The Sport Commitment Model: measurement development for the youth-sport domain. *Journal of Sport and Exercise Psychology*, **15**, 16–38.

**Scanlan, T., Stein, G. and Ravizza, K.** (1989). An in-depth study of former elite figure skaters. II. Sources of enjoyment. *Journal of Sport and Exercise Psychology*, **11**, 65–83.

**Seifriz, J., Duda, J. and Chi, L.** (1992). The relationship of perceived motivational climate to achievement-related affect and cognitions in basketball. *Journal of Sport and Exercise Psychology*, **14**, 375–91.

**Simons-Morton, B., O'Hara, N., Parcel, G., Huang, I., Baranowski, T. and Wilson, B.** (1990). Children's frequency of participation in moderate to vigorous physical activities. *Research Quarterly for Exercise and Sport*, **61**, 307–14.

**Sonstroem, R.** (1988). Psychological models. In R.K. Dishman (ed.), *Exercise adherence: its impact on public health*, pp. 125–54. Champaign: Human Kinetics.

**Stucky-Ropp, R. and DiLorenzo, T.** (1993). Determinants of exercise in children. *Preventive Medicine*, **22**, 880–89.

**Tappe, M., Duda, J. and Menges-Ehrnwald, R.** (1990). Personal investment predictors of adolescent motivational orientation toward exercise. *Canadian Journal of Sport Sciences*, **15**, 185–92.

**Taylor, W., Baranowski, T. and Sallis, J.** (1994). Family determinants of childhood physical activity: a social-cognitive model. In R. Dishman (ed.), *Advances in exercise adherence*, pp. 319–42. Champaign: Human Kinetics.

**Theodorakis, Y., Doganis, G., Bagiatis, K. and Gouthas, M.** (1991). Preliminary study of the ability of reasoned action model in predicting exercise behavior in young children. *Perceptual and Motor Skills*, **72**, 51–8.

**Treasure, D. and Roberts, G.** (1994). Cognitive and affective concomitants of task and ego goal orientations during the middle school years. *Journal of Sport and Exercise Psychology*, **16**, 15–28.

**Trost, S., Pate, R., Dowda, M., Saunders, R., Ward, D. and Felton, G.** (1996). Gender differences in physical activity and determinants of physical activity in rural fifth grade children. *Journal of School Health*, **66** (4), 145–50.

**Trost, S., Pate, R., Saunders, R., Ward, D., Dowda, M. and Feldon, G.** (1997). A prospective study of the determinants of physical activity in rural fifth-grade children. *Preventive Medicine*, **26**, 257–63.

**Tuorila, H.** (1990). The role of attitudes and preferences in food choice. In J. Somogyi and E. Koskinen (eds.), *Nutritional adaptation to new life-styles*, pp. 108–16. Bibliotheca Nutritio et Dieta, 45. Basel: Karger.

**Vlachopoulos, S., Biddle, S. and Fox, K.** (1996). A social-cognitive investigation into the mechanisms of affect generation in children's physical activity. *Journal of Sport and Exercise Psychology*, **18**, 174–93.

**Wankel, L.** (1997). 'Strawpersons,' selective reporting and inconsistent logic: a response to Kimiecik and Harris's analysis of enjoyment. *Journal of Sport and Exercise Psychology*, **19**, 98–109.

**Wankel, L. and Kreisel, P.** (1985). Factors underlying enjoyment of youth sports: sport and age group comparisons. *Journal of Sport Psychology*, **7**, 51–64.

**Wankel, L., Mummery, K., Stephens, T. and Craig, C.** (1994). Prediction of physical activity intention from social psychological variables: results from the Campbell's Survey of Well-Being. *Journal of Sport and Exercise Psychology*, **16**, 56–69.

**Warshaw, R. and Davis, F.** (1985). Dissenting behavioral intention and behavioral expectation. *Journal of Experimental Psychology*, **21**, 213–28.

**Weiss, M., McAuley, E., Ebbeck, V. and Wiese, D.** (1990). Self-esteem and causal attributions for children's physical and social competence in sport. *Journal of Sport and Exercise Psychology*, **12**, 21–36.

**Williams, L. and Gill, D.** (1995). The role of perceived competence in the motivation of physical activity. *Journal of Sport and Exercise Psychology*, **17**, 363–78.

**Wurtele, S. and Maddux, J.** (1987). Relative contributions of protection theory components in predicting exercise intentions and behavior. *Health Psychology*, **8**, 453–66.

**Yordy, G. and Lent, R.** (1993). Predicting aerobic exercise participation: social cognitive, reasoned action, planned behavior models. *Journal of Sport and Exercise Psychology*, **15**, 363–74.

**Zakarian, J., Hovell, M., Hofstetter, C., Sallis, J. and Keating, K.** (1994). Correlates of exercise in a predominantly low SES and minority high school population. *Preventive Medicine*, **23**, 314–21.

# Social and environmental factors associated with physical activity in young people

Bente Wold[1] and Leo Hendry[2]

[1]Research Director, Research Centre for Health Promotion, Bergen University, Norway

[2]Professor of Education, University of Aberdeen

Physical activity contributes significantly to the development of the physical, mental and social health of young people. There are several reasons why promoting physical activity is regarded as an important field in adolescent health promotion and these have been outlined in some detail in the previous chapters.

In order to be effective, interventions aimed at promoting physical activity among young people need to be based on knowledge about the determinants of participation in such activities. Such knowledge may be sought by looking at how the level of physical activity among young people may be explained as a result of certain characteristics of the persons involved, their social and physical environment and the behaviour (i.e. physical activity) in question. The main aim of this chapter is to review the research regarding the social and environmental factors associated with physical activity in youth, mainly adolescents aged 11–18 years. The data bases included in the search for literature were MEDLINE, PsychLit and SPORT DISCUS, using combinations of key words such as youth, physical activity, sports, social influences, environmental influences, parental physical activity and social inequalities. The main criteria for

selecting papers were that they had to have been published after 1985 and that the studies were based on relatively large and representative samples.

## Theories explaining participation in physical activity

When studying social influences on physical activity among young people, it is important to recognise that the typical adolescent activities generally are of a social nature (Wold, 1989; Sallis, 1993). Adolescents tend to perform much of their physical activity in group settings and team sports are very popular (Sallis, 1993). Thus, to a large extent, physical activity should be regarded as a social activity among young people.

In order to gain knowledge about how physical activity is influenced, it is useful to apply a socialisation perspective. Socialisation is defined as 'the lifelong process by which the individual acquires the attitudes, beliefs, customs, values, roles and expectations of a culture or a social group' (Craig, 1976: 12). Habitual leisure-time physical activity may be regarded as a custom in a particular culture or social group. The main socialising agents influencing the individual in this process of acquiring this habit are the family, the school and the peer group. Other socialising agents of great importance include the mass media, health professionals and various institutions and activities for children and young people, for example sport clubs.

Several theories and concepts from social and developmental psychology may help to understand how the process of socialising young people to engage in physical activity occurs, notably the ecological theory of development (Bronfenbrenner, 1979), the Social Cognitive Theory (Bandura, 1986) and the Problem Behaviour Theory (Jessor and Jessor, 1977; Jessor, Donovan and Costa, 1991). This review also utilises concepts and perspectives from social reproduction theory (Bourdieu, 1984) and cross-cultural psychology (Berry *et al.*, 1992).

The *ecological theory* of development (Bronfenbrenner, 1979) underlines the importance of studying how the various structures of society affect the development of habits of physical activity, beginning with the innermost structure – the micro-level settings. At this level, the immediate influences of socialising agents in the settings involving the person are studied, such as how family, peers, school and neighbourhood influence the person. At the next level, the meso-level, interaction between the micro-level settings are studied. In general, development is enhanced if there is a compatibility between settings. Thus, it is more likely that a child will take part in physical activity if he or she is encouraged to do so in a similar fashion both in the family, peer and school setttings. The next level, the exo-level, focuses on the influence of settings not involving the person, such as

various formal community groups making decisions about what kind of activities and facilities should be offered to children and young people in their area. At the highest level, the macro-level, cultural factors, such as values, norms and legislation, are significant in setting the boundaries for individual development in a community. The structures at these different levels also influence each other, which underlines the need to undertake complex analyses of why and how young people take part in physical activity.

Berry *et al.* (1992) have proposed an *ecocultural model* to guide the study of cultural influences on human behaviour such as physical activity. In this model three types of variables are suggested:

■ Contextual variables, which include ecological and socio-political variables.

■ Process variables, which include biological and cultural adaptation and transmission to individuals.

■ Psychological outcomes (in the context of this chapter this could refer to physical activity among young people).

This is a conceptual scheme rather than a theoretical model from which testable hypotheses can be derived. It is a general guide to classes of variables and their relevance for the explanation of similarities and differences in human behaviour and experience that can be found across cultures.

## ◻ Social factors associated with physical activity

### Demographic variables

In discussing the likely influence of key demographic variables, we shall consider age, gender and socio-economic status.

## Age

Levels of physical activity begin to decline at about six years of age and continue to decline throughout life (Kemper, 1994). Several types of physical activity also appear to be age-related, such that play-like activities are more widespread in childhood, organised sports in early adolescence and more instrumental and 'commercial' activities (e.g. working out in gyms and studios) during adulthood (Wold, 1989; Hendry *et al.*, 1993).

According to Bourdieu (1978), youth sports developed historically because of the need to occupy adolescents during school hours in the late nineteenth century English public schools. Bourdieu maintains that sport is an 'extremely economical means of mobilising, occupying and controlling adolescents' (1978: 831), which may explain the popularisation of youth sport and the growth of sport associations. Thus, the popularity of organised sport in this age group may be understood as a result of socio-political forces, as well as reflecting the predominant orientation typical of this age towards activities that can be undertaken together with peers.

Further, Bourdieu (1978) maintains that the relationships between the different sports and age is complex, which is defined within the relationship between a sport and a social class. He argues that 'the most important property of the "popular sports" is the fact that they are tacitly associated with youth, which is spontaneously and implicitly credited with a sort of provisional licence expressed, among other ways, in the squandering of an excess of physical (and sexual) energy and are abandoned very early (usually at the moment of entry into adult life, marked by marriage). By contrast, the "bourgeois" sports, mainly practised for their functions of physical maintenance and for the social profit they bring, have in common

the fact that their age-limits lies far beyond youth and perhaps comes correspondingly later the more prestigious and exclusive they are (e.g. golf)' (Bourdieu, 1978: 837).

## Gender

Most studies have found that boys are more physically active than girls (Godin and Shephard, 1986; Dishman, 1991; Wold and Anderssen, 1992; Hendry *et al.*, 1993; Sallis, 1993; King *et al.*, 1996). This gender difference may be explained as a result of sex role patterns in society (Greendorfer, 1978; Fasting, 1987). The male role is traditionally characterised by an orientation towards society, work and instrumental activities, while the female role is characterised as family-oriented and expressive. This implies that boys and girls are socialised to take on different roles and that they learn at a very early age that physical activity is valued more positively for males than for females.

Thus, children learn that the expectations associated with the role of the athlete are very different from those associated with the role of the female. Values underlying sport activities are often related to competition and achievement, which may be considered more consistent with values associated with the male than the female role (Wold and Kannas, 1993). Girls may therefore feel less attracted to the achievement-oriented aspects of sports. Moreover, girls are probably not rewarded for physical activity as much as boys (Sallis and Faucette, 1992).

## Socio-economic status

Several studies have found social inequalities in participation in sport and physical activity among adults (Aaroe, 1987; Dishman, 1991). Persons in higher socio-economic groups report engaging in physical activity more often than do persons in lower socio-economic status groups. Knowing that social inequalities tend to be reproduced in the next generation (Bourdieu, 1984), it is likely that this social inequality in physical activity among adults will also be reproduced (Wold *et al.*, 1994a).

This reproduction of social relationships from parents to children is due to social positions playing an influential role in the reproduction of social inequalities. Bourdieu (1984) uses the concept 'habitus' when decribing why people in different social positions have distinct lifestyles. Habitus refers to a system of dispositions that enable people to cope with the social world. This indicates that people learn to think and act in correspondence with what is recognised as valuable within their social class. Leisure-time physical activity is an element of people's habitus, which contributes to the reproduction of the social system.

The process of social reproduction is not only limited to the link between children and parents; education also plays an influential role. Parental position is positively associated with children's education, that is, children having parents in higher social positions are more likely to enter into a type of education that may result in a high social position in adulthood. Thus, the educational system reinforces social inequalities (Bourdieu, 1984).

The reproduction of social inequalities may be regarded as an underlying process influencing the physical activity of young people (Wold *et al.*, 1994a), firstly because of the relationship between the parents' social positions and their levels of physical activity and secondly, by its influence on the relationship between education and peer groups/youth organisations (e.g. sports clubs) as regards physical activity.

Few studies have focused on these meso-level influences on physical activity among young people, such as the combined effects of experiences at home, at school and with peers (Dishman and Dunn, 1988; Biddle and Mutrie, 1991). The findings indicate that high levels of physical activity among 13- and 15-year-olds in Austria, Norway and Wales are positively and additively associated with the physical activity levels of their parents and best friend, and they find it easy to make new friends and like school (Wold, Aaroe and Smith, 1994b).

According to Bourdieu (1978), 'the probability of practising different sports depends, to a different degree for each sport, primarily on economical capital and secondarily on cultural capital and spare time; it also depends on the affinity between the ethical and aesthetic dispositions characteristic of each class or class fraction and the objective potentialities of ethical or aesthetic accomplishment which are or seem to be contained in each sport.' As already mentioned, physical activities of the higher classes tend to progress into adulthood, while the activites of lower social classes tend to be more associated with youth itself and thus to be abandoned on entry into adulthood. This pattern of physical activity related to social class implies that children and adolescents from a higher social status background are more likely to take up physical activity as a lifetime habit, while those from lower social status background are more likely to participate in physical activity mainly during adolescence.

## Family influences

From a theoretical point of view, socialisation into sport and physical activity may be considered a modelling process in which significant others, such as family

owents

members, constitute available and powerful role models. Bandura (1986), in his social cognitive theory, has described the principles of this modelling process, but little is known about the role of modelling in the development of physical activity among adolescents (Biddle and Goudas, 1996).

Several studies have found that physically active parents tend to have physically active children (Dishman, 1991; Freedson and Evenson, 1991; Anderssen and Wold, 1992; Sallis *et al.*, 1992; Wold and Anderssen, 1992; Hendry *et al.*, 1993). The physical activity levels of siblings are also related (Wold, 1989; Sallis *et al.*, 1992; Taylor, Baranowski and Sallis, 1994). The findings from a World Health Organization cross-national study on health behaviours among school-age children aged 11, 13 and 15 years in 10 European countries indicate that when three or more significant persons (best friend, parents and/or siblings) take part in physical activity, 84% of boys and 71% of girls are found to take part in sport twice a week or more (Wold and Anderssen, 1992). When none of these significant others are involved in physical activity, 52% of boys and 30% of girls report that they are sports active. These data suggest a strong influence from significant others.

In a representative sample from the United States, it was found that fewer than 30% of mothers and fathers of children in the first four years of school participate in appropriate physical activity (Ross *et al.*, 1987). Further, mothers and fathers exercised with their children less than once a week, on average. Though mothers exercised with equal frequency with sons and daughters, fathers clearly spent more time exercising with sons. This imbalance was most profound in the fourth year of school when boys in large

numbers turned to competitiv sports. According to Ross *et al.* (1987), this suggests the start of a pattern that may be perpetuated throughout the school years.

Parents also influence the physical activity of their children through direct support for exercise, such as verbal encouragement, assistance in organising exercise sessions (e.g. transportation) and economic help (Anderssen and Wold, 1992; Hendry *et al.*, 1993; Biddle and Goudas, 1996). Some of these influences may also be negative, such as parents arranging transport and thus retarding physical activity of children.

## Peer influences

As stated, physical activity is very much a social activity in adolescence. Young people tend to perform these activities together and studies consistently show that physically active adolescents have friends who are also active (Anderssen and Wold, 1992; Wold and Anderssen, 1992; Hendry *et al.*, 1993). The peer group influence could conceivably function in a number of ways:

- Adolescents mutually influence each other into starting exercise.

- An adolescent may engage in sport because his or her best friend is already active.

- Friendships are established between adolescents who are already engaged in sports.

These types of interpersonal influence can arise out of two processes: imitation, in which one person copies the behaviour or values of another, or social reinforcement, in which one person adopts the values of another, which in turn affects his or her behaviour (Kandel, 1986). Physical activity, thererfore, may be considered an arena for making and keeping friends. Several studies confirm that making friends is an important reason for adolescents to take part in physical activity (e.g. Wold and Kannas, 1993).

## School factors

As stated by Pate *et al.* (1987) and Sallis *et al.* (1992), school is the setting with the most promise for having a public health impact, because virtually all adolescents can be reached in school and an existing infrastructure is devoted to physical education (PE) and health education. The way in which education could influence participation in physical activity is not clear. Studies have found that students tend to be rather inactive while in PE classes and that the skills emphasised in these classes seem to have little value for participation in adult physical activities (Sallis and McKenzie, 1991). Lack of participation in leisure-time physical activity among young people has been found to be related to negative memories of PE, especially among girls (Coakley and White, 1992). According to Biddle and Mutrie (1991), such experiences are, in accordance with self-efficacy theory (Bandura, 1986), likely to alter efficacy expectations in those activities experienced in school PE which may then generalise, to differing degrees depending on the activities, to other exercise modes.

The influence of other aspects of adolescents' experiences with school have largely been neglected (Biddle and Mutrie, 1991; Dishman, 1991). There seems to be a strong association between regular smoking, use of alcohol, food habits and oral hygiene and alienation from school, such that the more positive the relationship to school and education, the more positive the health behaviour (Jessor and Jessor, 1977; Nutbeam, Aaroe and Catford, 1989; Jessor *et al.*, 1991; Nutbeam and Aaroe, 1991; Aaroe, Laberg and Wold, 1995). Physical activity has consistently been found to be associated with these other health behaviours (Blair, 1988; Nutbeam, Aaroe and Wold, 1991) and appears to be negatively related to school alienation; those who have more positive attitudes towards school take part in physical activity more often than those who hold negative attitudes (Hendry *et al.*, 1993; Wold *et al.*, 1994b). However, the relationship between physical activity and school alienation appears weaker than that for the previously mentioned health behaviours (Nutbeam *et al.*, 1989; Nutbeam *et al.*, 1993).

Coggans and McKellar (1994: 24), in discussing school-based health education, wrote that educational interventions should be aimed at 'developing preference for healthy lifestyle choices ... engage the whole person with the [social] context ... reassert the role of the individual in their own development. Issues of choice and motivation have to be taken into account which also pay heed to the dynamic and reciprocal relationship between individuals and peers'. The fundamental challenge facing physical educators in school is how this can be done in relation to physical activity.

## Sport associations

Outside of PE, the major structured activity for youth is provided by sport associations – the most popular activities being team sports. As stated by Sallis (1993), there are many benefits to this emphasis on organised sports, such as regular activity, enhanced physical skills and socialisation. Several risks are also evident, most notably that reliance on team sports for physical activity may not prepare the adolescent to be active later in life. Some studies show, however, that the probability of being active as an adult increases with organised sport involvement in youth (Engstrom, 1986).

As Ingham (1987) has suggested, leisure activities such as sports may be significant in creating opportunities for identity development, social meaning, levels of competence and intrinsic satisfaction in adolescence. This is possible because alternative forms of self-presentation and style can be tried out without major consequences should they fail to impress. At the same time these individualistic aspects of behaviour are carried out within institutionally defined roles, with relatively predictable behaviours and rules. Adolescents need to learn a range of social skills in planning, self-orientation and organisation in the social and leisure domains as well as in cognitive and work-related spheres in order to develop a clear personal and social identity.

## Mass media

There is little systematic knowledge about the possible influences of mass media on physical activity among young people. Information and attention about sport and physical activity in TV, radio and printed media may have a strong influence on young people's attitudes and activity levels. It is possible that the increasing popularity of elite sports in mass media may result in more positive attitudes towards physical activity in general and thereby increase the level of physical activity, as has been suggested by the findings of Hofstetter *et al.* (1995). However, it is just as possible that the focus on elite sports in mass media may decrease the level of activity through its function as entertainment to be consumed passively via TV (Sallis, 1993). It is

also possible that some elite sports models may be unrealistic for many and hence demotivate young people to take up sports. These notions require further study.

Several community-wide programmes that have used mass media and community events with the aim of increasing exercise participation have demonstrated increased awareness of the campaign message and an increase in intentions to exercise (Aaroe, 1991; Nutbeam and Catford, 1991; Powell *et al.*, 1991; Donovan and Owen, 1994). In the Class of 1989 Study, part of the Minnesota Heart Health Programme, the results suggested that multiple intervention components, such as behavioural education in schools and complementary community-wide strategies involving mass media campaigns, can produce lasting improvements in adolescent physical activity, particularly with female students (Kelder, Perry and Klepp, 1993).

## Cultural factors

Little systematic cross-cultural research has been conducted on physical activity among young people. The macro-level factors suggested by Bronfenbrenner (1979) define the ultimate boundaries for physical activity among young people. The prevailing norms and values of a society have a profound effect on the behaviour of the members of that society. Nations and countries differ in the value and meaning attached to physical activity in their culture and these differences are expected to result in different activity levels.

Culture can be defined as 'the set of attitudes, values, beliefs and behaviours, shared by a group of people, communicated from one generation to the next via language or some other means of communication' (Barnouw, 1985). A more anthropological definition of culture is, for example, 'the man-made part of the environment' (Georgas and Berry, 1995). According to Georgas and Berry (1995), there has been an inability to construct a concept of culture for operational use and that what is needed is a system of classification, a taxonomy of nations and of cultural and ethnic groups, in terms of specific ecological and social indicators. This model could be employed to select nations that differ or are similar in regard to ecological and social indicators and to enable the interpretation of the health variables in terms of these indicators. Georgas and Berry (1995: 127) propose that 'one way to proceed is to abandon culture as a theoretical concept in cross-cultural research as a sampling unit and to adopt some more operational concepts, such as some specific dimensions of national units'.

In a survey of 105,000 students aged 11, 13 and 15 years from 25 countries and regions (mainly Europe), responses indicating participation in physical activity two or more times per week were found to vary from 28% among 15-year-old Spanish girls to 92% among 11- and 13-year-old Austrian boys (King *et al.*, 1996). In this study, the variable measuring physical activity was phrased: 'Outside school: How many times a week do you usually exercise in your free time so much that you get out of breath or sweat?' In all countries the data showed that consistently more boys than girls reported to exercise.

One should, of course, be cautious about comparing the actual levels of reported physical activity, especially since the survey was carried out at different times of the year. For example, it was conducted in December in Norway, the time of the year with the lowest activity level in that country and in May in Austria, which would be a season of more physical activity. There are also other problems in cross-national comparisons of this kind (Smith, Wold and Moore, 1992). The methods for sample selection, questionnaire administration and data preparation are defined in a common survey protocol (Wold *et al.*, 1994b). However, the variety of school systems included in the survey makes it impossible both to achieve homogeneity in the ages of the sampled children and to collect data at the same time of the year in each of the countries. Other structural problems concern variations in the wording of questions – translation of the English standard question may have resulted in differences as to how the concept of physical activity was presented in the national questionnaires.

An interesting finding from this study, which may be due to cultural factors, is that the gender differences tend to be lower in the Nordic countries than in other European countries (King *et al.*, 1996). Perhaps this can be attributed to the effect of gender equity, in which the Nordic countries – Denmark, Norway and Sweden – are usually perceived as having achieved more in this field than most other countries. The physical activity levels of Norwegian girls have increased over the period 1983–93 (Wold *et al.*, 1995). One of the activities that has gained in popularity among girls during this period is soccer, which traditionally has been viewed as a boys' sport.

## Availability and proximity

In this review of the factors influencing physical activity among young people, the main focus has been on social factors. Obviously, factors related to the physical environment are of paramount importance in enabling young people to be physically active. Opportunities for physical activity can be conceptualised as the availability of relevant facilities, supplies or programmes (Sallis, 1993). Sallis *et al.* (1990) found that in the United States there was an association between proximity of exercise facilities and frequency of exercise among adult San Diego residents. Several Norwegian studies show that if the distance to exercise facilities exceeds 700–800 metres, or 10 minutes of walking, their use is strongly reduced (Stroemme, Harlem and Vellar, 1983). This is particularly important to children and adolescents, who may need transportation. Anderssen and Wold (1992) found that direct support from parents concerning transport to exercise sessions was positively related to physical activity levels among 13-year-old Norwegians. Their study shows that direct help from parents in exercising vigorously related more strongly than any other single item to students' physical activity. This may reflect that children and young adolescents need help from their parents in organising participation in physical activities. One could hypothesise that this could be part of a trend in which involvement in physical activities requires the capacity to organise such activities (e.g. the capacity to organise transport to training sessions). However, parents should be encouraged to be cautious about pressuring their children to exercise vigorously. Such pressure could have the opposite effect and destroy children's pleasure in being physically active, as indicated by McGuire and Cook (1986).

## ▨ Conclusion

When assessing the reported influences of social and environmental factors on physical activity levels among young people, it is important to acknowledge that it is the combined effect of these influences that determines whether habitual physical activity will be developed as a lifelong habit (Sallis and Owen, 1996). Living in a physically active family seems to increase the probability of getting involved in physical activity, as does a positive attitude towards school and PE. Mass media may support the positive influences of other socialising agents and cultural factors such as gender equity also affect physical activity. The main challenge to promoters of physical activity among young people is to find ways of dealing with the fact that it is a major contributor to the reproduction of social inequality.

It is evident that more research is needed before any final conclusions about the impact of social and environmental factors can be drawn. The influence of schooling, including physical education, is still not clear (see Chapter 7). Moreover, cross-cultural studies may contribute further to our understanding of the determinants of physical activity. From this review, one suggestion would be to include perspectives including the influence of social structures, such as social reproduction theory, in order to understand how participation in youth sports may be carried over into adult habitual physical activity.

It is possible to suggest a framework of elements around which comparisons between organised (adult-led) and casual (peer oriented) physical activity might be conducted. For instance, power relationships, feelings of companionship, rule-making, enjoyment levels, social networks, peer preferences and types of motives and motivations. An interactionist research perspective that focuses on how individuals make sense of and interpret the social world in which they live, might provide an appropriate orientation to investigators in this field.

Furthering research in this way would enable us to examine how groups or sub-cultures of active and inactive youths develop, how they perceive various settings and their potential for physical activity, how they experiment with different forms of self-presentation and social identity, what social reinforcers shape developing social identities and the importance of physical activity to their self-presentational 'styles'. This important area of health research has been virtually ignored to date.

## ■ **What we know**

Based on the evidence presented, it is possible to provide several statements about what we know:

■ Young people growing up in families who are physically active, are more likely to be physically active themselves.

■ Physically active role models such as parents, siblings and peers influence young people to participate in physical activity.

■ Physical activity is first and foremost a social activity among young people (peer dependent).

■ Cultural norms and values define the gender differences in physical activity. Participation of girls is higher in countries with high equality between men and women than in countries low on gender equality.

■ Young people from lower socio-economic status are less likely to engage in lifetime physical activity. Physical activity contributes to the production of social inequality and thus to the social inequalities in health.

## ■ **What we need to know**

■ What types of exercise facilities promote physical activity among young people?

■ How much does the distance to exercise facilities influence physical activity?

■ How can physical education promote lifelong habitual physical activity?

■ How can organised sport activities promote lifelong habitual physical activity?

■ How does mass media influence physical activity among young people?

■ How can physical activity among lower socio-economic adolescents be promoted?

## ■ **References**

**Aaroe, L.E.** (1987). *Health behaviour and socioeconomic status: a survey among the adult population in Norway.* Unpublished doctoral dissertation. Faculty of Psychology, University of Bergen, Norway.

**Aaroe, L.E.** (1991). Fitness promotion programs in mass media – Norwegian experiences. In P. Oja and R. Telama (eds.), *Sport for all*, pp. 193–200. Amsterdam: Elsevier.

**Aaroe, L.E., Laberg, J.C. and Wold, B.** (1995). Health behaviour among adolescents: towards a hypothesis of two dimensions. *Health Education Research*, **10** (1), 83–92.

**Anderssen, N. and Wold, B.** (1992). Influences on leisure-time physical activity in young adolescents: behaviour, support and values of parents and peers. *Research Quarterly for Exercise and Sport*, **63**, 341–8.

**Bandura, A.** (1986). *Social foundations of thought and action*. Englewood Cliffs: Prentice-Hall.

**Barnouw, V.** (1985). *Culture and personality*. Chicago: Dorsey Press.

**Berry, J.W., Poortinga, Y.H., Segall, M.H. and Dasen, P.R.** (1992). *Cross-cultural psychology: research and applications*. Cambridge: Cambridge University Press.

**Biddle, S. and Mutrie, N.** (1991). *Psychology of physical activity and exercise*. London: Springer Verlag.

**Biddle, S. and Goudas, M.** (1996). Analysis of children's physical activity and its association with adult encouragement and social cognitive variables. *Journal of School Health*, **66**, 75–8.

**Blair, S.N.** (1988). Exercise within a healthy lifestyle. In R.K. Dishman (ed.), *Exercise adherence: its impact on public health*, pp. 75–89. Champaign: Human Kinetics.

**Bourdieu, P.** (1978). Sport and social class. *Social Science Information*, **17**, 819–40.

**Bourdieu, P.** (1984). *Distinction: A social critique of the judgement of taste*. Cambridge, Mass.: Harvard University Press.

**Bronfenbrenner, U.** (1979). *The ecology of human development*. Cambridge, Mass.: Harvard University Press.

**Coakley, J.J. and White, A.** (1992). Making decisions: gender and sport participation among British adolescents. *Sociology of Sport Journal*, **9**, 20–35.

**Coggans, N. and McKellar, M.** (1994). Drug use amongst peers: peer pressure or peer preference? *Drugs: Education, Prevention and Policy*, **1** (1), 15–26.

**Craig, G.J.** (1976). *Human development*. New Jersey: Prentice-Hall.

**Dishman, R.K.** (1991). Determinants of participation in physical activity. In C. Bouchard, R.J. Shephard, T. Stephens, J.R. Sutton and B.D. McPherson (eds.), *Exercise, fitness and health*, pp. 75–101. Champaign: Human Kinetics.

**Dishman, R.K. and Dunn, A.L.** (1988). Exercise adherence in children and youth: implications for adulthood. In R.K. Dishman (ed.), *Exercise adherence: its impact on public health*, pp. 155–200. Champaign: Human Kinetics.

**Donovan, R.J. and Owen, N.** (1994). Social marketing and population interventions. In R.K. Dishman (ed.), *Advances in exercise adherence*, pp. 249–90. Champaign: Human Kinetics.

**Engstrom, L.M.** (1986). The process of socialisation into keep-fit activities. *Scandinavian Journal of Sport Sciences*, **8**, 89–97.

**Fasting, K.** (1987). Sports and women's culture. *Women's Studies International Forum*, **10** (4), 361–8.

**Freedson, P.S. and Evenson, S.** (1991). Familial aggregation in physical activity. *Research Quarterly for Exercise and Sport*, **62**, 384–9.

**Georgas, J. and Berry, J.W.** (1995). An ecocultural taxonomy for cross-cultural psychology. *Cross-Cultural Research*, **29** (2), 121–57.

**Godin, G and Shephard, R.J.** (1986). Psychosocial factors influencing intentions to exercise of young students from grades 7 to 9. *Research Quarterly for Exercise and Sport*, **57**, 41–52.

**Greendorfer, S.L.** (1978). Socialisation into sport. In C.A. Oglesby (ed.), *Women and sport: from myth to reality*. Philadelphia: Lea and Febiger.

**Hendry, L.B., Shucksmith, J., Love, J.G. and Glendinning, A.** (1993). *Young people's leisure and lifestyles*. London: Routledge.

**Hofstetter, C.R., Hovell, M.E., Sallis, J.F., Zakarian, J., Beirich, H., Mulvihill, M., Keating, K. and Emerson, J.** (1995). Exposure to sports mass media and physical activity characteristics among ethnically diverse adolescents. *Medicine, Exercise, Nutrition and Health*, **4**, 234–42.

**Ingham, R.** (1987). Psychological contributions to the study of leisure. *Leisure Studies*, **6**, 1–14

**Jessor, R., Donovan, J.E. and Costa, F.M.** (1991). *Beyond adolescence: problem behaviour and young adult development*. Cambridge: Cambridge University Press.

**Jessor, R. and Jessor, S.L.** (1977). *Problem behaviour and psychological development*. New York: Academic Press.

**Kandel, D.B.** (1986). Processes of peer influences in adolescence. In R.K. Silbereisen, K. Eyferth and G. Rudinger (eds.), *Development as action in context*, pp. 203–27. Berlin: Springer Verlag.

**Kelder, S.H., Perry, C.L. and Klepp, K.I.** (1993). Community-wide youth exercise promotion: long-term outcomes of the Minnesota Heart Health Program and the Class of 1989 Study. *Journal of School Health*, **63**, 218–23.

**Kemper, H.C.G.** (1994). The natural history of physical activity and aerobic fitness in teenagers. In R.K. Dishman (ed.), *Advances in exercise adherence*, pp. 293–318. Champaign: Human Kinetics.

**King, A., Wold, B., Smith, C.T. and Harel, Y.** (1996). *The health of youth: a cross-national survey*. Copenhagen: WHO Regional Publications, European Series, 69.

**McGuire, R.T. and Cook, D.L.** (1986) The influence of others and the decision to participate in youth sports. *Journal of Sport Behavior*, **6**, 9–16.

**Nutbeam, D. and Aaro, L.E.** (1991). Smoking and pupil attitudes towards school: the implications for health education with young people. *Health Education Research*, **6**, 415–21.

**Nutbeam, D., Aaroe, L.E. and Catford, J.** (1989). Understanding children's health behaviour: the implications for health promotion for young people. *Social Science and Medicine*, **29**, 317–25.

**Nutbeam, D. and Catford, J.** (1991). Promoting physical activity in the community–experiences from the Heartbeat Wales programme. In P. Oja and R. Telama (eds.), *Sport for all*, pp. 175–83. Amsterdam: Elsevier.

**Nutbeam, D., Smith C., Moore L. and Bauman, A.** (1993) Warning! Schools can damage your health: alienation from school and its impact on health behaviour. *Journal of Paediatrics and Child Health*, **29**, 25–30.

**Nutbeam, D., Aaroe, L.E. and Wold, B.** (1991). The lifestyle concept and health education with young people: results from a WHO international study. *World Health Statistics Quarterly*, **44**, 55–61.

**Pate, R.R., Corbin, C.B., Simons-Morton, B.G. and Ross, J.G.** (1987). Physical education and its role in school health promotion. *Journal of School Health*, **57**, 445–50.

**Powell, K.E., Stephens, T., Marti, L., Heinemann, L. and Kreuter, M.** (1991). Progress and problems in the promotion of physical activity. In P. Oja and R. Telama (eds.), *Sport for all*, pp. 55–73. Amsterdam: Elsevier.

**Ross, J.G., Pate, R.R., Caspersen, C.J., Damberg, C.L. and Svilar, M.** (1987). Home and community in children's exercise habits. *Journal of Physical Education, Recreation and Dance*, Nov–Dec, 85–95.

**Sallis, J.F.** (1993). Promoting healthful diet and physical activity. In S.G. Millstein, A.C. Petersen and E.O. Nightingale (eds.), *Promoting the health of adolescents*, pp. 209–41. New York: Oxford University Press.

**Sallis, J.F., Simons-Morton, B.G., Stone, E.J., Corbin, C.B., Epstein, L.H., Faucette, N., Iannotti, R.J., Killen, J.D., Klesges, R.C., Petray, C.K., Rowland, T.W. and Taylor, W.** (1992). Determinants of physical activity and interventions in youth. *Medicine and Science in Sports and Exercise*, **24**, 248–57.

**Sallis, J.F. and McKenzie, T.L.** (1991). Physical education's role in public health. *Research Quarterly for Exercise and Sport*, **62**, 124–37.

**Sallis, J.F. and Faucette, N.** (1992). Physical activity. In H.M. Wallace (ed.), *Principles and practices of student health*: vol. 1, *Foundations*, pp. 213–27. Oakland: Third Party.

**Sallis, J.F., Hovell, M.F., Hofstetter, C.R., Elder, J.P., Hackley, M., Caspersen, C.J. and Powell, K.E.** (1990). Distance between homes and exercise facilities related to frequency of exercise among San Diego residents. *Public Health Reports*, **105**, 179–85.

**Sallis, J.F. and Owen, N.** (1996). Ecological models. In K. Glanz, F.M. Lewis and B.K. Rimer (eds.), Health behaviour and health education. *Theory, research and practice*, pp. 403–24. San Fransisco: Jossey-Bass.

**Smith, C., Wold, B. and Moore, L.** (1992). Health behaviour research with adolescents: a perspective from the WHO Cross-National Health Behaviour in School-Aged Children Study. *Health Promotion Journal of Australia*, **2**, 41–4.

**Stroemme, S.B., Harlem, O.K. and Vellar, O.D.** (1983). Physical activity for health and well-being. *Tidsskrift for Den norske lægeforening* [Journal of the Norwegian Medical Association], 4B (Special issue). (In Norwegian.)

**Taylor, W.C., Baranowski, T. and Sallis, J.F.** (1994). Family determinants of childhood physical activity: a social-cognitive model. In R.K. Dishman (ed.), *Advances in exercise adherence*, pp. 319–42. Champaign: Human Kinetics.

**Wold, B.** (1989). *Lifestyles and physical activity: a theoretical and empirical analysis of socialisation among children and adolescents*. Unpublished doctoral dissertation, Faculty of Psychology, University of Bergen, Norway.

**Wold, B., Aasen, H., Aaroe, L.E. and Samdal, O.** (1995). *Health and lifestyles among children and adolescents in Norway*. HEMIL-report series, 14. Research Centre for Health Promotion, University of Bergen, Norway. (In Norwegian.)

**Wold, B., Aaroe, L.E. and Smith, C.** (1994b). *Health behaviour in school-aged children: a WHO cross-national survey. Research protocol for the 1993–94 study*. HEMIL-report series, 4, Research Centre for Health Promotion, University of Bergen, Norway.

**Wold, B. and Anderssen, N.** (1992). Health promotion aspects of family and peer influences on sport participation. *International Journal of Sport Psychology*, **23**, 343–59.

**Wold, B. and Kannas, L.** (1993). Sports motivation among young adolescents in Finland, Norway and Sweden. *Scandinavian Journal of Medicine and Science in Sports*, **3**, 283–91.

**Wold, B., Oeygard, L., Eder, A. and Smith, C.** (1994a). Social reproduction of physical activity: implications for health promotion in young people. *European Journal of Public Health*, **4**, 163–8.

# Interventions to promote health-related physical education

Len Almond[1] and Jo Harris[2]

[1]*Senior Lecturer in Physical Education, Loughborough University*
[2]*Lecturer in Physical Education, Loughborough University*

From a review of the papers in this chapter there is clear evidence that a commitment to regular physical activity can result in health gains and is an essential component of a healthy lifestyle. Nevertheless, it is important to recognise also that some young people are at risk from a number of specific diseases and conditions, such as coronary heart disease, obesity, asthma and diabetes, all of which are amenable to exercise intervention. In addition, Mutrie, (see Chapter 3) makes a strong claim for mental health gains and proposes that such concerns should be part of health promotion initiatives in schools and within physical education (PE).

These concerns indicate that teachers need to recognise the importance of a general programme aimed at all young people. PE has the advantage over voluntary youth sport contexts, such as sports clubs, of being able to offer programmes to virtually all children. Also appropriate interventions need to be targeted directly at young people at risk and teachers need to be able to tailor their interventions to meet the needs of specific groups of individuals. This is an important therapeutic role for PE.

In England there have been few attempts to document the aspirations of

PE. One exception is the interim document leading up to the inauguration of the National Curriculum in England and Wales (DfE and WO, 1995). In this document there is a clear indication that PE has an important part to play in physical development and promoting the benefits of an active lifestyle. More recently, in the government-initiated review of the National Curriculum led by Sir Ron Dearing, it was proposed that 'we must encourage our young people to develop a fit and healthy lifestyle' (Dearing, 1994: 45).

In another recent document, the English Sports Council (1997) identified what they see as the main roles of a school in promoting physical activity. One of these roles highlights the need to establish a 'whole school' approach towards health, exercise, sport and the promotion of an active lifestyle for all young people. In addition, the English Sports Council emphasises the need to move beyond the curriculum and promote more physical activity through extra-curricular and out of school activities. These statements are taken from important, authoritative and public documents; therefore it seems reasonable to claim that the promotion of physical activity as part of an active lifestyle is accepted as an important role of PE in the UK.

The role of PE in public health promotion has been debated extensively in the United States (Sallis and McKenzie, 1991; Pate and Hohn, 1994a) and the UK (Armstrong and Biddle, 1992; Biddle, 1987). Although historically PE has not been viewed from a public health perspective, there has been a much greater emphasis in recent years on health-related exercise (HRE) in the PE curriculum in the UK (see Biddle, 1987; Harris, 1995, 1997; Harris and Cale, 1997). However, the explicitness of HRE in the relatively new National Curriculum in England and Wales is not always as obvious as some would like. In the United States, the Department of Health and Human Services (DHHS, 1997) has provided clear guidelines for school and community programmes for promoting physical activity with young people. Specifically, they recommend that PE should 'implement ... curricula and instruction that emphasize enjoyable participation in physical activity and that helps students develop the knowledge, attitudes, motor skills, behavioural skills and confidence needed to adopt and maintain physically active lifestyles' (DHHS, 1997: 12). However, the DHHS also suggest that evaluation of programmes is needed.

The purpose of this chapter, therefore, is to review the evidence for the effectiveness of health-related physical education (HRPE) programmes in promoting health-related outcomes. To do this, a number of selection criteria were drawn up for the literature search. Only intervention studies in which there were experimental and control groups and which had undergone peer review for publication as full papers in journals were selected. This meant that a large number of small-scale research projects, case studies of HRPE and research published only as abstracts were excluded. In addition, qualitative studies of HRPE were excluded on the grounds that it was difficult to determine the rigour of their research approach and their interpretations could not be traced back to their data. Consequently, the review includes only those HRPE programmes in primary and secondary schools that have been formally evaluated.

# ▣ The effectiveness of HRPE programmes in schools

In this section, a number of outcomes are considered including physiological measures (aerobic capacity, muscular strength and endurance, flexibility), clinical measures (body composition, blood pressure, blood lipids), behavioural aspects (activity levels and dietary habits), cognitive measures (knowledge and understanding) and affective measures (attitudes towards physical activity, physical education or school). The studies reporting HRPE programmes that have been implemented and evaluated in primary schools are presented in Table 7.1 and those in secondary schools are detailed in Table 7.2. This distinction is considered important for at least two main reasons: (1) the age differences between children in primary and secondary schools may be a factor in the effectiveness of programmes; and (2) teachers of PE in primary schools, at least in the UK, are usually general classroom teachers without the specialised knowledge of the subject attributed to PE teachers in secondary schools. Again, this could affect the outcomes of intervention studies.

**Table 7.1.** *Intervention studies in primary schools*

| Study | Study details all have at least one experimental and control groups. Variations specified | Physiological (HRF) and clinical outcomes | Behavioural outcomes (physical activity and diet) | Cognitive outcomes (academic performance; knowlege and understanding | Affective outcomes (attitudes) |
|---|---|---|---|---|---|
| **MacDonald** (1961) | France; daily PE; *n*=64 (11–12 years of age) | Increases in a range of physical measures | | Increase in academic performance | Positive increase in attitudes |
| **Shephard** *et al.* (1980) | Canada; daily PE; *n*=546 (10–12 years); 6-year intervention | Increase in aerobic capacity and muscular strength | Increase in vigorous weekday and weekend PA | | |
| **Geenen** *et al.* (1982) | USA; *n*=79 (6–7 years); 8-month intervention | Higher mean heart rates; increase in left ventricular mass | Increase in vigorous PA | | |
| **MacConnie** *et al.* (1982) | USA; *n*=59 (6–7 years); 8-month intervention | | Increase in vigorous PA | | |
| **Duncan** *et al.* (1983) | USA; *n*=34 (10 years); 9-month intervention | Increase in aerobic capacity/performance, flexibility and strength | | | |
| **Dwyer** *et al.* (1983) | Australia; daily PE; *n*=500 (10 years); 3 groups: fitness, skill and control. 14-week intervention with 2-year follow-up | Increase in aerobic capacity and decrease in body fat for fitness group; no change in blood lipids or BP after 14 weeks but decreased BP for boys after 2 years | | No evidence of loss of academic performance | |
| **Siegel and Manfredi** (1984) | USA; *n*=109 (8 years); 10-month intervention | Increase in aerobic capacity | | | |
| **Worsley and Coonan** (1984) | Australia; daily PE; *n*=420 (10 years); 3 experimental and one control group; 6-month intervention | The combined treatment group (daily PE + self-monitoring of diet and activity + health knowledge) showed a decrease in body fat | | Increases in health and body knowledge for treatment groups with health knowledge | |

**Table 7.1.** *continued*

| Study | Study details all have at least one experimental and control groups. Variations specified | Physiological (HRF) and clinical outcomes | Behavioural outcomes (physical activity and diet) | Cognitive outcomes (academic performance; knowlege and understanding | Affective outcomes (attitudes) |
|---|---|---|---|---|---|
| **Simons-Morton et al. (1988a)** | USA; $n=1293$ (8–9 years); 2-year intervention on PA and diet | | Increase in fitness activity time and dietary behaviour (after 1-year follow up) | | |
| **Walter et al. (1988)** | USA; $n=3388$ (9–10 years); 5-year intervention | No change in aerobic capacity, body mass or BP. Favourable trends for cholesterol | Favourable trend in dietary intake | Increase in health knowledge | |
| **Werner and Durham (1988)** | USA; $n=130$ (9–11 years); 9-week intervention | Increase in aerobic capacity, strength, flexibility and body composition measures | | | |
| **Pollatschek and O'Hagan (1989)** | UK; daily PE; $n=399$ (10–11 years); 1-year intervention | Increases in aerobic performance, muscular power/endurance (upper body), but not in sit-ups or flexibility | | Non-significant increase in academic achievements | Non-significant increase in positive attitude to school |
| **Ignico and Mahon (1995)** | USA; $n=28$ low fit children (8–10 years); 10-week intervention | Increases in aerobic performance and flexibility, but not body fatness, blood lipid levels or cardiorespiratory fitness (assessed on treadmill) | | | |
| **McKenzie et al. (1993, 1997)** | USA: 28 classes (9 years); 3 conditions: trained classroom teachers, PE specialists, control; 12-month (1993) and 4-year (1997) intervention. 1997 results showed that when specialist teachers were withdrawn, quantity and quality of PE was reduced. | Children in specialist and trained groups performed better on fitness measures (aerobic performance and sit-ups) | Children in specialist and trained groups were engaged in more activity during PE lessons | | |

**Table 7.1.** *continued*

| Study | Study details all have at least one experimental and control groups. Variations specified | Physiological (HRF) and clinical outcomes | Behavioural outcomes (physical activity and diet) | Cognitive outcomes (academic performance; knowlege and understanding | Affective outcomes (attitudes) |
|---|---|---|---|---|---|
| **Shephard and Lavallee (1993, 1994)** | Canada; daily PE; n=546; 5-year intervention | Increases in aerobic capacity and strength | | | |
| **Pieron et al. (1994, 1996)** | Belgium; daily PE; 14 schools, n=3000+ (5–11 years); 3-year intervention | Children in experimental schools achieved better performances in most fitness and motor performance tests | Children in experimental schools were less involved in out-of-school sports clubs | | More favourable attitude to PE and school by pupils; teachers had more positive perceptions of PE |
| **Westcott et al. (1995)** | USA; n=25 overfat children (9–10 years); 8-week intervention | Significant increase in lean muscle mass | Improvements in eating and PA habits (self-reported) | | |
| **McKenzie et al. (1996)** | USA; 96 schools, 2096 PE lessons, n=4000+; 2.5-year intervention | Non-significant improvement in 9-min run test by children in intervention schools | Children engaged in ore moderate-to-vigorous PA in PE lessons; children reported more daily vigorous PA | | |
| **Sallis et al. (1997)** | USA; 7 schools, n=955; HRPE taught in 3 types of groups: specialist PE teachers, trained classroom teachers and control group. 2-year follow-up. | After 2 years, girls taught by PE specialists were superior to girls in control condition in abdominal strength/endurance and cardiorespiratory endurance | More time spent in physical activity in lessons taught by PE specialists and trained classroom teachers in comparison with controls. No effects on PA outside of school. | | Positive attitude to programme reported by pupils, teachers and parents |

HRF: health-related fitness; PE: physical education; PA: physical activity; BP: blood pressure.

**Table 7.2.** *Intervention studies in secondary schools*

| Study | Study details (all have at least one experimental and control groups. Variations specified) | Physiological (HRF) and clinical outcomes | Behavioural outcomes (physical activity and diet) | Cognitive outcomes (academic performance; Knowlege and understanding | Affective outcomes (attitudes) |
|---|---|---|---|---|---|
| **Cooper et al.** (1975) | USA; daily PE; n=1215 boys (15 years of age); 15-week intervention | Increases in aerobic capacity/performance | | | |
| **Green and Farrally** (1986) | UK; 2 classes (12 years), 1 year group (15 years); 2x10 week interventions | Increases in aerobic performance and sport skill (15-year-olds only) | Feedback from parents suggested increases in physical activity (12-year-olds) | Increased understanding of the importance of aerobic fitness (12-year-olds) | Increased positive attitude to physical fitness (12-year-olds) |
| **Dragevick et al.** (1987) | New Zealand; daily PE; n=275 (11–12 years); 12-month intervention | Improvements in 500 m run and flexibility (boys and girls) and in speed (boys) and strength (boys). No differences when programme was not maintained | | | |
| **Phillipp et al.** (1989) | USA; daily PE; n=136 (14–17 years); 12-week intervention | Increase in aerobic performance, but no difference in composite fitness scores | Little improvement in self-reported health risk factors and behaviours | | |
| **Jones** (1990) | UK; n=442 (13–14 years); 12-week intervention | No improvement in aerobic performance | No increase in self-reported activity levels | | Significantly more positive attitude to PE (girls only) |
| **Goldfine and Nahas** (1993) | USA; n=90 (14–16 years); 12-week intervention | | No significant change in physical activity | Significant improvements in HRF knowledge | Significantly more positive attitude to physical activity, but not towards PE |

HRF: health-related fitness; PE: physical education.

Selected characteristics of the studies are presented in Tables 7.1 and 7.2. However, it is often difficult to ascertain the exact nature of interventions, particularly in regard to the time spent in the lessons or an overall programme. The most obvious distinction that can be made, however, is between 'daily' PE programmes and 'standard' programmes, sometimes with extra time allocation. Daily PE, as it suggests, is when PE lessons take place on each of the school days. This is nearly always the result of a special intervention; rarely, if ever, is PE performed at this level of frequency as normal practice in the UK. 'Standard' PE programmes usually comprise between one and three lessons per week. Some interventions offered more than this, but the main point to be made is that the interventions vary greatly in time, facilities, type of teacher and programme content. In addition to time devoted to PE, studies and programmes have a wide diversity of characteristics. PE programmes may be supplemented with after-school activities and some programmes have a classroom component to promote physical activity outside of school. Lessons can be taught by PE specialists or by classroom teachers using curricula that vary in specificity, standardisation and underlying objectives. Programmes also differ in their access to facilities and equipment. Because of this diversity and the relatively small number of studies, it is not possible to compare results across studies to isolate the effects of particular characteristics.

# The effects of HRPE programmes in primary schools

Daily HRPE programmes in primary schools have resulted in a wide range of positive outcomes, including increased aerobic capacity or performance (Shephard *et al.*, 1980; Dwyer *et al.*, 1983; Pollatscheck and O'Hagan, 1989; Shephard and Lavallee, 1993; Pieron, Delfosse and Cloes, 1994; Pieron *et al.*, 1996), muscular strength and endurance (Shephard *et al.*, 1980; Pollatscheck and O'Hagan, 1989; Pieron *et al.*, 1994, 1996; Shephard and Lavallee, 1994), flexibility (Pieron *et al.*, 1994, 1996), reduced body fat (Dwyer *et al.*, 1983; Worsley and Coonan, 1984) and lowered blood pressure (Dwyer *et al.*, 1983). In addition, daily programmes have been found to result in increased activity levels (Shephard *et al.*, 1980), more favourable attitudes towards school and PE (Pieron *et al.*, 1994, 1996) and an increased ability to understand and retain advanced health concepts (Worsley and Coonan, 1984). Further, there has been no evidence of a loss of academic performance due to daily PE despite a loss of classroom teaching time (MacDonald, 1961; Dwyer *et al.*, 1983; Pollatschek and O'Hagan, 1989; for a review see Shephard, 1997). However, studies in this area have not shown consistent findings.

Pollatschek and O'Hagan (1989) found no significant differences in sit-up and flexibility measures between daily and non-daily PE groups and Dwyer *et al.* (1983) found no change in blood lipids from a daily PE programme. Pieron *et al.* (1994, 1996) reported that daily PE favourably influenced fitness and motor performance and pupil and teacher attitudes towards PE, yet it negatively affected pupils' involvement in out-of-school sports clubs.

A number of positive outcomes have been found with less frequent HRPE programmes with young children. When extra time was allocated to PE and in comparison to standard PE provision, improvements have been found in aerobic capacity or performance (Duncan *et al.*, 1983; Siegel and Manfredi, 1984; Werner and Durham, 1988; Ignico and Mahon, 1995), muscular strength and endurance (Duncan *et al.*, 1988; Werner and Durham, 1988), flexibility (Duncan *et al.*, 1983; Werner and Durham, 1988; Ignico and Mahon, 1995) and body composition measures (Werner and Durham, 1988; Westcott, Tolken and Wessner, 1995). In addition, following an eight-month aerobic activity programme, prepubescent children have been found to exhibit changes in cardiac structure and function (Geenen *et al.*, 1982). In the SPARK study (Sallis *et al.*, 1997; and see Table 7.1), girls taught by specialist PE teachers had greater abdominal strength and endurance and cardiorespiratory fitness after two years of the study than control group girls.

In terms of behavioural, cognitive and affective outcomes, HRPE programmes in primary schools, when some extra time has been allocated, have resulted in increased physical activity levels (Geenen *et al.*, 1982; MacConnie *et al.*, 1982; Simons-Morton, Parcel and O'Hara, 1988a; Westcott *et al.*, 1995) and improved dietary behaviour (Simons-Morton *et al.*, 1988a; Walter, Hofman, Vaughan and Wynder, 1988; Westcott *et al.*, 1995), more favourable attitudes towards physical activity (Westcott *et al.*, 1995) and increases in children's knowledge of health and fitness concepts (Walter *et al.*, 1988). Sallis *et al.* (1997) also found that physical activity in lessons

was greater for children taught by PE specialists (and lasting 40 min) compared to those taught by trained classroom teachers (lasting 33 min) and those in control classes (lasting 18 min).

Some programmes, however, have reported equivocal findings. A vigorous activity programme improved aerobic performance and flexibility but did not improve body fatness, blood lipids or cardiorespiratory fitness as measured during treadmill exercise (Ignico and Mahon, 1995).

Some programmes attempt to utilise existing PE time differently. McKenzie *et al.* (1993, 1997) evaluated the effect of both the teacher and the curriculum on the quantity and quality of PE lessons. They found that specialist PE teachers had more frequent and longer PE lessons and involved their pupils more actively than did in-service trained classroom teachers, who in turn were more effective than classroom teachers. Another study by McKenzie *et al.* (1996), in 96 schools in four US states, revealed that the implementation of a standardised curriculum and staff development programme increases pupils' activity levels in primary PE lessons.

There are three studies (one from Belgium and two from North America) that deserve to be highlighted in greater detail. In 1991, the Ministry of Education for the French-speaking community in Belgium launched a pilot programme increasing the time allocated to PE in kindergarten and primary schools. A comprehensive overview of this and the following implementation phase has been reported by Pieron *et al.* (1996). A number of principles were outlined for the project:

- At the primary school level, every child should engage in physical activity for at least one daily session.

■ Motor development should be embedded in a process of total education.

■ Teaching tasks should be set up by a team involving a qualified PE teacher, who would work in close collaboration with the classroom teacher.

■ Information should be provided to parents as well as other members of the educational community.

The implementation phase of the project covered three years with 14 schools and more than 3000 pupils participating. Curriculum materials advised teachers on content and provided theoretical support for PE. The main focus for these materials was the theme of 'discovery' of basic skills in the first and second years of kindergarten, moving onto a focus on 'learning' in the third year, with a gradual progression in the knowledge base. For Years 3 to 4 and 5 to 6 the introduction of sports techniques aimed at improving physical and motor capabilities were introduced. In addition, there was clarification of the objectives and principles of application to ensure that there was consistency across the schools. The main objective of the research was to assess the effects of daily 40-minute PE lessons on children.

In terms of fitness and motor performance, children in the experimental groups achieved better performances in most tests than children in control classes, with their superiority more evident in motor skills than physical fitness. Other interesting findings were that girls were found to be particularly receptive to the programme.

Children who followed the daily PE programme showed significantly more favourable attitudes towards school, PE and homework, appeared to be in a better mood to complete their tasks and developed co-operative behaviour. In addition, the deterioration in attitudes observed in all pupils as age increased was less pronounced for those in the experimental group at each level, a finding that was highlighted in a previous analysis by Pieron *et al.* (1994). They pointed out that attitudes were more favourable in girls than in boys. A positive influence on teachers' perceptions of their children's school work was also observed and there appeared to be a more convivial atmosphere in pilot schools.

However, some negative aspects were identified related to the preparation of PE lessons and difficulties in terms of practical organisation. Children in the experimental group participated less in sport out of school than children from control schools.

In North America, Sallis *et al.* (1997) evaluated the effects of a HRPE programme ('Project SPARK') for 955 children in their fourth and fifth years of primary school. This project was designed to increase physical activity during PE classes and also outside-of-school hours. The classes were taught by both PE specialists and classroom teachers and in both cases students spent more time being physically active in PE classes than those in control classes, with the specialist-led classes showing the highest levels of activity. As reported earlier, after two years, girls in the experimental classes were found to be superior on abdominal strength and endurance as well as cardiorespiratory endurance assessed on a timed run. This study highlights that pupils' activity levels during PE lessons can be increased with the inclusion of a HRPE curriculum. However, activity levels outside of school were not affected.

The SPARK project has also highlighted the advantage of employing specialists to deliver PE in primary schools and the need for extensive professional development for classroom teachers involved in the delivery of PE (see McKenzie *et al.*,

141

1997). When assessing the effects of a HRPE programme on quantity and quality of lessons, specialists were found to have the best outcomes followed by trained classroom teachers, both of whom were better than non-trained colleagues. Maintenance-effects approximately 18 months after the intervention were also studied and it was found that classroom teachers maintained most of their gains. However, the withdrawal of specialists significantly reduced the quality and quantity of physical education because classroom teachers in those schools did not improve their teaching skills.

The Child and Adolescent Trial for Cardiovascular Health (CATCH) was a multicentre, randomised trial to test the effectiveness of a cardiovascular health promotion programme in 96 schools in the United States, a major part of which was an innovative HRPE programme. Over two and a half years, randomly selected schools received a standardised PE programme involving both staff and curriculum development. Intervention classes were taught by either specialist PE teachers or trained classroom teachers. Results indicated that pupils in intervention schools performed more moderate–vigorous physical activity in PE lessons and reported more daily vigorous activity throughout the day (McKenzie *et al.*, 1996). This large study shows that it is feasible to improve PE in a variety of contexts.

In summarising the results of intervention studies in primary schools, of the 19 studies reported in Table 7.1, all but one showed positive changes in either fitness or physical activity. More specifically:

- 15 of 17 studies documented positive changes in either physiological or clinical outcomes.

- All eight studies investigating physical activity, either in PE lessons or out of school, showed positive changes.

- One study reported a decrease in out-of-school physical activity for the experimental group.

- All three studies targeting dietary behaviour change showed favourable results.

- Five studies investigated cognitive change; two showed increases in health-related knowledge, one showed academic performance to increase significantly, one non-significantly and one study showed no evidence of any loss in academic performance despite increased time devoted to PE.

- Significant positive attitude change was demonstrated in three of four studies.

It should be noted, however, in interpreting these results that programmes vary greatly in a number of parameters, making it difficult to specify why some changes did or did not occur. Nevertheless, it is clear that HRPE programmes in primary schools can affect a number of important health-related variables and other outcomes.

## ■ The effects of HRPE programmes in secondary schools

A number of studies in secondary schools in North America and New Zealand have demonstrated that daily HRPE programmes have resulted in improved physical fitness in terms of aerobic capacity or performance (Cooper *et al.*, 1975; Dragicevick *et al.*, 1987; Phillipp *et al.*, 1989), muscular strength and endurance

(Dragicevick *et al.*, 1987) and flexibility (Dragicevick *et al.*, 1987).

Not all studies, however, have resulted in positive outcomes. Phillipp *et al.* (1989) found no significant improvements in composite physical fitness scores and little improvement in self-reported risk factors and behaviours and Dragicevick *et al.* (1987) found that fitness improvements only lasted while the programme was maintained. With respect to an HRPE programme where some extra time was allocated, Goldfine and Nahas (1993) found an increase in positive attitudes towards physical activity, but not towards PE and no significant improvements in physical activity behaviour.

Non-daily HRPE programmes in secondary schools have resulted in gains in aerobic capacity or performance, understanding of aerobic fitness and maintenance of skill levels (Green and Farrally, 1986), as well as improvements in attitudes towards physical activity (Green and Farrally, 1986) and PE (Jones, 1990) and positive changes in physical activity (Green and Farrally, 1986). Although the study by Jones (1990) revealed a significantly improved attitude towards PE (especially amongst girls), there was no improvement in aerobic capacity or in self-reported physical activity levels.

In summary, although the intervention studies in secondary schools are far fewer than those for primary schools, they essentially arrive at the same broad conclusions. The one exception appears to be that secondary school interventions are much less effective at changing activity levels. Specifically, the studies show:

■ Four of five studies document improvements in components of health-related fitness.

■ Only one of three studies reported increases in physical activity and this data was provided only by parents.

■ Two studies achieved an increase in health-related fitness knowledge.

■ All three studies assessing attitudes demonstrated favourable changes.

## ▦ What can be learnt from these studies of school-based HRPE programmes?

The review process has highlighted that most of the research studies are based in primary schools (children age 5–11 years) and that much is focused on PE programmes that have extra time allocated in comparison to standard PE programmes. This is most evident with daily PE within primary schools. Most of the investigations are short-term and there is limited information available using longitudinal studies. In effect, the review tells us little about the range of long-term effects of standard physical education, especially in secondary schools.

Whilst comparisons across studies are problematic, due to much variation in sample characteristics, study design, measurement tools and duration of intervention programmes, a number of positive physiological, clinical, behavioural, cognitive and affective changes have been reported following the implementation of HRPE programmes. As indicated within previous reviews (Simons-Morton *et al.*, 1988b; Sleap, 1990; Tinning and Kirk, 1991), many studies revealed positive outcomes, such as increased aerobic capacity, muscular strength and endurance and flexibility. In addition, the smaller number of studies that have explored behavioural, cognitive and affective outcomes mostly reported positive changes in activity and eating habits, in attitudes towards physical activity and in improved understanding of health-related fitness knowledge. Furthermore, some studies (Shephard *et al.*, 1980; MacConnie *et al.*, 1982; Sallis *et al.*, 1997) showed that increased activity at school did not negatively affect children's activity levels outside of school, although the large study in Belgium by Pieron *et al.* (1994, 1996) showed opposite findings. Results were equivocal for the effects of HRPE programmes on cardiovascular risk factors and clinical outcomes, such as body composition, blood pressure and lipid levels (Dwyer *et al.*, 1983; Worsley and Coonan, 1984; Walter *et al.*, 1988; Werner and Durham, 1988; Ignico and Mahon, 1995; Westcott *et al.*, 1995).

A limiting factor of the studies reviewed are that many are predominantly short-term and thus the longer-term effects of HRPE programmes, especially on behavioural, cognitive and affective measures, are not well documented. Many of the programmes within this review have been evaluated summatively following interventions lasting as little as 6 to 10 weeks (Green and Farrally, 1986; Phillipp *et al.*, 1989; Ignico and Mahon, 1995; Westcott *et al.*, 1995) and three to six months (Cooper *et al.*, 1975; Goldfine and Nahas, 1993). Longer-term programmes have included those lasting from six months up to one year (Geenen *et al.*, 1982; MacConnie *et al.*, 1982; Duncan *et al.*, 1983; McKenzie *et al.*, 1993; Siegel and Manfredi, 1984; Worsley and Coonan, 1984) and between one to five years (Dragicevick *et al.*, 1987; Simons-Morton *et al.*, 1988a; Walter *et al.*, 1988a; Pollatschek and O'Hagan, 1989; Shephard and Lavallee, 1993, 1994; Pieron *et al.*, 1994, 1996; Sallis *et al.*, 1997; McKenzie *et al.*, 1996, 1997). It may be that outcomes evidenced from short-term studies are not maintained in the long-term, as exemplified by the study by Dragicevick *et al.*

(1987) in which fitness improvements only lasted while the programme was maintained. Alternatively, some outcomes may not be revealed in the short-term but may become evident after a longer period of time. This scenario occurred with blood pressure measures in a study by Dwyer *et al.* (1983), which comprised a 14-week intervention with a follow-up two years later. At least one study shows that providing a HRPE curriculum and training to classroom teachers led to maintained improvements in teaching 18 months after the end of the study. This suggests improvements in PE can be institutionalised.

In addition, it is almost impossible to ascertain what kind of influences in a school can be associated with changes in behaviour, enhanced performance or improvement in knowledge. There is limited evidence available on teaching methods or learning approaches in the promotion of health-related physical activity. Few studies provide any detail about the type of experience that pupils encounter in PE. If we are to proceed in this important area, there is a need for the PE profession to clarify what outcomes or improvements they value as desirable indicators of success. Perhaps one of the most important outcomes that we should value is the role of the school, in stimulating further participation in physical activity beyond the school, as emphasised in policy documents cited at the beginning of this chapter. There is insufficient evidence to demonstrate that we can achieve this aspiration.

## ▪ **Issues Arising**

One of the issues arising from this review is the concern for increasing the amount of time devoted to PE, since it was largely programmes with extra time allocated over standard PE provision that achieved positive results. Nevertheless, it is quite clear that insufficient time is being provided for PE in curricular time. A number of studies have shown that time allocation for PE has been continually eroded (Harris, 1995, 1997; Fairclough and Stratton, 1997). If we look at this evidence of decreased time available for PE, we find that approximately 110 minutes, including changing time, is usually divided into two lessons per week. This is unlikely to bring about health benefits. As a result, many people have been prompted to advocate more active lessons so that young people get appropriate physical activity to stimulate health benefits. McKenzie *et al.* (1997) believe that modifications to PE are needed if schools are to provide the quantity and quality of physical activity in lessons that children need for health purposes. Similarly, Pate and Hohn (1994b) argue that the ineffectiveness of many programmes is attributable to the diverse aims of PE curricula. They advocate a strong emphasis on health-related physical education by stating that 'we believe that the mission of physical education should be to promote in youngsters adoption of a physically active lifestyle that persists through adulthood' (Pate and Hohn, 1994b: 4).

## ◼ Conclusion

In undertaking this review, our prime purpose was to elicit what can be learnt from published intervention studies. However, it was quite clear that current research does little to promote our understanding of what kind of programmes bring about health gains or outcomes that we value. If all of us are to enhance the role of schools in promoting HRPE, we believe that we need to go well beyond our current conceptions of school effectiveness studies. The starting point is to identify those outcomes that we value and to translate them into realistic and manageable indicators of success. When this is achieved, we can design procedures that enable us to monitor our best efforts in promoting HRPE.

### What we know

- Most of the intervention studies are based on non-standard PE programmes with additional time allocation, often with daily PE provision.

- Positive physiological, clinical and behavioural (physical activity) changes have been reported following the implementation of HRPE programmes.

- Behavioural and affective measures are represented in only a small number of studies, but most show positive changes.

- With additional time allocated to HRPE, academic performance remains largely unchanged

### What we need to know.

- What is the role of physical education in stimulating further participation within and beyond the school?

- What kind of influences in a school can be associated with changes in behaviour, enhanced performance or improvement in knowledge and understanding about health-related exercise?

- Which teaching methods or learning approaches best promote health-related physical activity?

- Research studies need to provide more detail about pupils' perspectives of the health experiences they encounter in PE.

- What types of in-service training for teachers enhance the quality of teaching health-related exercise?

- What form of teacher support is needed to enhance the promotion of health-related exercise?

- What health-related exercise outcomes do we value and can they be translated into realistic and manageable indicators of success?

## Acknowledgements

The comments of Dr Thomas McKenzie (San Diego State University) on an earlier version of this paper are gratefully acknowledged.

## References

**Armstrong, N. and Biddle, S.J.H.** (1992). Health-related physical activity in the National Curriculum. In N. Armstrong (ed.), *New directions in physical education*. vol. 2, pp. 71–110. Champaign: Human Kinetics.

**Biddle, S.J.H.** (ed.) (1987). *Foundations of health-related fitness in physical education*. London: Ling.

**Cooper, K.H., Purdy, J.G., Friedman, A., Bohannon, R.L., Harris, R.A. and Arends, J.A.** (1975). An aerobics conditioning program for the Fort Worth, Texas school district. *Research Quarterly*, **46** (3), 345–50.

**Dearing, R.** (1994). *The national curriculum and its assessment. Final report.* London: School Curriculum and Assessment Authority.

**Department for Education and the Welsh Office** (DfE and WO) (1995). *Physical education in the national curriculum.* London: HMSO.

**Department of Health and Human Services** (DHHS) (1997). Guidelines for school and community programs to promote lifelong physical activity among young people. *Morbidity and Mortality Weekly Report*, **46**, 1–35.

**Dragicevick, A.R., McN. Hill, P., Hopkins, W.G. and Walker, N.P.** (1987). The effects of a year of physical education on physical fitness in two Auckland schools. *New Zealand Journal of Health, Physical Education and Recreation*, **20** (1), 7–11.

**Duncan, B., Boyce, W.T., Itami, R. and Puffenbarger, N.** (1983). A controlled trial of a physical fitness program for fifth grade students. *Journal of School Health*, 53 (8), 467–71.

**Dwyer, T., Coonan, W.E., Leitch, D.R., Hetzel, B.S. and Baghurst, R.A.** (1983). An investigation of the effects of daily physical activity on the health of primary school students in South Australia. *International Journal of Epidemiology*, **12** (3), 308–13.

**English Sports Council** (1997). *England, the sporting nation: a strategy.* London: English Sports Council.

**Fairclough, S. and Stratton, G.** (1997). Physical education curriculum and extra curriculum time: a survey of secondary schools in the North West of England. *British Journal of Physical Education*, **28** (3), 21–4.

**Geenen, D.L., Gilliam, T.B., Crowley, D., Moorehead-Steffens, C. and Rosenthal, A.** (1982). Echo-cardiographic measures in 6- to 7-year-old children after an 8 month exercise program. *American Journal of Cardiology*, **49**, 1990–5.

**Godfine, B.D. and Nahas, M.V.** (1993). Incorporating health-fitness concepts in secondary physical education curricula. *Journal of School Health*, **63** (3), 142–6.

**Green, B.N. and Farrally, M.R.** (1986). Teaching health-related physical fitness (HRPF) in schools – some practical problems. In *Proceedings of the 8th Commonwealth and International Conference on Sport, Physical Education, Dance, Recreation and Health Education: Trends and Developments in Physical Education*, pp. 191-9. London: Spon.

**Harris, J.** (1995). Physical education: a picture of health? *British Journal of Physical Education*, **26** (4), 25–32.

**Harris, J.** (1997). *Physical education: a picture of health? The implementation of health-related exercise in the national curriculum in secondary schools in England and Wales*. Unpublished doctoral thesis, Loughborough University.

**Harris, J. and Cale, L.** (1997). How healthy is school PE? A review of the effectiveness of health-related PE pro-grammes in schools. *Health Education Journal*, **56** (1), 84–104.

**Ignico, A. A. and Mahon, A. D.** (1995). The effects of a physical fitness program on low-fit children. *Research Quarterly for Exercise and Sport*, **66** (1), 85–90.

**Jones, B.A.** (1990). Assessing the effect of a course in health-related fitness in changing the stated attitudes of pupils towards curriculum physical education. *British Journal of Physical Education Research Supplement*, **8**, 24–9.

**MacConnie, S.E., Gilliam, D.L., Geenen, D.L. and Pels, A.E. III.** (1982). Daily physical activity patterns of prepubertal children involved in a vigorous exercise program. *International Journal of Sports Medicine*, **3**, 202–7.

**MacDonald, A.** (1961). Experiments at Vanves and Brussels. *Australian Journal of Physical Education*, **21**, 25–30.

**McKenzie, T.L., Nader, P.R., Strikmiller, P.K., Yang, M., Stone, E. and Perry, C.L.** (1996). School physical education: effects of the child and adolescent trial for cardiovascular health. *Preventive Medicine*, **25**, 423–31.

**McKenzie, T.L., Sallis, J.F., Faucette, N., Roby, J.J. and Kolody, B.** (1993). Effects of a curriculum and in-service program on the quantity and quality of elementary physical education classes. *Research Quarterly for Exercise and Sport*, **64**, 178–87.

**McKenzie, T.L., Sallis, J.F., Kolody, B. and Faucette, F.N.** (1997). Long-term effects of a physical education curriculum and staff development program: SPARK. *Research Quarterly for Exercise and Sport*, **68**, 280–91.

**Pate, R.R. and Hohn, R.C.** (eds.) (1994a). *Health and fitness through physical education*. Champaign: Human Kinetics.

**Pate, R.R. and Hohn, R.C.** (1994b). A contemporary mission for physical education. In R.R. Pate and R.C. Hohn (eds). *Health and fitness through physical education*, pp. 1-8. Champaign: Human Kinetics.

**Phillipp, A., Piland, N.F., Seiden-wurm, J. and Smith, H.L.** (1989). Improving physical fitness in high school students: implications from an experimental course. *Journal of Teaching in Physical Education*, **9** (1), 58-73.

**Pieron, M., Cloes, M., Delfosse, C. and Ledent, M.** (1996). An investigation of the effects of daily physical education in kindergarten and elementary schools. *European Physical Education Review*, **2** (2), 116-32.

**Pieron, M., Delfosse, C. and Cloes, M.** (1994). Effects of daily physical education programmes on the attitude of elementary school pupils. In F.I. Bell and G.H. Gyn. (eds.). *Proceedings of the 10th Commonwealth and International Scientific Congress*, pp. 440–44. Victoria: University of Victoria.

**Pollatschek, J.L. and O'Hagan, F.J.O.** (1989). An investigation of the psychophysical influences of a quality physical education programme. *Health Education Research: Theory and Practice*, **4**, 341–50.

**Sallis, J.F. and McKenzie, T.L.** (1991). Physical education's role in public health. *Research Quarterly for Exercise and Sport*, **62**, 124–37.

**Sallis, J.F, McKenzie, T.L., Alcaraz, J.E., Kolody, B., Faucette, N. and Hovell, M.F.** (1997). The effects of a 2-year physical education programme (SPARK) on physical activity and fitness in elementary school students: sports, play and active recreation for kids. *American Journal of Public Health*, **87**, 1328–34.

**Shephard, R.J.** (1997). Curricular physical activity and academic performance. *Pediatric Exercise Science*, **9**, 113–26.

**Shephard, R.J., Jequier, J.-C., Lavallee, H., La Barre, R. and Rajic, M.** (1980). Habitual physical activity: Effects of sex, milieu, season and required activity. *Journal of Sports Medicine*, **20**, 55–66.

**Shephard, R.J. and Lavallee, H.** (1993). Impact of enhanced physical education in the prepubescent child: Trois Rivieres revisited. *Pediatric Exercise Science*, **5**, 177–89.

**Shephard, R.J. and Lavallee, H.** (1994). Impact of enhanced physical education on muscle strength of the prepubescent child. *Pediatric Exercise Science*, **6**, 75–87.

**Siegel, J.A. and Manfredi, T.G.** (1984). Effects of a ten-month fitness program on children. *The Physician and Sports Medicine*, **12** (5), 91–97.

**Simons-Morton, B.G., Parcel, G.S. and O'Hara, N.M.** (1988a). Implementing organizational changes to promote healthful diet and physical activity at school. *Health Education Quarterly*, **15** (1), 115–30.

**Simons-Morton, B.G., Parcel, G.S., O'Hara, N. M., Blair, S.N. and Pate, R.R.** (1988b). Health-related physical fitness in childhood: status and recommendations. *Annual Review of Public Health*, **9**, 403–25.

**Sleap, M.** (1990). Promoting health in primary school physical education. In N. Armstrong (ed.), *New directions in physical education*, vol. 1. pp. 17–36. Champaign: Human Kinetics.

**Tinning, R. and Kirk, D.** (1991). *Daily physical education: collected papers on health based physical education in Australia*. Geelong: Deakin University Press.

**Walter, H.J., Hofman, A., Vaughan, R.D. and Wynder, E.L.** (1988). Modification of risk factors for coronary heart disease: five year results of a school-based intervention trial. *The New England Journal of Medicine*, **318** (17), 1093–100.

**Werner, P. and Durham, R.** (1988). Health related fitness benefits in upper elementary school children in a daily physical education program. *The Physical Educator*, **45** (2), 89-93.

**Westcott, W.L., Tolken, J. and Wessner, B.** (1995). School-based conditioning programs for physically unfit children. *Strength and Conditioning*, **54** (5), 5–9.

**Worsley, A. and Coonan, W.** (1984). Ten year olds' acquisition of body knowledge – the Body Owner's programme 1980, 1981. *Health Education Journal*, **42** (4), 114–20.

# Family and community interventions to promote physical activity in young people

James Sallis

*Professor of Psychology, San Diego State University, USA*

Most studies of efforts to promote physical activity in young people have been based in schools. This approach has a strong public health rationale because virtually all children can be reached through schools, and the missions of physical education and health education are consistent with the promotion of physical activity. However, the vast majority of youth physical activity is done outside of schools (Ross *et al.*, 1985), and even the best physical education programmes do not provide adequate amounts of physical activity (Luepker *et al.*, 1996; Sallis *et al.*, 1997a). Other programmes to complement school-based interventions need also to be considered.

There is a substantial literature, based on observational studies, that provides an empirical rationale for family and community interventions to promote youth physical activity (see Chapter 6). A few further studies are highlighted below, because behaviour change interventions should be designed to change the factors that appear to control the behaviour.

## ■ Method of review

Articles cited to provide rationales for family and community interventions were taken from personal files, as were studies evaluating family and community interventions. Several Medline searches of the literature since 1990 revealed no additional articles. No published evaluation of a community intervention to promote youth physical activity could be located, despite Medline searches with a variety of index words.

## ■ Family interventions

Family interventions are particularly attractive because there are many mechanisms by which parents can promote health behaviours in their children, and long-term family bonds may lead to lasting changes (Sallis and Nader, 1988). The inconsistent association between parent and child physical activity levels (Taylor and Sallis, 1997) indicates that promoting parental modelling is not likely to be a reliable intervention approach. When different types of parental influence are examined, some appear more promising than others. For example, a study of 10-year-old children found that parental encouragement to be active and parental activity levels were unrelated to child activity and fitness levels. The frequency with which parents played with their children was inconsistently related to child physical activity. In this study, the only consistent parental association with child activity was taking the child to a place where he or she can be active (Sallis *et al.*, 1992a). This study suggests that the transportation function may be an important behaviour change target.

Studies of 4- to 5-year-old children have shown that direct encouragement of physical activity by parents is effective in promoting activity in the short-term (Taylor and Sallis, 1997). Children were less active in families with many rules that limited activity (Sallis *et al.*, 1993). These studies suggest that, at least with young children, it may be effective to teach parents to offer more frequent encouragement and to reduce family rules that have the effect of limiting children's play.

## Family-based programmes

The results of family-based programmes to increase children's physical activity levels are mixed. Less success is reported in educational programmes that attempt to change behaviour in healthy youth than in structured behaviour modification approaches for clinical samples. Nader and colleagues (1989) implemented a year-long structured nutrition and physical activity programme for families with pre-adolescents in school years 5 and 6. The intervention was intensive, based on social cognitive theory, and targeted improvements in family support for healthful behaviours. At the 24- and 48-month follow-ups, the programme was successful in changing dietary habits but

generally unsuccessful in increasing physical activity levels. There was an intervention effect in reported physical activity in only one of four sex/ethnic subgroups of children (Nader *et al.*, 1992). Baranowski and co-workers (1990) conducted a similarly intensive programme for African-American families at a community centre. This intervention was also not effective. The CATCH study (Child and Adolescent Trial for Cardiovascular Health) included a family intervention component that consisted of take-home materials and Family Fun Night in-person sessions at the schools. The family intervention did not enhance physical activity or other outcomes measured in the CATCH study (Nader *et al.*, 1996).

These three large studies of family interventions were all targeted at healthy families for health promotion purposes, and they were all ineffective in increasing physical activity. One of the likely reasons for the lack of effects is the difficulty of obtaining family participation. If families do not participate, there is no reason to expect behaviour change. In the Baranowski *et al.* (1990) study, participation rates were only 20%, and during the maintenance phase of the Nader *et al.* (1989) study, attendance rates were about 40%. Although over 90% of parents completed children's take-home assignments, student attendance at CATCH Family Fun Nights was less than 60%, and only 60% of those children were accompanied by a family member (Nader *et al.*, 1996). A significant association between family participation in the CATCH intervention and child physical activity (Nader *et al.*, 1996) indicates that there are benefits for those who attend the intervention. A critical challenge for these family programmes is increasing participation rates.

In contrast to the disappointing effects of cognitive-behavioural programmes for healthy families, there are several examples of successful programmes with samples of low-fit or obese children. In a small uncontrolled study, Taggart and colleagues (1986) enrolled families of children with low fitness levels in a 12-week programme. Parents were taught to apply behaviour modification principles and systematically reward children's physical activity. All children in this small sample increased both activity and fitness levels, with several children increasing physical activity over 100%.

A similar reinforcement-based approach was shown to be successful with obese children. Leonard Epstein and colleagues have published numerous studies with obese children showing that training parents to reinforce children for physical activity leads to reliable behaviour changes (Epstein, Koeske and Wing, 1984). These are intensive clinical programmes undertaken by clinically obese children with at least one obese parent. Parents are taught to provide rewards for changes in their children's eating and physical activity habits, and a variety of different interventions have produced substantial reductions in percentage overweight that have persisted for 10 years (Epstein *et al.*, 1994). Strategies with the best outcomes were those in which both parents and children were involved in the weight loss programme and were reinforced for behaviour change, and those that reinforced lifestyle rather than structured exercise (Epstein *et al.*, 1994).

Epstein and colleagues have investigated strategies for increasing physical activity of obese children that could be incorporated into family interventions. In laboratory studies, obese children who were reinforced for reducing sedentary behaviours or reinforced for being physically active both increased physical activity (Epstein, Saelens and O'Brien, 1995a).

Another study indicated that a benefit of reinforcing reductions of sedentary behaviours is a decreased liking of sedentary behaviours. Restricting access to sedentary behaviours increased liking of those behaviours (Epstein *et al.*, 1997). That is, rated enjoyment of sedentary behaviours increased when children were prohibited from doing them. This finding suggests that restricting such sedentary behaviours as television watching may not be the most effective strategy in the long term.

Finally, obese children who were reinforced for reducing sedentary behaviours lost more weight than those who were reinforced for increases in physical activity (Epstein *et al.*, 1995b). These findings are intriguing, but it is not clear how these findings apply to non-obese children, if physical activity can be reliably increased in non-laboratory settings, and whether families can adequately implement reinforcement for reducing sedentary behaviours. However, the strategy of teaching parents to reinforce decreases in sedentary behaviours needs to be evaluated.

### Comments on family-based programmes

There is substantial evidence from observational studies that families have strong influences on children's physical activity through multiple mechanisms, such as encouragement, transportation and reinforcement. Surprisingly, three large studies of family interventions for healthy families that relied on educational approaches were all ineffective in increasing children's physical activity. Until methods for enhancing participation are developed, and a new generation of family interventions is shown to be effective, family interventions cannot be recommended for broad implementation.

Studies with low-fit and obese children show that family interventions can be effective. It is possible that teaching families systematically to reinforce increases in physical activity or decreases in sedentary behaviours is more effective than the cognitive-behavioural interventions that were applied in the health promotion studies.

Given the disappointing results of the family-based interventions for healthy families, it may be useful to collect more extensive descriptive data that would be helpful in designing programmes that are more likely to appeal to children and parents. The meaning of being physically active as a family or participating in family programmes could be explored, so interventions could emphasise benefits that are most attractive to potential participants. Although quantitative surveys could be useful for this purpose, in-depth interviews and focus groups with youth and parents could also contribute to the development of a better understanding of how to improve recruitment, participation and behaviour change outcomes (Ingham, 1994).

In summary, there are no family-based interventions that have been shown to be effective in increasing children's physical activity in the general population. The feasibility and effectiveness of training parents in behaviour modification methods should be studied.

## ▧ Community interventions

There is evidence from observational studies of strong environmental influences on physical activity, but there is limited empirical support for the effectiveness of community-based programmes for youth physical activity pro-

motion. The vast majority of children's physical activity occurs outside of school, and much of this is in organised sports or other activities (Ross *et al.*, 1985 ; Simons-Morton *et al.*, 1990). If children are to be physically active, these findings strongly imply that access to facilities and/or programmes in the community is necessary.

Further support for environmental influences is provided by an association of children's physical activity with the number of different types of outdoor places to play within a short walk from the child's house and the amount of time the child spends in those places (Sallis *et al.*, 1993). Parents are able to identify factors they use in selecting play areas for their children. Parents of young children identified safety as the most important consideration. Other highly rated factors were such conveniences as toilets, drinking water, lighting and shade (Sallis *et al.*, 1997b). Improving the amenities in parks could be part of a strategy to increase the use of parks for children's play.

Three studies have shown that the most powerful correlate of young children's physical activity is the amount of time they spend outdoors (Klesges *et al.*, 1990; Baranowski *et al.*, 1993), with correlations observed as high as 0.74 (Sallis *et al.*, 1993). Taken together, these observational studies lead to a tentative conclusion that children need supportive environments in which to be physically active. If a child is to be regularly active, they need access to these environments daily. It should be a goal of community interventions to provide supportive environments for children and adolescents of all ages.

The literature on associations between environments and physical activity in youth indicates strong effects, but there are many gaps in knowledge. Characteristics of supportive environments are not well-defined, and because the previous studies were conducted on young children, essentially nothing is known about environmental influences on physical activity of adolescents. There is a large literature on youth sports (Seefelt, Ewing and Walk, 1993), but the relevance of youth sports to physical activity in the population is not well known.

Knowing more about the characteristics of environments and programmes that facilitate or hinder youth physical activity, is a first step in developing an empirical basis for community interventions. A second step is to determine the distribution of facilities and programmes within communities. Further studies should define factors that affect access to, or use of, those facilities and programmes. These kinds of preliminary data can be used to target efforts to change facilities and programmes to those that are most relevant to increasing physical activity levels in the community's young people.

## Community-based programmes

In a 1992 review of the literature on youth physical activity promotion, no studies evaluating programmes in community settings were found (Sallis *et al.*, 1992b). There are still no published evaluations of community programmes that could be located. This section presents a framework for conceptualising community physical activity interventions, offers ideas for research and practice and summarises relevant consensus guidelines.

In developing new community interventions to promote physical activity, it is useful to apply ecological models of health behaviour. These models assert that health behaviours are influenced by intrapersonal, social and cultural and physical environment variables; and interventions will be most effective when

they operate at multiple levels of influence (Sallis and Owen, 1996). A particularly relevant concept from these models is 'behaviour setting', which is the physical and social environment in which the behaviour takes place. Physical activity must be done in specific places. Some places, such as parks, sports fields, gymnasium, playgrounds and cycling paths, are specifically designed for physical activity. Other behaviour settings are either designed for sedentary behaviours or present barriers to physical activity. Examples include school classrooms, streets, homes, movie theatres and department stores and shops.

One hypothesis, derived from ecological models, is that communities with many behaviour settings that are conducive to physical activity should stimulate more physical activity than communities with few activity-related behaviour settings. To test this hypothesis, it is necessary to compile an inventory of 'activity behaviour settings'. Before such an inventory can be conducted, characteristics of behaviour settings that are believed to facilitate physical activity need to be defined. For example, parks with open spaces may encourage physical activity among nearby residents, but parks with football goals and climbing apparatus may be more effective in enhancing physical activity among children. It is a reasonable community intervention to increase the number and quality of activity-enhancing behaviour settings, although it is not known at this time how effective such a strategy would be.

Even if activity-enhancing behaviour settings are common and well distributed in a community, their effectiveness in promoting physical activity could be affected by limited access. Access can be limited by space, time, cost and policies. Access is limited to even free facilities when they are located far from the homes of poor children who have no transportation. If swimming pools are reserved for elite swim teams in the after-school hours, then non-team members do not have access during the times they are most likely to use the pools. Financial costs to use facilities have a great impact on children from low socio-economic status families. Policies can affect all of the previous factors. For example, many schools have policies that prohibit them being used as community recreation centres in the evenings and on weekends, although most schools have indoor and outdoor facilities that are designed for physical activity. This leads to a situation in which schools are the most widely available physical activity facilities, but they are the least used for physical activity by people in the community (Sallis *et al.*, 1990).

The value of behaviour settings for physical activity can be enhanced by providing a supportive social environment. One way of doing this is having supervised activities, either for competitive sport or recreation. Many organisations are involved in youth activity or sport programmes. In Belfast, Northern Ireland, there is some evidence from a quasi-experimental study (Roberts *et al.*, 1989) that increasing facilities may improve activity levels. Over the course of seven years, 14 new public leisure centres were built in Belfast, making it one of the best-served cities in the UK. There was some indication of increased participation in sports and physical activity of adults across all socio-economic strata. Although methodologically flawed and not reporting effects on youth, this study suggests that improved access to facilities can stimulate increased activity levels.

The effectiveness of sport and activity programmes in promoting physical activity in youth depends on the number of youth who participate, the frequency of contact, the months the programme is in operation and the amount of activity provided during each contact. Programme characteristics that lead to low public health impact include: restricted to elite athletes; meet infrequently; offered for part of the year; include little physical training; and emphasise sports with low activity levels.

Ecological models suggest several types of interventions on a community level that can be attempted to increase youth physical activity:

- Increase the number of behaviour settings that are conducive to youth physical activity.

- Enhance access to, and attractiveness of, behaviour settings that are conducive to youth physical activity.

- Promote increased use of activity-enhancing behaviour settings through communication media, special events or incentives.

- Increase the number of supervised programmes for youth physical activity.

- Enhance access to, and quality of, programmes for youth physical activity.

- Promote increased use of youth activity programmes through communication media, special events, or incentives.

Because community interventions can occur at different levels of influence, involve a wide range of individuals and organisations and use a variety of methods, they are difficult to plan, implement and evaluate. Several theories can be applied to the conduct of community interventions, including community organisation models (Minkler and Wallerstein, 1997), communication theory (Finnegan and Viswanath, 1997) and social marketing models (Donovan and

Owen, 1994; Lefebvre and Rochlin, 1997). There are books to guide those who plan community health promotion programmes (Bracht, 1990; Green and Kreuter, 1991), but few specific guidelines are generally known to lead to effective programmes. Those who plan community interventions for physical activity must rely on their ability to apply multiple theories, the best available data, input from members of the community and creativity.

# Consensus guidelines for community programmes to promote youth physical activity

A recent publication from Centers for Disease Control and Prevention (1997) in the United States summarised the results of a consensus development effort that was designed to develop recommendations for promoting youth physical activity. In the absence of data from programme evaluations, this is the best resource for programme planning for promoting youth physical activity. Many of the guidelines are related to school programmes. The guidelines related to family and community interventions are presented in Table 8.1, which includes 8 of the 10 general guidelines, plus the most relevant specific guidelines. Further discussions on these guidelines can be found in Chapter 9.

# What we know

### Family interventions

- Observational studies suggest there are many ways in which parents can pro-

mote their children's physical activity. These findings suggest strong potential for family-based interventions to be effective.

- Family-based health promotion programmes have been ineffective in increasing children's physical activity, due in part to low family participation in the intervention.

### Community interventions

- Observational data show that young people need suitable and accessible facilities and programmes that provide opportunities for activity, which implies the need for environmental and policy interventions to increase these opportunities.

- No studies evaluating community interventions to promote youth physical activity could be located.

# What we need to know

### Family interventions

- What are the effects of new strategies for family interventions that are based on findings from descriptive studies? Potential strategies include encouraging parents to transport children to facilities and programmes and reducing family rules that limit physical activity.

- What strategies can be used for enhancing family participation in interventions?

- What are the effects on youth physical activity of programmes in which parents are trained to reinforce reductions in children's sedentary behaviours?

**Table 8.1.** *Extracts from 'Guidelines for School and Community Programmes to Promote Lifelong Physical Activity among Young People' (Centers for Disease Control and Prevention, 1997) that are most relevant to family and community interventions*

*Recommendation 1. Policy: Establish policies that promote enjoyable, lifelong physical activity among young people*

■ Require that adequate resources, including budget and facilities, be committed for physical activity instruction and programmes.

■ Require that physical activity instruction and programmes meet the needs and interests of all students.

*Recommendation 2. Environment: Provide physical and social environments that encourage and enable safe and enjoyable physical activity*

■ Provide access to safe spaces and facilities for physical activity in the school and the community.

*Recommendation 5. Extracurricular activities: Provide extracurricular physical activity programmes that meet the needs and interests of all students*

■ Provide a diversity of developmentally appropriate competitive and noncompetitive physical activity programmes for all students.

■ Link students to community physical activity programmes, and use community resources to support extracurricular physical activity programmes.

*Recommendation 6. Parental involvement: Include parents and guardians in physical activity instruction and in extracurricular and community physical activity programmes, and encourage them to support their children's participation in enjoyable physical activities*

■ Encourage parents to advocate for quality physical activity instruction and programmes for their children.

■ Encourage parents to support their children's participation in appropriate, enjoyable physical activities.

■ Encourage parents to be physically active role models and to plan and participate in family activities that include physical activity.

*Recommendation 7. Personnel training: Provide training for education, coaching, recreation, health care, and other school and community personnel that imparts the knowledge and skills needed to effectively promote enjoyable, lifelong physical activity among young people*

■ Train school and community personnel how to create psychosocial environments that enable young people to enjoy physical activity instruction and programmes.

■ Train school and community personnel how to involve parents and the community in physical activity instruction and programmes.

■ Train volunteers who coach sports and recreation programmes for young people.

**Table 8.1.** *continued*

*Recommendation 8. Health services: Assess physical activity patterns among young people, counsel them about physical activity, refer them to appropriate programmes, and advocate for physical activity instruction and programmes for young people*

■ Regularly assess the physical activity patterns of young people, reinforce physical activity among active young people, counsel inactive young people about physical activity, and refer young people to appropriate physical activity programmes.

■ Advocate for school and community physical activity instruction and programmes that meet the needs of young people.

*Recommendation 9. Community programmes: Provide a range of developmentally appropriate community sports and recreation programmes that are attractive to all young people*

■ Provide a diversity of developmentally appropriate community sports and recreation programmes for all young people.

■ Provide access to community sports and recreation programmes for young people.

*Recommendation 10. Evaluation: Regularly evaluate school and community physical activity instruction, programmes, and facilities*

■ Evaluate the implementation and quality of physical activity policies, curricula, instruction, programmes, and personnel training.

## Community interventions

■ What factors influence access to and use of facilities and programmes?

■ An empirical literature needs to be generated to provide guidance for the design of large-scale community programmes. Based on theories and models, three types of community interventions are recommended as high priorities for research:

(1) Increase the number of activity facilities and programmes that are relevant for youth of all ages.

(2) Enhance access to, and attractiveness of, facilities and programmes by all youth.

(3) Promote increased use of facilities and programmes through communication media, special events or incentives.

## ▨ References

**Baranowski, T., Simons-Morton, B., Hooks, P., Henske, J., Tiernan, K., Dunn, J.K., Burkhalter, H., Harper, J. and Palmer, J.** (1990). A center-based program for exercise change among Black-American families. *Health Education Quarterly*, **17**, 179–96

**Baranowski, T., Thompson, W.O., Du Rant, R.H., Baranowski, J. and Puhl, J.** (1993). Observations on physical activity in physical locations: age, gender, ethnicity, and month effects. *Research Quarterly for Exercise and Sport*, **64**, 127–33.

**Bracht, N.** (ed.) (1990). *Health promotion at the community level*. Newbury Park: Sage.

**Centers for Disease Control and Prevention.** (1997). Guidelines for school and community programmes to promote lifelong physical activity among young people. *Morbidity and Mortality Weekly Report*, **46** (No. RR-6), 1–36.

**Donovan, R.J. and Owen, N.** (1994). Social marketing and population interventions. In R.K. Dishman (ed.), *Advances in exercise adherence*, pp. 249–90. Champaign: Human Kinetics.

**Epstein, L.H., Koeske, R. and Wing, R.R.** (1984). Adherence to exercise in obese children. *Journal of Cardiac Rehabilitation*, **4**, 185–95.

**Epstein, L.H., Saelens, B.E., Myers, M.D., and Vito, D.** (1997). Effects of decreasing sedentary behaviors on activity choice in obese children. *Health Psychology*, **16**, 107–13.

**Epstein, L.H., Saelens, B.E. and O'Brien, J.G.** (1995a). Effects of reinforcing increases in active versus decreases in sedentary behavior for obese children. *International Journal of Behavioral Medicine*, **2**, 41–50.

**Epstein, L.H., Valoski, A.M., Vara, L.S., McCurley, J., Wisniewski, L., Kalarchian, M.A., Klein, K.R., and Shrager, L.R.** (1995b). Effects of decreasing sedentary behavior and increasing activity on weight changes in obese children. *Health Psychology*, **14**, 109–15.

**Epstein, L.H., Valoski, A., Wing, R.R. and McCurley, J.** (1994). Ten-year outcomes of behavioral family-based treatment for childhood obesity. *Health Psychology*, **13**, 373–83.

**Finnegan, J.R. and Viswanath, K.** (1997). Communication theory and health behavior change: the media studies framework. In K. Glanz, F.M. Lewis, and B.K. Rimer (eds.), *Health behavior and health education: theory, research, and practice*. 2nd edn, pp. 313–41. San Francisco: Jossey-Bass.

**Green, L.W. and Kreuter, M.W.** (1991). *Health promotion planning: An educational and environmental approach*, 2nd edn, Mountain View: Mayfield.

**Ingham, R.** (1994). Some speculations on the concept of rationality. In G. Albrecht (ed.), *Advances in medical sociology*, vol. 4, *A reconsideration of health behavior change models*, pp. 89–112. Greenwich: JAI Press.

**Klesges, R.C., Eck, L.H., Hanson, C.L., Haddock, C.K. and Klesges, L.M.** (1990). Effects of obesity, social interactions, and physical environment on physical activity in preschoolers. *Health Psychology*, **9**, 435–49.

**Lefebvre, R.C. and Rochlin, L.** (1997). Social marketing. In K. Glanz, F.M. Lewis and B.K. Rimer (eds.), *Health behavior and health education: theory, research, and practice*, pp. 384–402, 2nd edn. San Francisco: Jossey-Bass.

**Luepker, R.V., Perry, C.L., McKinlay, S.M., Nader, P.R., Parcel, G.S., Stone, E.J., Webber, L.S., Elder, J.P., Feldman, H.A., Johnson, C.C., Kelder, S.H. and Wu, M.** (1996). Outcomes of a field trial to improve children's dietary patterns and physical activity: The Child and Adolescent Trial for Cardiovascular Health (CATCH). *Journal of the American Medical Association*, **275**, 768–76.

**Minkler, M. and Wallerstein, N.** (1997). Improving health through community organization and community building. In K. Glanz, F.M. Lewis and B.K. Rimer (eds.), *Health behavior and health education: theory, research, and practice*, pp. 241–69. 2nd edn. San Francisco: Jossey-Bass.

**Nader, P.R., Sallis, J.F., Abramson, I.S., Broyles, S.L., Patterson, T.L., Senn, K., Rupp, J.W. and Nelson, J.A.** (1992). Family-based cardiovascular risk reduction education among Mexican- and Anglo-Americans. *Family and Community Health*, **15**, 57–74.

**Nader, P.R., Sallis, J.F., Patterson, T.L., Abramson, I.S., Rupp, J.W., Senn, K.L., Atkins, C.J., Roppe, B.E., Morris, J.A., Wallace, J.P. and Vega, W.A.** (1989). A family approach to cardiovascular risk reduction: results from the San Diego Family Health Project. *Health Education Quarterly*, **16**, 229–44.

**Nader, P.R., Sellers, D.E., Johnson, C.C., Perry, C.L., Stone, E.J., Cook, K.C., Bebchuk, J. and Luepker, R.V.** (1996). The effect of adult participation in a school-based family intervention to improve children's diet and physical activity: The Child and Adolescent Trial for Cardiovascular Health. *Preventive Medicine*, **25**, 455–64.

**Roberts, K., Dench, S., Minten, J. and York, C.** (1989). *Community response to leisure centre provision in Belfast*. London: Sports Council.

**Ross, J.G., Dotson, C.O., Gilbert, G.G. and Katz, S.J.** (1985). After physical education: physical activity outside of school physical education programmes. *Journal of Physical Education, Recreation and Dance*, **56** (1), 77–81.

**Sallis, J.F., Alcaraz, J.E., McKenzie, T.L., Hovell, M.F., Kolody, B. and Nader, P.R.** (1992). Parent behavior in relation to physical activity and fitness in 9-year-olds. *American Journal of Diseases of Children*, **146**, 1383–8.

**Sallis, J.F., Hovell, M.F., Hofstetter, C.R., Elder, J.P., Caspersen, C.J., Hackley, M. and Powell, K.E.** (1990). Distance between homes and exercise facilities related to the frequency of exercise among San Diego residents. *Public Health Reports*, **105**, 179–85.

**Sallis, J.F., McKenzie, T.L., Alcaraz, J.E., Kolody, B., Faucette, N. and Hovell, M.F.** (1997a). The effects of a 2-year physical education programme (SPARK) on physical activity and fitness in elementary school students. *American Journal of Public Health*, **87**, 1328–34.

**Sallis, J.F., McKenzie, T.L., Elder, J.P., Broyles, S.L. and Nader, P.R.** (1997b). Factors parents use in selecting playspaces for young children. *Archives of Pediatrics and Adolescent Medicine*, **151**, 414–17.

**Sallis, J.F. and Nader, P.R.** (1988). Family determinants of health behavior. In D.S. Gochman (ed.). *Health behavior: emerging research perspectives*, pp. 107–24. New York: Plenum.

**Sallis, J.F., Nader, P.R., Broyles, S.L., Berry, C.C., Elder, J.P., McKenzie, T.L. and Nelson, J.A.** (1993). Correlates of physical activity at home in Mexican-American and Anglo-American preschool children. *Health Psychology*, **12**, 390–8.

**Sallis, J.F. and Owen, N.** (1996). Ecological models. In K. Glanz, F.M. Lewis and B.K. Rimer (eds.), *Health Behavior and health education: theory, research, and practice*, pp. 403–24. 2nd edn. San Francisco: Jossey-Bass.

**Sallis, J.F., Simons-Morton, B.G., Stone, E.J., Corbin, C.B., Epstein, L.H., Faucette, N., Iannotti, R.J., Killen, J.D., Klesges, R.C., Petray, C.K., Rowland, T.W. and Taylor, W.** (1992). Determinants of physical activity and interventions in youth. *Medicine and Science in Sports and Exercise*, **24**, S248–S257.

**Seefelt, V., Ewing, M. and Walk, S.** (1993). *Overview of youth sports programmes in the United States.* Washington, DC: Carnegie Council on Adolescent Development.

**Simons-Morton, B.G., O'Hara, N.M., Parcel, G.S., Huang, I.W., Baranowski. T. and Wilson, B.** (1990). Children's frequency of participation in moderate to vigorous physical activities. *Research Quarterly for Exercise and Sport*, **61**, 307–14.

**Taggart, A.C., Taggart, J. and Siedentop, D.** (1986). Effects of a home-based activity programme: a study with low-fitness elementary school children. *Behavior Modification*, **10**, 487–507.

**Taylor, W.C. and Sallis, J.F.** (1997). Determinants of physical activity in children. In A.P. Simopolous and K.N. Pavlou (eds.), *Nutrition and fitness: metabolic and behavioural aspects in health and disease. World review of food and nutrition*, vol. 82, pp.159–67. Basel: Karger.

# Critique of existing guidelines for physical activity in young people

Russell Pate[1], Stewart Trost[2] and Craig Williams[3]

[1]Professor and Chairman, Department of Exercise Science,
University of South Carolina, USA
[2]Graduate Research Assistant,
University of South Carolina, USA
[3]Senior Lecturer in Sport and Exercise Science,
University of Brighton, UK

The health benefits of a physically active lifestyle are now well established in adults. It is known that physically active adults, as compared with their sedentary counterparts, are at substantially reduced risk for premature development of an array of chronic diseases (Department of Health and Human Services, 1996) and for death from all causes (Paffenbarger *et al.*, 1986, 1993; Blair *et al.*, 1989b, 1995;). This extensive scientific documentation of the health benefits of physical activity has prompted a number of prestigious medical and public health authorities to issue recommendations concerning the types and amounts of physical activity needed for health (American College of Sports Medicine [ACSM], 1990; Pate *et al.*, 1995; Fletcher *et al.*, 1996). Although many of these official documents have alluded to the physical activity needs of children and youth, until recently, specific guidelines on physical activity have been directed only toward adults.

The importance of physical activity during childhood and adolescence, though well accepted by professionals and the public, is not as extensively documented as is the case for adults. It seems certain that regular physical activity is required to support normal growth and development,

but the minimum amount needed is unknown (Parizkova, 1996). Regular exercise may reduce chronic disease risk in youngsters, but documenting this is difficult because chronic diseases, such as coronary heart disease, rarely manifest themselves prior to the middle adult years and the physiological risk factors for these diseases are generally observed to be at rather favorable levels in children and youth (Pate and Blair, 1978; Baranowski *et al.*, 1992). Higher levels of physical activity early in life may well carry into adulthood, but to date the childhood predictors of a physically active lifestyle during adulthood are largely unknown (Sallis *et al.*, 1992; Malina, 1996).

Because of the aforementioned limitations in the scientific literature, there has been uncertainty concerning the types and amounts of physical activity that should be recommended for children and adolescents. In some cases guidelines developed primarily for adults have been applied to younger persons as well (Riopel *et al.*, 1986; ACSM, 1988; Public Health Service, 1990). However, the appropriateness of this practice is highly questionable. Youngsters differ markedly from adults in both physical and behavioural characteristics related to exercise, and indeed, within the younger age range, children are quite different from adolescents. In recent years some efforts have been made to develop physical activity guidelines that are designed specifically for children and adolescents. This chapter is intended to summarise and analyse these existing guidelines. In addition, some modifications to existing guidelines will be proposed.

## Background – guidelines on physical activity and physical fitness

Only in recent years have efforts been made to develop specific recommendations concerning the types and amounts of physical activity that are needed by children and adolescents. Historically, physical fitness has received more attention than *physical activity*, and throughout most of the twentieth century both scholarly and professional groups have given great attention to issues of definition, measurement and standards for *physical fitness* in young people (AAHPER, 1958; AAPHERD, 1988; Freedson and Rowland, 1992). Over the past two decades operational definitions and measurement protocols for physical fitness have moved away from an emphasis on motor or performance-related fitness toward an emphasis on so-called health-related physical fitness (Pate, 1983; Armstrong, 1984; Simons-Morton *et al.*, 1987). Concurrent with this transition, physical fitness standards that are based on health criteria have become more accepted than the traditional norm-referenced standards. These trends seemingly reflect an increasing concern for the short- and long-term health consequences of physical activity and fitness early in life.

While for children and youth most of the earlier attention was focused on physical fitness rather than physical activity, the opposite has been true for adults. Organisations such as the YMCA have established standards for health-related physical fitness for adults of both genders and various age groups (YMCA, 1989). However, to date this practice has not been adopted by medical or public health authorities. In contrast, physical activity recommendations for adults have been promoted on a large scale for over 20 years. In the mid-1970s the American College of Sports Medicine published the first edition of *Guidelines for exercise testing and prescription* (ACSM, 1975) and its first Position Stand, entitled *Position statement on the recommended quantity and quality of exercise for developing and maintaining fitness in healthy adults* (ACSM, 1978). These documents and others that followed over the ensuing decade recommended regular performance of structured, vigorous exercise, for example 20–60 minutes of continuous aerobic exercise performed at 60% or more of individual $\dot{V}_{O_2 max}$ on three or more days of the week. Such recommendations were supported by an extensive body of scientific literature demonstrating that the standard 'exercise prescription' produced significant gains in physical fitness (usually operationalised as $\dot{V}_{O_2 max}$) in initially sedentary adults (Pollock, 1973).

During the 1980s and early 1990s the emerging discipline of physical activity epidemiology produced impressive data on the effects of physical activity during adulthood on morbidity and mortality from coronary heart disease and other chronic diseases (Berlin and Colditz, 1990; Department of Health and Human Services, 1996). This documentation that sedentary lifestyle carries an enormous public health burden in the developed societies became the launching pad from which recently initiated large-scale public health efforts to promote physical activity have been projected (Department of Health, 1992; McGinnis, 1992; McGinnis and Foege, 1993; Department of Health and Human Services, 1996). A key aspect of these public health education and promotion efforts has been a re-examination of the traditional recommendations for physical activity during adulthood. The most recent adult guidelines, while reaffirming the benefits of performing structured, vigorous exercise, have also endorsed accumulation of moderate intensity physical activity. In 1995, the US Centers for Disease Control and Prevention and the American College of Sports Medicine recommended that, 'Every US adult should accumulate 30 minutes or more of moderate-intensity physical activity on most, preferably all, days of the week' (Pate *et al.*, 1995). This recommendation was reaffirmed in the US Surgeon General's report on physical activity and health released in 1996 (Department of Health and Human Services, 1996) and forms the basis for current guidelines and promotional activities in England through the Health Education Authority's *ACTIVE* for LIFE campaign.

# ■ **Recommendations on types and amounts of physical activity in children and youth**

Perhaps because of the traditional focus on physical fitness, or possibly because of limitations in the relevant scientific evidence, efforts to establish physical activity

recommendations for young persons have lagged behind the efforts with adults. Some official statements, directed primarily toward adults, have mentioned the physical activity needs of children – though usually in rather general terms (American Academy of Pediatrics, 1987; Public Health Service, 1990; American Medical Association, 1994; UKK Institute for Health Promotion Research, 1996). More attention has been paid to recommendations for promotional activities, and these guidelines are summarised in a later section of this chapter. A good example of these tendencies was a position statement of the American Heart Association published in 1986 (Riopel *et al.*, 1986). This statement focused primarily on promotion of physical activity in school, home and health care settings. Also, it included reference to the American Heart Association's previously published exercise recommendations for adults (see Fletcher *et al.*, 1996), which essentially mirrored the previously cited 'exercise prescription' guidelines of the American College of Sports Medicine (ACSM, 1990). No specific physical activity guidelines for children or youth were made, however, the following statement (Riopel *et al.*, 1986) was prominently presented:

> The major goal is to develop in the child a desire to be physically active that will persist through adolescence and adult years. Exercise habits should lead to the maintenance of a more efficient cardiovascular system and reduce other atherosclerotic risk factors.

The concepts communicated in this statement have been common themes in official statements and expert opinions published on this issue for at least two decades.

The recent emergence of physical activity as a priority of the public health community has given impetus to efforts to establish physical activity guidelines for young persons. In the United States, national health objectives were first published in 1980 and then revised in 1990. Both documents have included physical activity objectives that were applied to young persons as well as adults. Table 9.1 lists the applicable physical activity objectives as stated in *Healthy people 2000* (Public Health Service, 1990). The differ-

ent objectives endorse rather different types and amounts of physical activity, and all of them are applied to the entire range of ages, beginning at six years. While there seems to be little doubt that each of the objectives is, in the broad sense, 'appropriate' for children and youth, it is not clear that the physical activity objectives included in *Healthy people 2000* are targeted to meet the unique and specific needs of children or

**Table 9.1.** *The objectives relating to physical activity in children and adolescents taken from* Healthy people 2000

---

1.3 Increase to at least 30 percent the proportion of people aged 6 and older who engage regularly, preferably daily, in light to moderate physical activity for at least 30 minutes per day

1.4 Increase to at least 20 percent the proportion of people aged 18 and older and to at least 75 percent the proportion of children and adolescents aged 6 through 17 who engage in vigorous physical activity that promotes the development and maintenance of cardiorespiratory fitness 3 or more days per week for 20 or minutes per occasion.

1.5 Reduce to no more than 15 percent the proportion of people aged 6 and older who engage in no leisure-time physical activity

1.6 Increase to at least 40 percent the proportion of people aged 6 and older who regularly perform physical activities that enhance and maintain muscular strength, muscular endurance, and flexibility.

1.7 Increase to at least 50 percent the proportion of overweight people aged 12 and older who have adopted sound dietary practices combined with regular physical activity or attain appropriate body weight.

1.8 Increase to at least 50 percent the proportion of children and adolescents in 1st through 12th grade who participate in daily school physical education.

1.9 Increase to at least 50 percent the proportion of school physical education class time that students spend being physically active, preferably engaged in lifetime physical activities.

1.11 Increase community availability and accessibility of physical activity and fitness facilities.

1.12 Increase to at least 50 percent the proportion of primary care providers who routinely assess and counsel their patients regarding the frequency, duration, type and intensity of each patient's physical activity practices.

---

Source: Public Health Service (1990).

adolescents. In the UK similar objectives are being pursued in *The health of the nation* (Department of Health, 1992), which stresses the need for active lifestyles to be established as early as possible.

A novel approach to setting a physical activity standard for children and youth was proposed by Blair *et al.* (1989). Working from the epidemiological studies that link physical activity to health in adults, they estimated that a daily energy expenditure in physical activity of 12.6 kJ·kg⁻¹ of body weight (3 kcals·kg⁻¹·day⁻¹) was an appropriate target. This level of activity, when extrapolated to children, corresponds to 20–40 minutes of moderate to vigorous physical activity per day (Cureton, 1994) – an amount not unlike that called for in Objective 1.3 of *Healthy people 2000*. If one assumes that some decline in physical activity is inevitable between childhood and adulthood, the adult standard of 12.6 kJ·kg⁻¹ of body weight per day could be factored up to a higher level in younger people. Blair and co-workers suggested applying a 33% adjustment, and this yielded a target of 16.8 kJ·kg⁻¹ of body weight (4 kcals·kg⁻¹·day⁻¹) (Blair *et al.* 1989a). This method of establishing a physical activity recommendation for young people has the advantage of being linked, albeit indirectly, to adult health outcomes. However, since the vast majority of children and youth meet both the 12.6 and 16.8 kJ·kg⁻¹day⁻¹ standards, one is left to wonder if either standard is high enough to provide the desired short and long term benefits.

After reviewing existing guidelines for physical activity in youth, Corbin *et al.* (1994) proposed a 'lifetime physical activity' guideline. In contrast to the traditional prescription-based guidelines that had previously been applied to youth, it recommended that, as a minimum, children and adolescents accumulate 30 minutes of moderate physical activity daily (3–4 kcal·kg⁻¹day or 12.4–16.8 kJ·kg⁻¹day⁻¹). For optimal functioning, the authors recommended an accumulation of 60 minutes of moderate to vigorous physical activity daily (6–8 kcal·kg⁻¹day⁻¹ or 25.2–33.6 kJ·kg⁻¹day⁻¹).

To date the most focused and extensive effort to develop guidelines on the types and amounts of physical activity needed by young people has been the International Consensus Conference on Physical Activity Guidelines for Adolescents. This conference and its products have been described in detail by Sallis and Patrick (1994). Briefly, an international panel of experts on physical activity in children and youth was commissioned to produce written reviews of the scientific literature on the various health effects of physical activity in adolescents. Based on this review of the pertinent scientific literature, the panel issued recommendations on physical activity participation during adolescence. Two guidelines were generated:

(1) All adolescents should be physically active daily, or nearly every day, as part of play, games, sports, work, transportation, recreation, physical education or planned exercise, in the context of family, school and community activities.

(2) Adolescents should engage in three or more sessions per week of activities that last 20 min or more at a time and that require moderate to vigorous levels of exertion.

Guideline 1 is similar to *Healthy people 2000* Objective 1.3 (Public Health Service, 1990) and other recently released adult guidelines in that it calls for daily physical activity (Pate *et al.*, 1995; Fletcher *et al.*, 1996). Also, it is progressive in that its phraseology makes reference to the wide range of forms and settings in which physical activity may be performed. This is consistent with the growing emphasis on 'lifestyle physical activity' (Simons-Morton *et al.*, 1987), an approach which is intended to be consistent with the body of knowledge on determinants of physical activity. A limitation associated with guideline 1 is its lack of quantification – that is, no specific amount of daily activity is recommended. In contrast, guideline 2 is presented in quite specific and quantified terms, and accordingly this guideline lends itself to use as a tool in evaluating physical activity participation in individuals, groups of various types and populations. However, a concern is that this guideline espouses the traditional adult exercise prescription, which may not be ideal from a behavioural perspective in either adults or adolescents (Riddoch and Boreham, 1995). Also, guideline 2 is based on a scientific literature that is limited by the tendency of investigators to use the traditional exercise as the only exercise treatment in controlled exercise training studies. So it is possible, perhaps even likely, that guideline 2, though consistent with the existing scientific literature, presents a recommendation that is narrower than necessary or appropriate. Only a marked expansion of our knowledge of the dose–response relationship for physical activity and health in adolescents will resolve this issue.

To summarise, our review of previously published recommendations on types and amounts of physical activity in children and youth points to three conclusions. The first is that there is no clear consensus across the various recommendations. Different authorities have adopted rather different approaches. Several of the earlier position statements essentially adopted existing adult guidelines, giving little attention to the specific characteristics of children and youth (Riopel *et al.*, 1986; ACSM, 1988). Others attempted to project the physical activity dose needed by children and youth by extrapolating back from the dose known to be effective in adults (Blair *et al.*, 1989a; Corbin *et al.*, 1994). Most statements have focused exclusively on whole-body, dynamic physical activity, but some have issued multiple guidelines directed at different specific types of physical activity (targeted at associated components of physical fitness) (Public Health Service, 1990). The recent International Consensus Conference (Sallis and Patrick, 1994), by recommending both daily physical activity and regular participation in structured moderate to vigorous exercise, seems to capture many but not all the attractive elements of previous statements.

A second conclusion is that each of the previously published recommendations manifests significant limitations. Most of the previous statements are limited to guidelines for dynamic physical activity, despite the fact that there is increasing concern for, and documentation of, the health benefits of resistance exercise (ACSM, 1990). Some of the published guidelines suffer from lack of specificity, a weakness that limits their utility in public health surveillance and promotion efforts. Also, as a group, previous recommendations give little attention to behavioural issues related to the types and patterns of physical activity that are recommended for young persons at various developmental stages. This may be particularly critical in young people, not only because of short-term developmental concerns but because the greatest health impact of a physically active (or sedentary) lifestyle is probably exhibited during middle or late adulthood.

Finally, it must be acknowledged that both the lack of consensus and limitations shown in previous physical activity rec-

ommendations for young people are likely
explained by glaring deficiencies in the
body of knowledge upon which guidelines
should be based. The nature of these deficiencies will be discussed in more detail
later in this chapter.

## ■ Recommendations for physical activity provision and promotion in children and youth

Many of the official statements on physical activity in young people issued by professional and scientific organisations have
focused primarily on recommended
actions for providing and/or promoting
physical activity. These statements
demonstrate considerable agreement
concerning the strategies that should be
used to provide youngsters with more
physical activity and to promote lifelong
participation in appropriate physical
activity. The US Centers for Disease
Control and Prevention recently published
*Guidelines for school and community
programs to promote lifelong physical
activity among young people* (Centers for
Disease Control and Prevention, 1997).
This document includes 10 recommendations, and these are consistent with the
earlier official recommendations of several other organisations (Riopel *et al.*,
1986; American Academy of Pediatrics,
1987; ACSM, 1988; British Association of
Sports Sciences, Health Education
Authority and Physical Education
Association, 1990; UKK Institute for
Health Promotion Research, 1996; all
Chapter 8).

The most common theme in the various
recommendations on provision of physi-

cal education is that school physical education curricula and teaching methods
should be changed to place more emphasis on participation in moderate to vigorous physical activity and mastery of
lifetime physical activities (Simons-
Morton *et al.*, 1987). Recommendation
three of the *Guidelines for school and
community programs to promote lifelong
physical activity among young people*
(Centers for Disease Control and
Prevention, 1997) calls upon physical
education to provide curricula and
instruction that emphasize enjoyable participation in physical activity and that help
students develop the knowledge, attitudes, motor skills, behaviour skills and
confidence needed to adopt and maintain
physically active lifestyles. The American
College of Sports Medicine recommends
that school physical education programmes provide greater emphasis on the
development and maintenance of lifelong
exercise habits (ACSM, 1988). In similar
fashion, the American Academy of
Pediatrics recommends that school programmes emphasise lifelong aerobic
activities and decrease time spent teaching skills used in team sports, such as football, basketball and baseball (American
Academy of Pediatrics, 1987). In contrast,
in the UK, the recently implemented
national curriculum has promoted
increased competition and this may have
a negative impact on enjoyment in the
physical education curriculum.

The American Heart Association calls
upon health educators to provide interesting and informative instruction relative to
the benefits of physical activity (Riopel *et
al.*, 1986), while the American College of
Sports Medicine emphasises the teaching
of cognitive, affective and behaviour skills
associated with exercise, health and fitness (ACSM, 1988).

Several documents provide recommendations regarding the role of physicians and other health care providers in promoting physical activity among children and adolescents. The American Medical Association *Guidelines for adolescent preventive services* (American Medical Association, 1994) recommends that primary health care providers regularly counsel adolescents about the benefits of physical activity. The American Academy of Pediatrics (1987) recommends that pediatricians interact with local school boards to ensure that physical education programmes emphasise lifelong fitness activities. Recommendation eight of the *Guidelines for school and community programs to promote lifelong physical activity among young people* (Centres for Disease Control and Prevention, 1997) calls upon health service providers to assess physical activity patterns among young people, counsel them about physical activity, refer them to appropriate programmes and advocate for physical activity instruction and programmes for young people. Similarly, the American College of Sports Medicine calls for the health care profession to become actively involved in promoting physical activity and physical fitness for children and youth (ACSM, 1988).

Finally, many of the official statements on physical activity in young people include recommendations regarding the role of family and community in facilitating opportunities for physical activity. Recommendation eight of the *Guidelines for school and community programs to promote lifelong physical activity among young people* (Centers for Disease Control and Prevention, 1997) asks communities to provide a range of developmentally appropriate community sports and recreation programmes that are attractive to all young people. Position statements from the American College of Sports Medicine and the American Heart Association both recommend that parents and other influential adults become active role models and advocates for a physically active lifestyle (Riopel *et al.*, 1986; ACSM, 1988).

## ■ Considerations in formulating physical activity guidelines in children and youth

In developing guidelines for participation in physical activity by children and youth, several considerations should be applied. First, there should be substantial scientific evidence that the amount of physical activity recommended is associated with desirable status of physiological risk factors for chronic disease, physical fitness, and/or other favorable health outcomes. Ideally, there should also be evidence that the amount of physical activity recommended is associated with continued participation in physical activity during adulthood and physiological and psychological health outcomes during adulthood. With regard to the latter point, it is acknowledged that existing research has not documented that physical activity behaviour tracks strongly from childhood or adolescence into adulthood.

Second, guidelines for participation in physical activity should be sound from a behavioural perspective. That is, the type and amount of physical activity recommended should be conducive to enhancing physical activity self-efficacy and favourable beliefs and attitudes regarding physical activity. Moreover, the amount of physical activity recommended should be consistent with maintenance of physical activity self-efficacy, attitudes and beliefs from childhood into adulthood.

Third, physical activity guidelines should be consistent with, but not driven by, the patterns of physical activity behaviour typically observed in children and adolescents. For example, objective monitoring studies completed in several countries indicate that relatively few children engage in continuous 20-minute bouts of physical activity. Conversely, the majority of youth exhibit numerous 5- and 10-minute bouts of physical activity (Armstrong *et al.*, 1990; Pate, Long, and Heath, 1994). Accordingly, a recommendation that emphasises the accumulation of intermittently performed moderate to vigorous physical activity would be more practical than a recommendation that emphasises participation in continuous bouts of structured moderate to vigorous physical activity.

We readily acknowledge that none of the aforementioned considerations can, at the present time, be applied in the strict data-based manner that would be preferred. At present our knowledge of dose–response relationships between physical activity and various health outcomes is limited in children and adolescents. Accordingly, it must be recognised that, while physical activity guidelines should be *consistent with* current knowledge, it is not now possible to use scientific evidence concerning dose–response relationships as extensively as has been the case in the development of adult guidelines.

Further, we acknowledge that the considerations indicated above mix physiological and behavioural issues, a combination that we feel is appropriate given that, in the long-term, the physiological benefits of regular physical activity accrue only to those who choose to participate. In theory, children and youth could be required or forced to participate in

some recommended amount of physical activity, but in our view such a coercive approach would risk behavioural consequences that would ultimately prove self-defeating. Hence, in our view, the manner in which a physical activity recommendation is met may be as or more important than simply meeting it. This viewpoint is consistent with the philosophical position adopted by many authors who have addressed this issue over the past two decades.

At the same time we wish to emphasise that the recommended type and amount of physical activity should be given considerable priority when physical activity programmes for young persons are designed. We consider it most unfortunate that many school physical education programmes provide little physical activity (Centers for Disease Control and Prevention, 1997). We feel that the behavioural and physiological objectives of physical activity programmes for young people are entirely compatible and can be successfully pursued through activities that provide both moderate to vigorous physical activity and experiences that enhance such psychosocial factors as physical activity self-efficacy. Such an approach has been shown to be effective in recent studies of modified physical education programmes (McKenzie *et al.*, 1996).

## ▪ Proposed physical activity guidelines for children and youth

Based on the review of existing physical activity guidelines presented above and with consideration being given to the body of scientific evidence regarding the physiological and behavioural bases of physical activity participation in young people, the following physical activity guidelines are proposed.

**Recommendation 1. All children and youth should participate in physical activity that is of at least moderate intensity for an average of one hour per day. While young people should be physically active nearly every day, the amount of physical activity can appropriately vary from day to day in type, setting, intensity, duration and amount.**

As used here, the term 'moderate intensity physical activity' refers to activity requiring energy expenditure at the rate of at least 5 METs extending to levels of up to 8 METs (1 MET = 3.5 milliliters of oxygen consumed per kilogram body weight per minute). In youth, this intensity corresponds to roughly 40–60% of $\dot{V}_{O_2max}$. Examples of activity of this level include brisk walking, steady bicycling, and playing outdoors (Saris, 1996). Consistent with the lifetime physical activity recommendation proposed by Corbin *et al.* (1994), activity may be performed in a continuous fashion or intermittently accumulated throughout the day (Bailey *et al.*, 1995). Also, it is emphasised that the target level of physical activity is presented as a daily average. While performance of some physical activity on a daily basis is desirable, it is recognised that an individual's physical activity behaviour will vary considerably from day to day. Ideally this recommendation would be supported by compelling epidemiological or experimental evidence that 60 minutes of physical activity on a daily basis provides important health benefits early in life and is associated with maintenance of a physically active lifestyle into adulthood. Though such evidence is not currently available, we feel that it is appropriate to recommend an average of 60 minutes of moderate-intensity physical activity per

day, twice the amount recommended in guidelines directed primarily toward adults. Available evidence indicates that the vast majority of children and adolescents would meet a recommendation of 30 minutes of at least moderate intensity physical activity per day (Pate *et al.*, 1994; Cale and Almond, 1997). Yet there are data to suggest that many youngsters exhibit at least one modifiable risk factor for cardiovascular disease (Baranowski *et al.*, 1992), that the prevalence of childhood obesity is on the rise (Troiano *et al.*, 1995; Hughes *et al.*, 1997;), and that physical activity habits established in childhood are not carried into adulthood (Department of Health and Human Services, 1996). Also, existing recommendations call for children and adolescents to be active on a daily or near daily basis. Recommendation 1 is consistent with this approach, but adds a quantifiable amount of daily physical activity. Based on the descriptive physical activity literature, a daily average of 60 minutes of at least moderate activity appears to be a reasonable target.

**Recommendation 2. All children and youth should participate at least twice per week in physical activities that enhance and maintain strength in the musculature of the trunk and upper arm girdle.**

As part of the recommended 60 minutes of daily physical activity (recommendation 1), children and youth should engage in activities that promote strength and muscular endurance. Strength promoting activities that are appropriate for young children include playground activities that involve climbing, gymnastics, and calisthenics. Where appropriate, adolescents may participate in supervised resistance training programmes (Blimkie and Bar-Or, 1996). This recommendation is clearly consistent with objective 1.6 of

*Healthy people 2000*, which calls for people aged six years and older regularly to perform activities that enhance and maintain muscular strength. Also, it is consistent with the growing body of evidence that participation in strength promoting activities is associated with increases in bone mineral density (Bailey and Martin, 1994). Strength in the musculature of the trunk and upper arm girdle is particularly important as it is required to perform the activities of daily living (i.e. lifting heavy objects and other household tasks). Furthermore, clinical experience suggests that trunk strength may be associated with reduced risk for back pain and injury (Plowman, 1992).

**Recommendation 3. All children and youth should meet physical activity recommendations 1 and 2 by participating in types, intensities and durations of physical activity that are developmentally appropriate from both physiological and behavioural perspectives.**

This recommendation concerns the manner in which young people meet recommendations 1 and 2. It acknowledges that the packaging of daily physical activity, the physiological consequences of that activity and the consequential behavioural outcomes associated with physical activity will change as children grow and develop. For example, young children may meet recommendation 1 by alternating short bouts of moderate to vigorous physical activity with rest periods throughout the day. Teenagers, however, may meet recommendation 1 in a more 'adult like' fashion by performing structured continuous bouts of moderate to vigorous physical activity. As mentioned above, young children may promote strength and/or muscular endurance (recommendation 2) through playground climbing activities or gymnastics, while older children may increase strength and muscular

endurance through structured resistance training programmes.

# ■ Summary

The rapidly expanding body of knowledge concerning the health implications of physical activity has heightened interest in the issuance of public health recommendations on physical activity participation. An impressive body of scientific evidence exists upon which to base physical activity guidelines for adults, however, the analogous evidence for children and youth is much less extensive. Early efforts focused on establishing physical fitness standards for children and youth, but more recently several organisations have issued physical activity recommendations for young people. These recommendations have adopted varying approaches and have presented rather variable guidelines. In this chapter the authors have proposed guidelines that are based on both physiological and behavioural considerations and which draw on the efforts of previous expert panels.

It is the position of the authors that the three recommendations presented in this chapter are consistent with the pertinent body of knowledge and with the relevant official positions of government, scientific and professional organisations. However, it is readily acknowledged that these recommendations are not supported by epidemiological or experimental research at nearly the desired level. Clearly, further research is needed to test the validity of these recommendations. In particular, more work is needed to identify the types, intensities and durations of physical activity needed to provide health benefits at each stage of development. Furthermore, much more longitudinal research is